Preface

On 1 May 1960, a traditional military parade was held in Moscow. It stood out from the previous ones due to the clear predominance of missiles over other weapons. Immediately after the latest self-propelled artillery guns, eight vehicles with silver double-tailed missiles mounted on them drove into Red Square. 'Anti-aircraft, … Class: 'ground-air' … knowledgeable people were talking. They were followed by eight larger rockets. The Soviet mass media described the parade: 'More and more new units are entering the square. On special tractors and self-propelled tracked installations rest massive missiles, differing from each other in configuration and size of the rocket body. Our missile forces, as you can see, have ballistic strategic missiles of various purposes with a firing range from tens to many hundreds and thousands of kilometres. How many rocket launchers have passed? On the spectator stands they count: twenty … twenty-five … thirty … thirty-five … The score is approaching fifty.'

There was nothing surprising in this predominance of missiles, against which the 'traditional' guns and tanks looked like poor relatives. Rocket troops were declared by Nikita Khrushchev to be the 'main branch of the armed forces', for the development of which the most funds and the best scientific specialists were allocated. There was no aviation parade in 1960 at all! After all, Khrushchev considered aircraft to be a 'dying species', which from now on were expected to play only an auxiliary role. And the events of that May morning seemed to confirm this opinion. The spectators and participants of the grandiose 'rocket' parade did not even suspect that one of the key events of the Cold War era had recently occurred. Khrushchev was already aware that an American reconnaissance plane had been shot down over the Urals by one of these missiles!

In the United States, the Aquaton project (secret reconnaissance flights over the USSR) was still considered to be peacekeeping in nature. Ostensibly, these risky missions made it possible to study Soviet military potential and prevent a possible threat of war. Francis Gary Powers, who was shot down over the Urals on 1 May 1960 and was captured, is today considered to be a US national hero. For example, in Steven Spielberg's film *Bridge of Spies* (2015), this pilot is shown being subjected to brutal interrogation and torture, but he allegedly did not tell the Soviets anything. At the same time, Powers was being asked questions, the answers to which had actually been known for a long time …

This book refutes the myths and legends and is an objective account of the U-2 flights from the Russian side. This work, based on the archives of the CIA, declassified documents of the USSR Ministry of Defence, archives of Soviet mass media, and memoirs of participants in the events, tells the true story of the preparation, implementation and consequences of the U-2 reconnaissance missions over the Soviet Union and

The U-2 Over
the Soviet Union

America's Famous Cold War Spy
Plane from a Soviet Perspective

The U-2 Over
the Soviet Union

America's Famous Cold War Spy
Plane from a Soviet Perspective

Dmitry Degtev

AIR WORLD

First published in Great Britain in 2025 by
Pen & Sword Airworld
An imprint of
Pen & Sword Books Ltd
Yorkshire - Philadelphia

ISBN 978 1 39906 739 3

Typeset in INDIA by IMPEC eSolutions
Printed and bound in England by CPI Group (UK) Ltd, Croydon, CR0 4YY

The Publisher's authorised representative in the EU for product safety is Authorised Rep Compliance Ltd., Ground Floor, 71 Lower Baggot Street, Dublin D02 P593, Ireland.
www.arccompliance.com

For a complete list of Pen & Sword titles please contact

PEN & SWORD BOOKS LIMITED
47 Church Street, Barnsley, South Yorkshire, S70 2AS, England
E-mail: enquiries@pen-and-sword.co.uk
Website: www.pen-and-sword.co.uk

or

PEN AND SWORD BOOKS
1950 Lawrence Rd, Havertown, PA 19083, USA
E-mail: uspen-and-sword@casematepublishers.com
Website: www.penandswordbooks.com

MIX
Paper | Supporting responsible forestry
FSC
www.fsc.org
FSC® C013604

Contents

Contents

Cuba in 1956–62. What was the true reliability and value of the information received? How did public opinion in the Soviet Union perceive information about the flights of American reconnaissance aircraft? Also, readers will find out for the first time what objects were confiscated by the Russians from Powers? What brand of cigarettes did he smoke? Why was the U–2 pilot supplied with women's jewellery and watches before the mission? How great was the risk of nuclear war due to the U–2 flights?

Chapter 1

Hunting the Jaguar

On 9 July 1942, the weather was clear and sunny in the Moscow region. Russian air defence recorded the flight of a strange target that appeared from the west and flew over the Soviet capital at an altitude of 12km. It was out of range of the Russian 85-mm anti-aircraft guns. By that time, the 6th Fighter Aviation Air Defence Corps (6th IAK Air Defence) had 480 fighters, including 154 high-altitude MiG-3 interceptors, 111 British Hurricanes and 19 American P-39 Airacobras. The Russians regularly intercepted German Junkers Ju-88D reconnaissance aircraft flying at an altitude of 6,000–7,000m in the Moscow area. In the summer of 1942, fighters of the 6th IAK Air Defence managed to shoot down four Ju-88Ds, while four more were hit and made emergency landings on German territory. However, none of the Russian fighters could climb to a height of 12,000m. On 9 July, the Soviets could not even identify the target, and in the combat diary of the 6th IAK Air Defence it was written: 'It is necessary to have a special type of lightweight fighter for operations at altitudes 10,000–12,000m.'

The next similar episode occurred on 12 August 1942. From 13.59 to 15.11, an unidentified aircraft was recorded flying at an altitude of 10–11km along the route Mikhnevo–south-east and south of Moscow–Zvenigorod–Mozhaysk. At 14.22, a pair of MiG-3s from the 177th Fighter Aviation Regiment (177th IAP) took off to intercept, but they could not climb to such a high altitude. The pilots said that it was probably a Ju-88, but they couldn't really see the mysterious target.

On 24 January 1943, Russian radar stations again recorded a target flying near Moscow at a very high altitude. A pair of MiG-3s of Senior Lieutenant Kryukov and Junior Lieutenant Yakovenko took off from the Central Airfield of the capital. Seeing an vapour trail high in the sky, they climbed to an altitude of 9,000m and established visual contact with the target. However, it was flying 2–2.5km higher! The Russians followed the UFO to Volokolamsk, after which the fuel in their tanks began to run out and the fighters turned to the base.

By that time, Moscow's air defence had become very powerful, and German Ju-88D reconnaissance aircraft no longer risked flying over the huge city. They usually flew over the railway lines encircling the Soviet capital and observed railway traffic. When Russian fighters appeared, the Germans usually immediately changed course and altitude, hid in the clouds and used other tricks. But not everyone managed to escape. In September 1942, the Russians shot down three Ju-88Ds in the Moscow area at once, then two more in November, and two in February 1943.

The next appearance of the mysterious plane happened on 9 February. From 14.58 to 16.37, the aircraft, again identified as a 'Ju-88', flew along the route Uvarovka–Mozhaysk–Zvenigorod. However, unlike conventional reconnaissance aircraft, it did not turn in front of Moscow, but continued on.

Russian air surveillance posts calculated that the target's altitude was 11,000m. After passing over Kuntsevo, where Joseph Stalin's country residence was located, the plane turned south. Anti-aircraft regiments fired sixty-four shells at it. Russian fighters 'escorted' the target from Mozhaysk to Moscow and further to Maloyaroslavets, but none of them were able to climb to 11km.

The morning of 26 March 1943 began routinely. From 11.42 to 12.08, a Ju-88D, which appeared from the Valdai upland, passed along the route Staritsa–Pogoreloye Gorodische–Zubtsov–Rzhev and further west. Then, at 13.35, another reconnaissance aircraft appeared in the area of Volokolamsk, and then followed the railway to Toropets. At 14.06, a third target appeared from Smolensk. It flew over Vyazma, Gzhatsk, Uvarovka, Mozhaysk, and then through Kubinka, hading straight for Moscow. After passing over the fire zone of eight anti-aircraft regiments and directly over the city centre, the plane reached the eastern outskirts of the capital at an altitude of 12km. It then turned around twice and flew over the Kremlin and other areas, after which it departed on the same course at 16.01. After interviewing pilots and ground observers who saw the 'ghost', it was concluded that presumably it was a Messerschmitt Jaguar! In the diary of combat operations, it was written: 'The enemy aircraft by its actions is flying over our fighters, going towards them, causing a ceiling limit to be set in order to reveal the maximum height of our fighters ... It can be assumed that the height margin gives it the opportunity to take a load of about 300kg. The possibility of dropping bombs on the city from a height of 11,000 metres is not excluded.'

The Messerschmitt Jaguar was one of the 'phantom' German planes that the Russians regularly saw, but which never fell into their hands. Among these were the Heinkel He 113, Focke-Wulf Fw 187 and Focke-Wulf Fw 198 fighters. At the same time, the first two actually existed in the form of prototypes, but the Fw 198 was entirely invented by the Russians! In 1935, the Bf 161 and Bf 162 Jaguar aircraft were developed by order of the German Reich Aviation Ministry (RLM). The first was created as a reconnaissance aircraft, and the second as a high-speed bomber. Externally, they resembled the Bf 110 heavy fighter (Zerstörer), but had a wider fuselage, and the Jaguar was equipped with an internal bomb bay. The Bf 161V1, serialled D-AABA, made its first flight in 1938. In the autumn of the same year, a second prototype was ready, which had a different form of cockpit glazing. Outwardly, it resembled the ugly French bombers of that time. In 1939, the Bf 161V3 was built, after which flight tests began. However, by that time it was already clear that the faster Bf 110 could be used as a reconnaissance aircraft, so the need for a specialised Bf 161 aircraft simply disappeared. The same fate befell the Jaguar, which did not go beyond flying prototypes. Exact data on the dimensions of the aircraft are unknown, except for the length, which was 16.25m. However, in the Soviet Union, the Messerschmitt Jaguar was noticed and even remembered and carefully studied. And after the flight of a mysterious plane with something similar to it (a twin tail and two engines) over Moscow, they thought that the Germans had completed the Bf 161/Bf 162 family, turning it into a secret high-altitude reconnaissance aircraft.

The next time the mysterious Jaguar flew near Moscow was on 13 April 1943. From 12.11 to 13.40 the plane appeared from the direction of Vyazma at an altitude of 6,000m on a route Gzhatsk–Kubinka–Kuntsevo–Tushino–Zvenigorod. When the reconnaissance aircraft approached Moscow, several pairs of fighters were scrambled to intercept it, some of which rose to 9,500–10,000m. But then it turned out that the height of the target was 12,000m. 'The air battles did not take place due to the difference in altitude,' one combat diary reported.

Early in the morning of 2 June, at 07.33 in the area of Vyazma, the flight of another reconnaissance aircraft was recorded, which passed along the route Gzhatsk–Mozhaysk–Zvenigorod. It became clear that, most likely, this was the mysterious Jaguar. On this day, the weather contributed to high-altitude reconnaissance: it was a clear and warm summer day, slightly cloudy, and visibility was 10–15km. The plane flew slowly over Moscow at 12,500–13,000m, remaining in the zone of anti-aircraft artillery fire for almost an hour. However, the artillery did not fire and the fighters could not engage either as they could barely climb to 11,600m. Various fighters were scrambled to intercept, among which was the Yak-9PD No. 01-29 of the pilot inspector of the 6th IAK Air Defence, Lieutenant Colonel Lev Sholokhov, who took off from the Central Airfield. After reaching 6,000m, the pilot looked at the instruments: the water temperature was 105°C, and the engine oil temperature was 95°C. After that, Sholokhov continued climbing and soon reached an altitude of 8,500m. At that time, a message came over the radio: 'The target has passed Vnukovo.' At that moment, the pilot realised that the enemy was somewhere nearby. Looking around, Sholokhov saw a 'ghost' ...

A thick contrail was visible in the clear sky, at the end of which a small black dot could be seen approaching the southern outskirts of Moscow. The Yak-9PD immediately turned towards the city. After a fifteen-minute race with simultaneous climb, the fighter caught up with the enemy. The altimeter read 11,650m! Then Sholokhov looked up and saw the silhouette of a twin-engine aircraft directly above him at a distance of 1.5km. The lieutenant colonel clearly saw the yellow engines and the vague outlines of crosses. At that moment, he realised that he was seeing the same Jaguar that he had heard so much about. However, he did not long to admire the sight.

Soon, the fuel pressure dropped to almost zero, and Sholokhov had to descend almost a kilometre. After that, he made a second attempt to climb and again reached 11,400m. But then the pilot saw steam pouring out from under the engine cover, and the cockpit glass began to become covered with ice. It was clear that it would not be possible to reach the target, and as a result he was forced to end his pursuit and land. Other fighters also failed to intercept the target. After studying the drawings of various German aircraft, Sholokhov, who saw the target at close range for the first time, said that it looked most like an old German Ju-86 bomber.

The Soviets began developing the Yak-9PD high-altitude interceptor in the autumn of 1942, specifically to combat the mysterious Jaguar. A special M-105PD engine with two-stage E-100 superchargers was installed in the fighter. Only one 20-mm cannon with 120 rounds of ammunition was installed.

The first experimental interceptors were manufactured at Saratov Aircraft Factory No. 292, being completed on 20 April 1943. The first five aircraft were delivered to the 12th Guards IAP of Major K.V. Marenkov. The pilots completed sixty-nine flights, thirty-nine of them at altitudes from 10,000 to 11,500m.

However, it was discovered that a continuous climb in the Yak-9PD was impossible. At an altitude of 7km, the water temperature of the engine cooling system reached 120°C and it began to boil. The engine lubricant (oil) was heated to 100°C. After that, it was necessary to suspend the ascent and temporarily fly horizontally, waiting until the overheating stopped. As a result, an ascent to 11,650m took at least twenty-five minutes, too long to successfully intercept a target. In addition, it was not possible to reach 12,000m.

On the afternoon of 4 June, in conditions of good visibility, a high-altitude reconnaissance aircraft again appeared in the Moscow area. This time it took the route Yukhnov–Medyn–Detchino–Maloyaroslavets–Borovsk–Vereya–Kaluga. The plane was over Soviet territory for about three hours and calmly soared at an altitude of 12,000m. All attempts to intercept it again ended in failure.

On 22 August came the culmination of the Jaguar hunt. Russian air defence spotted a high-altitude target at 07.52 in the area of Vyazma. Then it followed the route Vereya–Zvenigorod–Lyubertsy and then straight to Moscow. The reconnaissance aircraft soared slowly in the zone of anti-aircraft artillery fire for almost two hours, while it passed over the Kremlin four times and flew over the suburbs of the capital; Vnukovo, Lyubertsy, Khimki, Kuntsevo, etc. At 10.17 the aircraft flew Naro-Fominsk–Mozhaysk–Gzhatsk–Vyazma to the west on a course of 270°.

The Soviets scrambled fifteen fighters to intercept: six Yak-1s, three Yak-9PDs, two MiG-3s, two Bell P-39s and two Spitfires. Of these, nine were able to climb to a sufficiently high altitude and get close to the target. At 08.08, a pair of Yak-9PDs flown by Lieutenant Zhuravlev and Second Lieutenant Nalivaiko took off from the Central Airfield in Moscow. The pilots managed to climb to 11,000m and establish visual contact with the target directly over Moscow. Then the fighters chased it to Mozhaysk, but could not climb higher. At 08.37 in the area of Istra, the target was spotted by a pair of Yak-1s piloted by Second Lieutenants Polkanov and Bushlov from the 562nd IAP, although they did not manage to climb higher than 9,500m.

At 08.20 a pair of P-39 Airacobras flown by Junior Lieutenants Mikhail Abramov and Evdokimov from the 28th IAP climbed to 9,000m and met the target over the northern outskirts of Moscow. The fighters failed to climb higher. A pair of MiG-3s of Junior Lieutenants Krupenin and Klimov, who took off from Kubinka airfield, managed to climb to 10,800m and in the Vnukovo area they observed the target, which simply passed directly over them.

As a result, only one interceptor, the Spitfire of Senior Lieutenant Semenov from the 16th IAP, managed to get close to the high-altitude reconnaissance aircraft. Being at an altitude of 10,000m south of Moscow, the pilot saw a vapour trail and then the enemy aircraft itself. The Spitfire went to intercept and at that moment the target began to turn on a 270° course, slightly sideways to Semenov, and he was able to examine it carefully. The pilot saw that it was really an old Ju-86 bomber! However, it was very different to the 1936 model aircraft. The plane had a rounded cabin and incredibly long, very thin wings. It seemed to Semenov that the target was painted in bright white. South of Moscow, Semenov was able to climb to an altitude of 11,500m, after which he opened fire vertically with his guns and machine guns. The Ju-86 began an evasive manoeuvre, periodically lurching to the left, and from somewhere in the rear of the fuselage a tracer machine gun burst appeared. Semenov was very close to victory, but after the second burst the Spitfire's guns froze and jammed. Then two of his machine guns iced over. With the last of his strength, Semenov pursued the target to Kubinka, firing his remaining two machine guns. However, after that his fuel and oxygen began to run out and Semenov had to return to base. Subsequently, it was determined that the Spitfire had fired 450 rounds and 30 shells at the Ju-86 from a distance of 600–650m while 500m below the target.

The Russians recorded the last flight of the elusive reconnaissance aircraft over Moscow on 5 September 1943.

The Ju-86P reconnaissance aircraft was developed from the Ju-86 bomber in 1940. A new two-seat pressurised cabin was attached to the aircraft and diesel engines were installed, which made it possible to reach an altitude of 10,000m. The aircraft made several reconnaissance flights over the UK, remaining out of reach of fighters and anti-aircraft artillery. In May 1941, in preparation for the invasion of the USSR, they began flying over Russian territory. Later, German designers further improved this aircraft, increasing the wingspan to 32m, installing powerful four-bladed propellers and the GM-1 system in the engines to improve high-altitude performance. This made it possible to increase the maximum operational height to 14,400m! The modified type was designated Ju-86R-1, and the Germans used these reconnaissance aircraft over Great Britain and over Egypt. However, the British quickly learned how to intercept such elusive aircraft. Over the Suez Canal, Spitfires managed to attack them even at an altitude of 12,800m, that is, almost 13km. The first Ju-86Rs arrived on the Eastern Front in June 1942 and became part of the first Staffel of the elite long-range reconnaissance air group Aufklärungsgruppe Oberbefehlshaber der Luftwaffe (Aufkl.Gr.Ob.d.L). Taking off from Orsha air base, Ju-86Rs periodically flew over Moscow with impunity for almost a year and a half, and all Russian attempts to shoot them down ended in failure.

Just thirteen years would pass and the Soviet Union would face the same problem again. A mysterious reconnaissance aircraft flying at a great height would again invade the country's airspace. And the Russian air defences would have to fight the 'ghost' again …

Chapter 2

The Spiders Attack and the Storming
of the Stratosphere

Speed Requires Sacrifice

The history of the creation of the famous U-2 aircraft is well known. Therefore, we will not repeat ourselves here, limiting ourselves to the most important aspects relative to its Soviet Union flights.

In 1933, a young graduate of the University of Michigan, Clarence 'Kelly' Johnson, was hired by Lockheed Aircraft Corporation. His first mission was to participate in aerodynamic tests of the new Lockheed Model 10 aircraft. The engineer almost immediately concluded that the type would be unstable along its axis, which was quickly confirmed. 'We can do better,' Johnson promised his colleagues and radically changed the design and construction of the aircraft, which later turned into the famous Electra. The talented designer was then the sixth member of the design bureau team, but by 1938 he had risen to chief designer.

In 1936, the USAF issued a specification for a twin-engined, long-range fighter with a maximum speed of at least 367mph. At that time, the Americans had not yet thought about a major war in Europe, and what was an exotic aircraft for its time was needed primarily for the Pacific. As a result, Johnson's team created the famous P–38 Lightning, which surpassed all American fighters of that time in speed and range. Along with the British Mosquito and the German Bf 110, this aircraft entered the top three twin-engine fighters of the Second World War.

In 1941, the command of the US Army Air Corps came to the conclusion that a high-speed reconnaissance aircraft was required, capable of flying missions into the deep rear of the enemy at a distance of 1,500km. It would be required to conduct aerial photography of industrial and military facilities, and in case of danger, get away from air defence fighters. To meet the requirement, Johnson installed four K–17 cameras in the nose of the P–38. After testing, the variant was put into mass production under the designation F–4. Later, the aircraft was modified and given the new name F–5. In 1942–45, these aircraft became the most common USAF reconnaissance aircraft in Europe and the Pacific. For long-range flights, the F–7 (a modification of the B–24 bomber) and F–13 (modified B–29) scouts were also used.

An epoch-making event in the history of aviation came on 25 July 1944. On that day, Mosquito PR.XVI MM273 of 554 Squadron, RAF, was suddenly attacked over the Alps by a twin-engine aircraft without propellers, which easily caught up with it, even at maximum speed, and carried out four attacks. The crew was barely able to hide from an unknown opponent in the clouds at low altitude. At the same time, the aircraft received serious damage, not from shells and bullets, but due to stress overloads. The pilot eventually managed to fly to Fermo air base in Italy, where he reported that the Germans had probably started using jet fighters. And it was true. Most likely, the Mosquito was attacked by Me 262S-12 W.Nr. 130017 flown by Lieutenant Alfred Schreiber of the air group 'Commando Lechfeld'. Already, on 8 August, the unit had won the type's first confirmed victory, shooting down a Mosquito from 540 Squadron over Lake Ammersee. Who would have thought then that piston aircraft, the creation and improvement of which so much effort and money had been spent on, would give way to jet aircraft in just a few years. And in the next serious war – in Korea – jet planes would play the main role.

Of course, the United States and the UK also worked on jet aircraft. The first US type, the XP-59, developed by the Bell Aircraft Corporation, turned out to be completely unsuccessful, with its top speed only slightly higher than that of conventional piston-engined fighters. In parallel, Clarence Johnson also designed a jet fighter commissioned by the US Army Air Corps. He managed to meet the deadline in 143 days instead of the 176 set by the contract. The first prototype of the XP-80, called the Shooting Star, flew on 8 January 1944. It became the first American aircraft to break the 500mph (800km/h) barrier. However, because of the tight deadlines, the aircraft was still very raw and did not enter service in any numbers before the end of the war.

Johnson developed a modification of the reconnaissance aircraft based on the XP-80, simply integrating the camera compartment from the F-4 into its fuselage. The aircraft was put into production shortly before the Korean War under the designation F-14A (later changed to RP-80A/RF-80A). However, it was this conflict, which became the first real battle of the jet age, that showed the vulnerability of the reconnaissance aircraft available to the USAF, especially during deep reconnaissance. The widely used RB-45 Tornado proved to be an easy target for Russian MiG-15 interceptors.

After a year of large-scale military operations, accompanied by a high number of casualties and destruction, a relative lull was established in Korea from the summer of 1951, and the warring sides sat down at the negotiating table. Meanwhile, a propaganda war unfolded on an unprecedented scale, during which the sides accused each other of truly unthinkable crimes, including those related to the use of aviation. So, in the spring of 1952, the Chinese and North Korean media reported the terrifying news about the beginning of a hitherto unprecedented 'large-scale bacteriological war'. The reports that appeared in the newspapers shocked people. Moreover, the greatest fear was caused not by the very fact of using bacteria, but by a rather original method allegedly developed by the insidious American military!

The newspapers wrote:

During the period from 11 to 21 March, the American interventionists, ignoring the just and resolute protests of the peoples of the whole world, spread a large number of insects infected with bacteria in the rear of the Democratic People's Republic of Korea and at the front, including in the vicinity of the neutral zone of Panmunjoy. On 6 March, at 9 a.m., 6 enemy jets flew over Sukcheon. One of them dropped a paper bag with spiders. On 9 March, two enemy aircraft dropped bacteria-infected fleas over Muncheon ... on 10 March, 42 American aircraft flew in eight groups over Andong, Changdianhekou and Baichuzi and dropped infected insects over these points. On the same day, a large number of bacteria-infected leaves were found in the vicinity of Andong, and many infected flies, mosquitoes, ants, spiders, grasshoppers, bedbugs and fleas were found in Lingjiang and other places. At 5 pm, 8 enemy light bombers appeared near Kuchaan and released a large number of birds similar to crows infected with deadly bacteria. On 11 March, an enemy aircraft dropped spiders, flies, sand flies and other insects over Suncheon ... on 16 March, one enemy fighter jet dropped cotton balls west of Koksan, in which rats and rat excrement were found. Two enemy P-51 fighters, flying north-east of Namkhonjom, dropped a large number of infected frogs ... on 17 March, an enemy aircraft dropped butterflies, ants and other insects north of Pyongyang and south of Sukchon.

Of course, people were horrified to hear these details. With not enough atomic bombs, nor enough napalm and phosphorus bombs, they had already switched to spiders, fleas, bedbugs, rats and rat droppings!

History was silent about how, say, a paper bag with spiders could be dropped from jet planes flying at transonic speed and how these spiders reached the surface safely. Similarly, it was not made clear how the valiant army of the DPRK had caught thousands of fleas, flies and bedbugs allegedly dropped by the Americans. Chinese and Korean newspapers also reported on artillery attacks using shells filled with flies and ants.

In such conditions, Clarence Johnson arrived in Korea. His task was to interview American fighter pilots who had to fight with Soviet MiG-15s. The pilots believed that the American planes were superior to the enemy, nevertheless the F-86 suffered serious losses. It was not possible to achieve complete air supremacy over North Korea, even despite the regular massive bombing of airfields. Johnson, who was distinguished by his adventurism and bold, unconventional views on aircraft design, flew back to America with a lot of ideas and plans. He conceived the idea of creating such an interceptor fighter that would obviously surpass all modern jets in speed, including those that would be created in the near future.

It is no secret that the designers of the Third Reich had a huge influence on post-war aviation. Johnson probably borrowed a number of ideas and developments from them, in particular, concerning missile interceptors of the Me 163 type. And what happens if you combine all the advantages of a 'rocket plane' and a turbojet engine in one plane? This fighter will be difficult to control and have a small range, but this is compensated for by incredible speed characteristics. This is how the famous L-246 interceptor was born, later called the XF-104, then the F-104 Starfighter. Johnson formulated the concept of an interceptor simply: take off quickly, quickly catch up and shoot down the enemy, and then quickly disappear. For this purpose, an aerodynamic profile of an aircraft with a small wing was chosen. Suffice it to say that with a length of 16.7m, the aircraft had wings with a span of only 6.6m! For comparison, the small German fighter Bf 109F had a wingspan of almost 10m. To improve aerodynamics, the powerful J-79 turbojet engine was built directly into the fuselage, flanked by two semicircular air intakes. The thickness of the wings did not exceed 10cm, and their edges were made so thin that they resembled a knife blade.

The project as a whole turned out to be not very successful and very difficult. The first USAF unit, the 83rd Fighter Interceptor Squadron (FIS), only received its Starfighters in January 1958. The flight characteristics of the F-104 turned out to be fantastic (it reached a speed of 2,200km/h and soared up into the stratosphere in a few seconds, like a rocket). But as a fighter, the F-104 turned out to be ineffective. Due to poor manoeuvrability and high speed, pilots often simply did not have time to catch the target, while the aircraft had weak armament (due to its small size, there was simply nowhere to hang missiles). However, the combat career of another Johnson aircraft, created on the basis of the Starfighter, turned out to be much more successful and vivid.

Secret Flights

After the end of the Second World War, during which humanity suffered huge losses and many cities were virtually destroyed, many people hoped that now the appropriate conclusions would be drawn and people would realise that war was not the best way to sort out differences. Germany, which for many years dreamed of 'living space' and expanding its possessions, eventually lost all the lands east of the Oder, which the Germans had conquered and cultivated for several centuries. The Japanese Empire, which also terrified the whole of Southeast Asia for many years and carefully and methodically increased its possessions, also lost almost everything. However, the fallen empires were replaced by new ones and Europe from the Baltic to the Adriatic Sea was divided by the Iron Curtain, and the former allies in the East and West promptly began to develop plans for war against each other. Soon, third parties appeared. In 1946–47 there was a short period of what was then called a tense lull, and in the summer of 1948 the first serious crisis broke out, the Soviet blockade of West Berlin. The Russian occupation forces cut off all communications between the Western zone of occupation and Berlin, which was divided into four parts. In response, the British and Americans organised an airlift to West Berlin. All this not only resembled the events of recent years, but also clearly smelled of a new war.

In 1949, several key events took place at once, defining world politics for the next forty years. The NATO military bloc and the Federal Republic of Germany were formed. In response, the creation of the GDR was announced in the Eastern zone of occupation. Almost simultaneously, Chinese leader Mao Zedong announced the creation of the People's Republic of China, while the remnants of the nationalist forces led by Chiang Kai-shek, supported by the United States, 'temporarily' evacuated to the island of Taiwan. Events developed rapidly, and in June 1950, the North Korean army unexpectedly attacked South Korea. The former was actually openly supported by the USSR and the PRC, and the latter by the UN countries, which for the most part represented the United States. By that time, it was already known that the USSR had an atomic bomb, as well as strategic bombers.

In the spring of 1949, the United States and Great Britain began conducting secret reconnaissance flights over the USSR. On 10 May, an RF-84 aircraft from the 8th Tactical Reconnaissance Squadron (8th TRS), based at Yokota air base in Japan, made its first flight over the Kuril Islands. Later, RF-80FB, F-84, RB-45C, RB-50, P-2V and B-47B reconnaissance aircraft were used for flights over the Soviet Far East, and the Spitfire Mk XIX was used over China (with a high-altitude pressurised cabin and increased wingspan). The first reconnaissance flight over the western part of the Soviet Union was made by RAF pilots. On the night of 18 April 1952, three RB-45Cs took off from Sculthorpe air base in Norfolk, entered the airspace of the USSR and conducted reconnaissance in three divergent directions: the Baltic States, Ukraine and the Moscow region. All three aircraft completed the mission and returned safely to base. The altitude of the RB-45Cs was 11,000–12,000m, and the Soviet air defence did not detect the intruders.

Periodic short-range flights were combined with unexpected raids deep into Soviet territory. At the end of August 1953, an RAF English Electric Canberra took off from Giebelstadt airfield in West Germany, flew over southern Poland, Kiev, and then all over Ukraine up to Kharkov. The Soviet air defences initially could not even identify the target, which was flying at an altitude of 14,500m. After Kharkov, the Canberra headed further east to Stalingrad, and then passed over the main target, the Kapustin Yar missile range. In this area, the plane was finally intercepted by MiG-17 fighters, one of which was able to fire a machine gun burst at it. The Canberra was damaged, but was nevertheless able to fly safely to Iran.

The next daring RAF operation took place on the night of 29 April 1954. Once again, an entire unit consisting of three RB-45CS took off from Sculthorpe, refuelled from an air tanker over Denmark and then invaded the airspace of the USSR on different courses. The planes flew the route Novgorod–Smolensk–Kiev, after which they turned back. This operation caused panic in the Soviet leadership, as all three targets were identified as American B-47 bombers with nuclear weapons on board. The Soviets decided that in this way NATO wanted to intimidate the Soviet Union and conducted nuclear attack training. On 8 May, an air battle took place over the Kola Peninsula between an RB-47E reconnaissance aircraft from the USAF and a pair of MiG-17s from the 161st IAP. The American aircraft was damaged, but was still able to return to base.

All these missions were very adventurous and risky, and they grossly violated international law. In addition, they forced the Soviets to increase the power of their weapons and accelerate work on the creation of anti–aircraft and ballistic missiles. On 14 June 1954, an order was issued by the Ministry of Defence of the USSR in relation to the reorganisation of the structure of the country's air defence forces. It provided for the organisation of the Moscow and Baku air defence districts, several air defence armies, and also required urgent strengthening of fighter aircraft, increased vigilance, etc.

Despite the success of the flights, it was clear to the Americans that a new-generation aircraft was required for aerial reconnaissance over the Soviet Union and other potential adversaries. On 27 March 1953, the defence department issued secret order No. 53WC-16507 for a reconnaissance aircraft capable of taking aerial photographs from 'extreme' heights inaccessible to fighters and other air defence systems. The general parameters were: subsonic speed, the ability to carry 700lb (226kg) of camera equipment, a range of more than 3,000 miles (4,800km), and a ceiling (maximum height) of over 70,000ft (21,300m). The aircraft should not be equipped with a catapult and carry weapons.

The experience of the Second World War showed that the vast majority of reconnaissance aircraft of all warring countries were created by simply modifying production bombers or fighters, and in some cases ground-attack planes and even passenger and transport aircraft. But there were also different examples. For example, the most famous Luftwaffe reconnaissance aircraft, the Fw 189, nicknamed Rama (Frame), was an ideal example of an aircraft designed specifically for aerial reconnaissance. Another famous aircraft, the jet Ar 234 Blitz, was also created as a long-range reconnaissance aircraft, and only then were bomber and night fighter versions created using the design. In fact, the war had not given a clear answer as to which concept was more optimal and effective.

Financing of the US programme was initiated under the code designation MX-2147. Several aviation companies received orders for the development of the reconnaissance aircraft at once: Martin Aircraft Corporation, Bell Aircraft and Fairchild. The latter's designers presented a single-engine aircraft project, but it seemed too exotic. Bell proposed its large, twin-engine X-16 aircraft. The designers at Martin chose the simplest option, which provided for the modernisation of the twin-engine B-57 jet bomber. This was a licensed copy of the British Canberra bomber that was already in use with the US Air Force. Martin decided to equip the aircraft with elongated wings and new engines. This project was recognised as a priority, while the Bell X-16 received the status of a promising one.

Meanwhile, an event occurred that, as it turned out, became a turning point in the history of American aviation. In the autumn of 1953, John Carter, a member of the board of directors of the Lockheed Aircraft Corporation, visited the Pentagon on company business. There he met his old friend, Eugene Kiefer, who served in the planning and development department of the USAF headquarters. Over a cup of coffee, Kiefer told Carter about a secret programme to create a high-altitude reconnaissance aircraft. Kiefer complained that the command wanted the impossible, trying to get a tactical and strategic reconnaissance aircraft in one project. He also hinted that the programme was generously funded.

When Carter returned to California, he immediately met with the vice president of the corporation and suggested that he create a new-generation reconnaissance aircraft. Like the designer Clarence Johnson, Carter believed that in the aircraft industry it was necessary to apply not 'standard' (literally and figuratively) solutions, but innovative and extraordinary ones;

to stay ahead of your opponents, and at the same time your competitors, not by a head, but by two or three heads at once. In general, Carter's idea looked something like this: the most lightweight airframe, a speed of Mach 0.8 and a flight altitude of 21,000m. With these ideas, he, having received the consent of his superiors, turned to Johnson.

In the shortest possible time, the design team, which had the nickname the Skunk Works, developed a draft aircraft, which received the code designation CL-282. It was based on the principle of maximum simplification, with the design following the principles of non-motorised gliders. The XF-104 fuselage, shortened by 5ft, was used as a base, and this was equipped with large, elongated wings with small positive transverse V. It was decided to equip the aircraft with one General Electric J-73 turbojet engine. The use of a pressurised cabin and an ejection seat was also abandoned, as well as standard landing gear. Having studied the experience of the German Me 163 and Ar 234 jet aircraft, the designers at the Skunk Works decided to equip the CL-282 with a wheeled trolley for take-off. The landing was to be carried out directly on the reinforced lower part of the fuselage. According to the calculated data, the reconnaissance aircraft could reach an altitude of 21,000m, carry reconnaissance equipment weighing 270kg and would have a range of 6,000km.

The CL-282 project was ready in February 1954, and early the following month Johnson personally presented it to the chief of development planning objectives of the USAF headquarters, General Bernard Adolph 'Bennie' Schriever. He liked the idea, and the general asked Johnson to provide a more detailed description. In early April, Schriever brought Johnson to the Pentagon, where he delivered a report on his project to the USAF command. However, this rejected the project on various pretexts. On 7 June 1954, Johnson received an official letter notifying him that his project had been rejected. It also cited the reasons for the failure, the main ones being its 'too unusual shape' and 'unreliability of the single-engine design'. After this failure, the CL–282 could well have suffered the fate of hundreds of other bold and exotic aircraft projects created by the imagination of engineers from different countries, but for one reason or another not approved by the military and officials. However, Johnson was lucky, because his brainchild appeared at the right time and in the right place.

When retired General Dwight Eisenhower won the presidential election in 1952, he, as a veteran of the Second World War, former commander-in-chief of Allied forces in Europe and an experienced planner of many major military operations, carried out major reforms in American intelligence. It was during his presidency that the Central Intelligence Agency (CIA), actually created by Eisenhower's friend Allen Dulles, turned into the intelligence agency that we know today. The main task of the agency was to conduct strategic intelligence around the world in the interests of national security. This meant not only collecting data and information about the military potential of potential opponents and their military preparations, but also assessing and preventing other potential threats, including the emergence and spread of potentially dangerous political regimes (primarily communist ones) in different parts of the world. Given that the world had changed dramatically after Pearl Harbor and threats, including a sudden military attack, had become more dangerous, Eisenhower believed that America needed a special service subordinate directly to the president, capable of responding quickly to the situation in a volatile world and even conducting its own military operations. And it also required special equipment. Eisenhower ordered the creation of an independent body responsible for increasing the offensive and defensive power of the United States. It became the Technological Capabilities Panel (TCP), formed in the summer of 1954 under the leadership of Professor James Killian, president of the Massachusetts Institute of Technology. The members of the group gained access to all state secrets and secret projects. One of the divisions of the TCP was the department of the Project Three study group, Project-3), which dealt with the effectiveness of methods for obtaining intelligence information. Its first driver was the famous scientist, designer, inventor of the widely known Polaroid instant photography device and millionaire Edwin Land.

In addition, at the initiative of Eisenhower, a number of various bureaux and committees were created. So, a little later, the so-called Committee on Secret Affairs, also known as 'Special Group 5412/2', was formed in the structure of the presidential administration. It was headed by the young Vice President Richard Nixon. The committee was intended to provide general guidance to all covert CIA operations and coordinate the department's actions with other security agencies and the army. All these measures allowed Eisenhower to carry out many activities, including military and intelligence, without the knowledge of Congress and the Joint Chiefs of Staff, even at his discretion to adopt new equipment and use it anywhere in the world.

One day, Clarence Johnson introduced CIA officer Philip Strong to his project. Strong lobbied the CL-282 project among the leadership of the CIA, convincing it of its advantage over other reconnaissance aircraft projects. This played a crucial role for the future of the aircraft. In early November 1954, President Eisenhower had already personally approved the CL-282 project, and on 24 November he officially signed the document on activation. Richard Bissell was appointed head of the CIA project, code-named Aquatone. During the Second World War, he served on the committee that coordinated the transportation of Allied fleets around the world. Bissell then returned to the Massachusetts Institute of Technology and became a professor in 1948. Being at the same time a teacher, a politician, a businessman and a millionaire, in January 1954 he participated in the development of one of the first major CIA operations – the overthrow of Guatemalan President Jacobo Árbenz, whom Washington suspected of having links with communists. The operation was successful, and Bissell was appointed deputy director of the CIA.

Having finally received the green light, Kelly Johnson selected the most experienced and capable designers for the new group. At first, this team consisted of only about fifty people, and eventually reached just over eighty employees. Johnson promised to prepare a prototype within eight months after signing the contract, that is by 2 August 1955, and this schedule was followed. The assembly of the first aircraft under the Aquaton programme was completed on 15 July 1955. The prototype was not painted and received only the internal number 001, although the CIA assigned it its own designation Product 341 (Article 341). In the early morning of 24 July, the aircraft was delivered to the secret Rancho test air base in the Nevada Desert. Later this place gained cult fame under the name Area 51.

The first flight of the CL-282 took place on 4 August. During the autumn, many tests were carried out, during which the design flight altitude of 21,000m was reached, and then the maximum ceiling of 22,700m. The test pilots also completed a ten-hour flight to a range of 8,000km, finally proving that the aircraft met all its design data. During the testing process, the aircraft received its new designation, which later became one of the most famous in the history of world aviation. Since the designations adopted for bombers, fighters and transport aircraft were not suitable, and because of the necessary secrecy it was impossible to use the designations adopted for reconnaissance aircraft. After studying many aviation reference books, they discovered a rare category of aircraft that came under the designation U for Utility. At that time, only two types of aircraft of this category were registered in the United States: the de Havilland U-1 and Cessna U-3. As a result, it was decided to fill this niche by assigning an inconspicuous and at the same time obscure designation to the new aircraft, Utility-2 (U-2).

Lockheed's initial proposal for the CL-282 project, drawn up in May 1954, provided for the construction of twenty aircraft with GE J-73 engines for $28 million. When the CIA became interested in the project, it was agreed that Lockheed would build twenty aircraft, a two-seat training aircraft and several sets of spare parts. The total amount of the contract was reduced to $26 million. Some sceptics then expressed doubts about the timing and money, believing that the CL-282 project would absorb much more funding. But in reality, Johnson not only met the budget, he even saved taxpayers money. During the final contract negotiations held in the spring of 1958, Lockheed Aircraft Corporation and the US government agreed on a price for the first batch of twenty aircraft in the amount of $17,025,542 plus a profit of $1,952,055. Thus, the total amount of the contract was less than $19 million, that is, less than $1 million for each aircraft. Since the design of the U-2 was largely based on the already developed F-104, the aircraft turned out to be relatively inexpensive, even despite manual assembly and a small production run.

Since the use of the U-2, at Eisenhower's request, was supposed to have the status of 'civilian', it was originally planned to recruit non-American citizens as pilots. Seven pilots from NATO countries were selected as the first candidates. Dulles and Bissell believed that if the U-2 was shot down over the Soviet Union, then the violation of airspace in this case could be explained by navigation errors or a malfunction of the aircraft. As a cover story, all candidates were officially sent to perform high-altitude flights within the framework of the international weather research programme. However, due to insufficient experience in high-altitude flying, as well as difficulties in mastering the aircraft, their training was halted after two weeks.

After that, it was decided to recruit American pilots associated with the CIA or with Lockheed, as well as pilots of fighter squadrons that were part of strategic aviation, to fly on the U-2. The pilot selection process was very thorough: in addition to confirming the pilot's high qualifications, it included various physical and psychological tests. In strategic aviation, preference was given to those pilots who expected to be transferred to other units, so the transition to the U-2 programme and the unexpected disappearance of a person did not arouse suspicion from colleagues. As a result, six pilots who had previously flown F-84 fighters were selected initially: Marty Knutson, Carmen Vito, Wilburn Rose, Glenn Dunaway, Carl Overstreet and Harvey Stockman.

Recruitment took place in the best traditions of spy blockbusters. Knutson and Carmen Vito were urgently called to their wing commander, who offered them a mysterious special mission. 'If you agree, you will find out the details at the Albany Hotel on the next night.' Both pilots were intrigued and agreed, and the fact that the mentioned institution had the fame of a brothel only added to the mystery. In one of the rooms, Knutson and Vito waited for mysterious people in civilian clothes, who offered them the dream of every hero: an unforgettable experience, the opportunity to do something important for their country (and even save the world) and, of course, good money. The salary of pilots enrolled in the Aquaton programme, compared with what they received in the USAF, increased fourfold ($2,500 per month), and after the end of the contract they could return to military service, receiving an extraordinary rank. During this 'business trip', they all retired, became reservists and signed a secret contract with the CIA as civilians.

As subsequent events would show, the psychological testing programme clearly turned out to be wrong.

In early 1956, the first group of volunteers arrived at Area 51. The candidates later recalled that they imagined flying on rockets or supersonic fighters and were surprised when they saw something in the middle of the desert that looked like a prehistoric glider with a steering wheel like a rocker in a cramped cabin. The pilots were even more amazed on the second day when they learned that they were going to fly over the USSR and its satellite states on this 'thing'.

With the start of training flights, the population of the Ranch increased dramatically (by spring 250 people already lived there), and in March 1956 there were already 9 U-2s on site. The intensity of flights also increased dramatically. In addition to Nevada, the geography of test flying spread to the entire northwestern part of the United States. The tests were supposed to show how visible the U-2s were to ground-based radars. The Americans assumed that Soviet radars were created using technologies that the USSR received from the Allies during the Second World War. Accordingly, if American radar stations had difficulties identifying objects located at an altitude of over 12,000m, then Soviet radars should have the same disadvantages. These arguments were generally confirmed during the tests. The CIA concluded that the Soviets would most likely be able to cross-target the target several times, but would not be able to clearly identify it and trace the entire flight route. According to calculations, this situation could persist for at least two more years. On 28 May, the CIA's Office of Scientific Intelligence (OSI) presented a report to Dulles and Eisenhower. It reported that the Soviets would not be able to achieve consistent tracking of the U-2 flight and would not be able to track its flight path.

Meanwhile, the training programme for the first group of pilots was over and the U-2s were ready to conduct secret missions.

Chapter 3

From Moscow to Cairo

Hunting for 'Bison'

At a meeting in Geneva in June 1955, President Eisenhower proposed to Soviet leader Nikita Khrushchev a plan called Open Skies. It provided for mutual permission for reconnaissance flights over the territories of the countries participating in the programme. The flights would be pre-coordinated, and their conduct would allow monitoring of the development of military potential and military preparations. Eisenhower offered to provide airfields in the United States for aerial photography of any military installations, if the Soviet Union would provide similar air bases for American aviation in return. The president sincerely hoped that Khrushchev would accept his offer, but he was also ready to refuse. 'I'll make one attempt. If they do not accept our proposals, we will fly the U-2,' he told his entourage.

Eisenhower's proposal was never accepted, and at the same time the launch programme of American reconnaissance air probes gave very modest results. And yet, the president doubted the need for flights to the last, fearing possible consequences. Studying the OSI report of 28 May 1955 only reinforced his doubts, but the main argument in favour of starting flights was the mysterious Soviet M-4 aircraft. The first such aircraft, which clearly resembled a jet strategic bomber, flew over Red Square during the May Day parade in 1954.

Back in the 1930s, the USSR had a tradition of showing the new products of its aviation industry during these events. This was supposed to demonstrate to the Soviet people the steady growth of the country's military power and show the whole world that 'you can't take Russians with your bare hands'. And for foreign intelligence agencies, it was a regular opportunity to assess the current military potential of the Soviet Union.

In 1955, the May parade was not held due to bad weather, but back in April, military attachés of Western countries received invitations to demonstration flights of new Soviet aircraft. There they saw thirty M-4s at once, as well as a new Tu-95 strategic bomber. The former were code-named 'Bison' according to the NATO classification, and the latter 'Bear'. Soon the CIA prepared a report stating that, allegedly, by the middle of 1958, the Russians would have 350 M-4s and 250 Tu-95s. And, consequently, the Soviets would be able to launch a nuclear strike on the United States at any moment, while the American programme to build new B-52 bombers was still unfolding.

In early February 1956, the Chief of Staff of the USAF, General Twining, made a report to Congress to the members of the Committee on Armaments. He pessimistically assessed the military power of his country, scaring congressmen with an alleged Soviet aviation breakthrough. And in May, *US News and World Report* magazine published two sensational articles under the headlines 'Are the Soviets gaining air supremacy?' and 'Is the U.S. really losing the sky?' It is clear that American military officials and industrialists were interested in increasing the military budget and were trying to influence the presidential administration with the help of a horror story about the Bison.

In addition to the bombers, the American military was also concerned about the lack of information about the Soviet missile programme. On 30 January 1956, *Time* magazine published an article in the spirit of the scandalous story of the Martian invasion in 1938. It described the near future, 1962, when the United States was subjected to a sudden Soviet missile attack and suffered a humiliating defeat, because it lagged behind the USSR in the development of guided missiles. And just two weeks after the publication appeared, it became known that the Russians had successfully tested a missile with a range of 900 miles (1,500km). All this caused another panic in the US, as a result of which Eisenhower was forced to give a press conference, during which he honestly admitted that the Soviet Union could indeed outpace the United States in some areas of the missile programme.

As a result, faced with growing concern from Congress and the public about Soviet offensive capabilities, on 19 June 1956, the president approved the CIA's proposed programme for the first U-2 flights. Meanwhile, the meteorological service had given a long-term forecast, according to which there would be clear weather over the European part of the USSR from 20 June to 10 July.

By this point, the CIA had already launched a developed cover story. In April, Weather Reconnaissance Squadron Provisional 1 (WSRP-1) was created. Further, on 7 May, the National Aeronautics and Space Administration (NASA) announced the launch of a research programme during which U-2 aircraft would collect data on atmospheric conditions at high altitudes.

As part of this 'partial disclosure', the CIA has developed the following disinformation. A fake instruction was drawn up for flights on the U-2, which indicated the maximum flight altitude of 16,700m, as well as the composition of the equipment, which included a set of instruments for studying the atmosphere and weather conditions. An additional trick was a set of images representing the instrument panel along with comments regarding maintaining the listed flight parameters. In total, four copies of the instructions were prepared, which were specially artificially aged (with traces of oil, cigarette ash and coffee) and, if appropriate, they were to be planted for Russian intelligence.

In fact, the unit equipped with the U-2 was named Detachment A (abbreviated Det. A).

During the negotiations between Secretary of State John Dulles and British Prime Minister Anthony Eden, an agreement was reached that Detachment A would be based in the UK, for which the Americans promised to share all the intelligence materials they received. Lakenheath air base in Suffolk was chosen for the flights. The first two aircraft were delivered there disassembled on 29 April by C-124 aircraft. By 4 May, all aircraft and equipment, as well as all personnel, arrived at the air base. However, the stay of the 'weather explorers' in England turned out to be short. Firstly, the U-2 quickly attracted the attention of the press. On 1 June, *Flight* magazine published an article entitled 'The Mysterious Stranger', describing the planes seen in Suffolk. Secondly, a scandal broke out in England related to the secret inspection of the Soviet cruiser *Sverdlov*, on which Khrushchev visited Great Britain. As a result, Eden revoked the mission's flight permit and gave the CIA twenty-four hours to remove the U-2 from the country. Then, on 11 June, Detachment A was transferred to Wiesbaden air base in West Germany, although the German government was not informed about this.

While preparations for the operation were under way, a specially created Flight Planning Committee was working on a list of targets; a list of objects, information about which was of paramount importance. After approval, it was transferred to a CIA department, which developed specific flight routes. Each flight plan received an individual number, for example, Mission 4016. The deadline for completing the task did not depend on the individual number. The first U-2 reconnaissance flight, Mission 2003, was conducted immediately after receiving Eisenhower's authorisation, on the night of 20 June 1956. The countries of Eastern Europe were chosen for it. The plane, carrying A-2 camera equipment, flew over Warsaw, and then returned to base via East Berlin.

The next flight had to be postponed for several days due to the fact that at that time the American delegation was at an aviation holiday in Moscow, as well as due to the need to inform German Chancellor Konrad Adenauer about the introduction of secret flights from his country. Then the weather intervened. In anticipation of favourable conditions, Detachment A performed two more test flights over Eastern Europe, both on 2 July. The first of them took place over Czechoslovakia, Bulgaria and Hungary, and the second over the GDR, Poland, Hungary and Romania. In both cases, contrary to expectations, the violators were spotted and tracked by the radars of the air defence of the USSR and the Warsaw Pact countries. However, neither the height nor the type of target could be determined. Several dozen MiG-15 and MiG-17 fighters were scrambled from Poland, Czechoslovakia, Hungary, Romania and the western military districts of the USSR. However, only a couple of MiG-17 pilots who took off from an airfield north of Košice managed to establish visual contact with the target. According to the pilots, it flew at an altitude of about 16,000m at a speed of 750–800km/h. At the same time, the intruder had a 'cruciform' appearance, silver colour and looked most like a B-57 Canberra.

The first flights were carried out along such a route so that in the event of an engine problem, the U-2 had the opportunity to plan to leave the borders of the Warsaw Pact countries. From an altitude of 21,000m, the aircraft could fly with a non-working powerplant for almost 600–700km, and even more under ideal weather conditions!

The scheme of the first flights over the USSR on 4–5 July 1956.

Meanwhile, on 3 July, President Eisenhower gave final permission for the U-2 to fly over the territory of the Soviet Union. The first stage of the operation was planned to be carried out within ten days, after which the flights were to be stopped for analysis of the results. On 4 July, U-2B No. 347, piloted by Harvey Stockman, took off from Wiesbaden. The flight was named Mission 2013. Interestingly, during the first flights over the 'evil empire', as Russia was often called in the West, the pilots took with them a special emergency kit, which, in addition to vital items, included 7,500 rubles, twenty-four gold coins and as a letter in fourteen languages asking for help and promising rewards for saving the pilot. In the future, the composition of these sets changed somewhat, as will be discussed below.

After take-off and climb, the plane flew over Berlin and headed across Poland to Bialystok, where it entered the airspace of the USSR. After reaching Bobruisk, the U-2 turned north towards Leningrad, which was the main objective of the mission. Heading north, Stockman flew in the area of Orsha, Vitebsk, then in the Pskov area turned north-east, reaching the Moscow–Leningrad railway. Further, heading north-east, the scout reached the former St Petersburg. After conducting aerial photography, the U-2 made an arc over Karelia up to the Finnish border, and then turned south. The plane crossed the Gulf of Finland near Narva and turned west, after which it passed over Tallinn, Riga, the coast of Latvia, Kaliningrad, and then headed for Germany. On this winding route, Stockman flew over several bases of Soviet long-range bomber aircraft to determine the number of M-4 bombers stationed there, and also photographed several airfields in the Baltic Sea area. After eight hours and forty-five minutes of flight, he landed back in Wiesbaden.

Radar stations of the Group of Soviet Forces in Germany detected the flight of the intruder at 08.18 Moscow time, when it crossed the border of the GDR 30km east of Kassel. The unidentified aircraft entered the airspace of the USSR at 09.30 60km south of Grodno, then its route was tracked only in the area of Minsk, Vilnius, Kaunas and Kaliningrad. The flight of the target up to the Leningrad area was not recorded, and it seemed simply unthinkable. More than 100 fighters (MiG-17s, MiG-19s and Yak-25s) were scrambled to intercept the mysterious target, but only a few of them managed to make visual contact. One MiG-17PF chased the intruder over Belarus for five to seven minutes. Being at an altitude of 15,100m, the pilot reported that the target was 1,500–2,000m above him. In the Vilnius area, a pair of MiG-17 pilots also observed a 'large jet plane' flying at high altitude. And in the area of Kaunas, the crew of a two-seat Yak-25M fighter flying at 14,400m discovered the intruder on the screen of their on-board radar station. Based on the pilots' reports, the aircraft type was again presumably identified as B-57, and the flight altitude was 16,000–17,000m.

Flight to the City of Brides

The departure of the Mission 2014, which was aimed at Moscow for the first time, was scheduled for 05.00 on 5 July. According to the established procedure, three coded signals, each consisting of only one word, were to be transmitted to Wiesbaden twenty-four, twelve and two hours before launch. If at least one of the signals did not arrive, it meant that the mission was cancelled. After receiving the second signal, the ground staff and pilots prepared for departure within twelve hours. The Lockheed, Pratt & Whitney and Kodak teams conducted thorough inspections of the aircraft, engine and cameras. The pilots put on their special suits, and after receiving the third signal, in the last two hours before departure, they performed a special procedure, the purpose of which was to purge nitrogen from the blood. Simply put, the pilots breathed pure oxygen for two hours. Meanwhile, the second signal, which was expected at the base at 17.00 on 4 July, was not received from the CIA. As a result, it was concluded that the flight had been postponed and the crew could relax at the Independence Day party. However, at 19.00, a message suddenly came from Washington that 'the mission is being activated'. At that time, the only still sober pilot turned out to be Carmen Vito, who had the honour to fly to Moscow. The pilot immediately went to bed, and three hours before departure he was woken up and called for breakfast, which for the U-2 pilots consisted of steak (meat chop) and scrambled eggs. Carmen Vito recalled: 'They always fed us steak and eggs before the flight. I didn't want meat and eggs at two in the morning at all, but they were on the checklist. So, I had to eat it.'

At 05.00 on 5 July, U-2B No. 347 took off. The route passed over the southern part of the GDR and Warsaw. In the Brest region, the aircraft entered the airspace of the Soviet Union and headed for Baranovichi and Minsk. In this area, the first

MiG-17 fighters were scrambled to intercept, although the pilots could not even see the target. After reaching the capital of Belarus, Vito headed towards Moscow, then following the Minsk–Moscow railway. This moment was symbolic in many ways. It has been almost thirteen years since 5 September 1943. That was the last time a Luftwaffe Ju-86R high-altitude reconnaissance aircraft flew in the Moscow area. Now the plane, developed using the technology of the infamously deceased Third Reich, flew 8km higher than its German predecessor!

However, the first part of the flight took place in cloudy conditions, and the pilot did not have the opportunity to admire the scenery for a long time. Vito recalled:

The sky was clear at an altitude of 3,000 to 4,000 feet, but I had cloudy weather halfway through. The sky cleared up as I followed the railway from Minsk to Moscow. At an altitude of over 66,000 feet, I listened to the song 'Peter and the Wolf', a Russian musical composition with narration, which was broadcast by a Soviet radio station. Small mosaic fields of collective farms could be seen below. They reminded me that Russian peasants cultivated the land by hand. I felt no malice towards those who were doing hard work there. I was never angry at the Soviet people themselves, but I hated their government.

In the Moscow area, the sky became completely clear, which exactly corresponded to the weather forecast for the mission, which was compiled by the Americans based on data from

Moscow radio. Upon reaching the huge city, Vito photographed the airfield in Ramenskoye, the aviation plant in Fili, where, according to American reports, M-4 strategic bombers were assembled, as well as a whole network of anti-aircraft missile launch sites. The pilot continued his story:

> Later I learned that the Soviets had scrambled at least five fighters to intercept me. The lead fighter aborted take-off, moved away from the runway and exploded. His wingman went through the flames and then exploded too. Two more planes took off and were refuelled in the air. These planes crashed or collided. The pilots ejected. The fifth plane could not find the tanker plane. He went down and has never been found to this day.

It is unknown where the Americans got such information from, although the Soviet air defence system did really turn out to be in complete disarray. At 07.42, Russian radar stations in the GDR recorded the flight of an unidentified aircraft, which was later recorded over Poland. At 08.54, an intruder aircraft was recorded entering the territory of the USSR. However, it was not possible to fully track the flight route of the target. Yuri Votintsev, at that time deputy commander of the 1st Air Defence Army of Special Purpose (1st AON PVO), stationed around Moscow, recalled:

> One of the long-range target detection stations east of Minsk, at an altitude of about 20,000m, detected a target. The target was moving through Minsk to Moscow ...

the specialists faced a difficult task – to identify the target. First of all, it was flying at a high altitude. Secondly, it was surprising that the target 'failed' – disappeared from time to time on the radar screen when it should not disappear. We called it 'failing'. The speed was also confusing, which in some areas differed sharply from the cruising speed of the aircraft and reached the flight speed of a bird. Experts believed that if there was an aircraft on the radar screen, then it should fall at that moment. At the same time, the mark from the target on the radar screen did not look like a flock of birds – they do not fly at such an altitude. A natural phenomenon? A balloon probe that was often launched by Western intelligence agencies at that time? But then how do you understand that the goal has reached a certain point, and then began to move in the opposite direction – to the West. There were more questions than answers. In short, the target was invisible.

There was complete confusion at the command posts, especially in the Belarusian Military District. As a result, the flight of the intruder towards Moscow remained almost unnoticed. Individual radar stations observed an unidentified target, but its mark was soon clogged by numerous marks from interceptor aircraft. One of the MiG-17 pilots reported that he visually observed a glider-like aircraft high above him, but no one believed him. The Soviet Air Defence Command could not imagine that there were planes capable of flying such long distances at an altitude inaccessible to fighters. Some recalled the events of thirteen years ago, when the elusive German Ju-86R flew over Moscow. But it was difficult to believe in a complete repetition of that story, and even in peacetime (not wartime).

The air defence units located around Moscow were already armed with the S-25 Berkut anti-aircraft missile systems, which (in theory) were designed to hit targets at an altitude of up to 25,000m, flying at speeds up to 1,250km/h. The U-2 photographed their positions, but the systems were still being installed and were not operational.

In general, everything went well for Vito. After photographing military installations in the Moscow region, he headed north-east towards the Volga. The extreme point of 'penetration' was the city of Ivanovo, located 1,100km from the border. From this point, only 180km remained from to the city of Gorky (now Nizhny Novgorod), which was one of the most important military industrial centres of the Soviet Union. Fighter planes, submarines, anti-aircraft missile systems, armoured personnel carriers, radars, radar stations and other numerous military equipment were produced there. However, for some reason, the CIA did not show interest in this goal, and aerial photography of the city of Gorky was not included in the flight task. Probably, American intelligence believed that there was enough detailed information about this city preserved in the archives of the Third Reich.

In the area of the 'city of brides' (as the city of Ivanovo is called in Russia because of the large number of women who work in textile factories there), the U-2 turned around and headed west. After that, it photographed the city of Kalinin (now Tver), where, according to the CIA, there was a rocket factory (this was not true), and headed north-west. Having reached the Vyshny Volochyok–Bologoye area, Vito headed over the Valdai upland towards the Baltic Sea. The U-2 flew over Latvia and Lithuania, after which it turned to base.

On 6 July, anxiety reigned again at the airfields of the Belarusian Military District. Immediately after the unpunished flight of this UFO, it was decided to form special groups within several fighter aviation regiments to intercept violators using supersonic MiG-19 fighters. They also created such a group in the elite 15th IAP 'Dzerzhinsky', which was based at Rumbula airfield in the Riga area. This aviation regiment began to receive new MiG-19s at the end of 1955. One of the pilots of the 15th IAP, Vasily Pikanov, later recalled:

The first aircraft began to be mastered by the leadership of the aviation division and the aviation regiment. I was a wingman for the deputy commander of the division, Colonel Pirogov, and therefore, in mastering the programme, I went 2–3 exercises ahead of my colleagues. Since the training programme was not completed by 5 July, the aviation regiment was not on combat duty. The planes were permanently parked – without outboard fuel tanks. In short, I repeat, we were preparing for scheduled training flights. But the day presented me with a more difficult test. When I was having breakfast in the regimental canteen, I was called out of the room. By order of the regiment commander, Colonel Yesin, I was taken by car to the parking lot where my plane was located.

I was surprised by the following: the MiG-19 was already ready to take off, there was a high-altitude compensating suit and a parachute lying next to it. By the decision of the Army Commander, a special group had been created to intercept the offending aircraft. We were supposed to be on duty at the air base of the Lithuanian city of Kedeniai. In order to manage our group more effectively, the Oak command post, in addition to radio communication, established a wire connection with us.

The scheme of action was supposed to be as follows. I was supposed to be the only one aiming to intercept the target, all other planes should be on the ground, so it's easier to control. Another plane was to be sent to intercept from the Air Force of the Carpathian Military District. On 5 July, it was established that the intruder was flying at an altitude of approximately 20,000 metres, and the maximum flight altitude of the MiG-19 was 17,800 metres. The task was set for me: to reach an altitude of 20,000 metres due to the so-called dynamic slide, that is, the plane after acceleration had to make a jump, as it were.

On the morning of 6 July, a message was received at the Kedenyai airfield that a high-altitude aircraft was flying over the territory of Germany, which might again fly towards the USSR. Then a signal was transmitted from radar stations about the appearance of a 'vaguely visible' target in the Brest area. It seemed that the situation of the previous day was repeating itself, and Pikanov's MiG-19 was scrambled to intercept. After climbing to 12,500m (the maximum height under afterburner) with a course of 180°, the pilot received data on the target's course. It was following the same altitude, but on an opposite course. Pikanov prepared to attack, but soon instead of an intruder he saw in the sky ... another MiG-19. It turned out that this was his partner from the air force of the Carpathian Military District. The interceptors were simply pointed at each other (fortunately, they did not shoot each other down!). In fact, there were no U-2 flights at all that day.

On the opposite side of the planet, in Washington, the first results of the operation were being summed up at that time. When Dulles arrived at work after the holidays, he immediately asked his assistant Bissell if there were any flights in the U-2 on Independence Day? In response, he was amazed to hear about those two flights over Leningrad, Moscow and other areas that took place at once, and the results exceeded all expectations. 'Oh my God, isn't this too much to start with?' the CIA director asked. 'On the contrary, the first attempt is the safest,' Bissell replied. The next day, the results were reported to Eisenhower, and within thirty-six hours of Carmen Vito's return, the CIA was able to compile a detailed report on the actions of the Soviet air defences. Based on the data of the radio interception, American experts concluded that the Russians could detect the U-2 flight, but only 'fragmentally', that is, not throughout the entire route. At the same time, the reconnaissance aircraft was not detected directly in the area of Moscow and Leningrad, but several unsuccessful interception attempts were made.

'Descendant of ANT-25'

Due to bad weather over Eastern Europe, no flights were conducted during 6–8 July. Meanwhile, the ten-day period during which Eisenhower's sanctioning of flights was in effect was coming to an end, so as soon as the clouds cleared, Bissell decided to conduct two flights at once, code-named Mission 2020 and Mission 2021.

On the morning of 9 July, two U-2s took off from Wiesbaden air base, one after the other. The route of the first one passed over the territory of the GDR, Poland and the Baltic States. The aircraft flew over Lithuania, Latvia, then the Minsk area, over Warsaw, then again over East Germany, after which it returned to Wiesbaden. Many fighters were scrambled, including several MiG-19s from the special air group of the 15th IAP from Kedenyai and Rumbula air bases. Among them was Vasily Pikanov's fighter. He recalled:

Information came from the GDR, from the Group of Soviet Forces in Germany: a high-altitude aircraft moving in the direction of the USSR. On command from the Oak command post, I started with a 180-degree course and gained an altitude of 12,500 metres. After that, I was turned on a course of 270 degrees ... After some time, a new command: 'Turn right at an angle of 30 degrees until the command is received.' I was immediately given the information: 'The intruder is located at a distance of 6 kilometres, altitude – 16,000–16,500 metres.' It was possible to carry out an interception with confidence. I was turned around by 60–70 degrees and given the command: 'Turn on the afterburner.' I prepared for the attack. But …

After turning on the afterburner, about 15–20 seconds later, an explosion occurred. The red light on the scoreboard announced 'fire in the left engine'. It was just abruptly reducing power. I reported the incident to the command post and turned left 45–50 degrees to make sure visually if there were signs of a fire. When I was sure that brown smoke was spreading behind the plane, I turned off the fire valve of the left engine. The warning light went out, and the smoke stopped. The offending plane flew towards Moscow with impunity again, because there were no more fighters in the air except mine …

Meanwhile, the second U-2, carrying out Mission 2021, travelled a long way over the central regions of the USSR. It flew over many targets, over Lviv, Kiev and Minsk, after which it returned to Germany via Belarus and Poland. More than 100 Soviet fighters were scrambled to intercept the 2 intruders, and in the Kiev area the target was even fired at by anti–aircraft artillery (shell explosions were observed by the U-2 pilot). MiG-17PF and MiG-19 aircraft were mainly trying to aim at the target. Vasily Pikanov recalled:

When the U-2 was returning, the most trained pilots of our regiment were scrambled to intercept it from the Rumbula airfield. These were squadron commander Major Sokolov, flight commanders Captains Korenev and Kapustin. To no avail: the first landed at the Shauliai airfield, the second in Poland. Captain Kapustin did not reach the runway of the Kedenyai airfield 500 metres away. He turned left into a meadow, rammed a flock of sheep on landing crashed into a destroyed house building at a fairly high speed and wrecked the plane. Kapustin himself remained alive, but became disabled – he injured his spine.

Some Russian interceptors were able to reach an altitude of 18,000m. At the same time, Soviet radar stations recorded the height of the target in the area of Bobruisk as 20km, in the area of Minsk it was 19.1km. Due to major errors in the operation of the stations, the actual location of the target, as a rule, differed significantly from the one indicated by the operators. Therefore, even with difficulty climbing to a high altitude, fighter pilots in most cases did not observe the intruder at all. At best, they did not see the target directly above them, but far away. According to the description of the pilots, it was a silver or white twin-engine aircraft with long wings, without identification marks. Most pilots identified the target as a B-66, a B-57, or an English Electric Canberra.

Meanwhile, the CIA did not let the Soviet air defence relax. On 10 July, the fifth flight was carried out. The main goal of Mission 2023 was Crimea. The U-2 again flew over the GDR, southern Poland, then south of Lviv, Romania and entered the airspace of the USSR over Moldova. Then the reconnaissance aircraft took aerial photographs of Odessa, Simferopol and Sevastopol, turned around over the Black Sea and returned to Wiesbaden via Romania and Czechoslovakia.

Soviet radar stations detected the target at 07.36, when it crossed the GDR border in the Würzburg area, and at 09.08 they detected an invasion of Soviet airspace in the Przemyśl area. The height of the target was set at 20,000m, and the speed was from 800 to 1,000km/h. Over more than sixty fighters, including thirteen MiG-19s, were scrambled to intercept. The reports of the pilots who visually observed the target turned out to be very diverse and contradictory. Some pilots claimed that the wings of the reconnaissance aircraft were straight, others that they were swept. Some of the pilots saw two engines on the plane, others did not note any engines (high-altitude glider?).

As for Pikanov's MiG-19, a commission found that the engine fire occurred after switching on the afterburner mode due to poor welding of the discharge tube from the high-pressure line. The fuel was supplied in the form of an emulsion into the space between the engine and the fuselage. However, for this type, which was built in a hurry, this failing was more the rule than the exception. As in the 1930s and during the Second World War, the government required design bureaux and factories to create and manufacture new aircraft at an accelerated pace, constantly referring to the 'difficult international situation'. The Soviets tried to compensate for the technical lag behind the leading aviation powers with high-speed work and slogans. The MiG-19 was put into production even before the completion of state flight tests. During the first test flights of production aircraft, which took place in early 1955, a lot of complex defects were identified that seriously affected flight safety. This concerned both the fuselage and the control systems, and especially the RD-9B engines. For example, failures of both turbines during landing, failures of the hydraulic system and jamming of the controls were recorded. It even went so far that the MiG-19 arbitrarily performed uncontrolled manoeuvres in flight.

There were many accidents and catastrophes. For example, on 13 July 1955, pilot P.Y. Gerbinsky died during factory tests. His aircraft suffered the destruction of the aerodynamic partition of the right wing, which led to a sudden stall into a spin. On 18 August 1955, MiG-19 No. 5921-0449 (produced by aircraft factory No. 153) spontaneously opened the rear lock of the cockpit canopy flap during a flight at an altitude of 10,000m. Test pilot A.A. Grishin ejected, and the plane crashed. On 19 December, after take-off from the airfield of aircraft factory No. 153, MiG-19S No. 0215310 crashed and exploded. Pilot I.A. Pritskau was killed. The accident occurred due to jamming of the hydraulic booster of the horizontal tail drive. A few days later, MiG-19 No. 0115301 crashed for the same reason. Nevertheless, the substandard fighter was already being delivered to aviation fighter regiments at an accelerated pace. In 1955, 139 MiG-19s were produced; in 1956, 619 units, of which 331 were manufactured at aircraft factory No. 21 in Gorky and 288 at aircraft factory No. 153 in Novosibirsk.

In aviation units, the development of the MiG-19 was also accompanied by numerous accidents. In flight, hydraulic amplifiers and automatic controls failed, and turbines were constantly stalling. Due to the rough assembly, small metal chips remained in the pipelines, which clogged the jets, which also led to failures of turbines and control systems. In some cases, this led to a rearrangement of the stabiliser, which immediately caused the nose of the fighter to be lifted up or, conversely, dive. At low altitudes, it almost always ended with the death of the pilots. In general, in 1956, the MiG-19 was still a substandard aircraft. However, such problems, as well as high accident rates, were typical for the entire initial era of jet aviation.

The worst thing was that, despite all the efforts, emergency work and sacrifices, the MiG-19 did not produce the characteristics that the country's leadership and especially the air defence command expected. First of all, it concerned the altitude of the flight. Even the lightweight modification of the MiG-19SV, the first thirty of which were assembled in the city of Gorky during 1956, the service ceiling did not exceed 18,500m instead of the required 20,000m. But this bar was achieved only due to forced engine operation, fuel overspending and was associated with a constant risk of engine failure. The fighter's armament (especially missile) and avionics also had many problems.

There were also purely subjective reasons why the MiG-19 did not receive as much widespread distribution as its successor, the MiG-21, and was only produced for four years. At the end of 1956, the Soviet Union became aware of the unprecedented breakthrough that was planned in the American aircraft industry. This was confirmed by the adoption of the F-104 Starfighter interceptor by the USAF. In December 1956, Deputy Minister of Defence of the USSR Marshal

Vasily Sokolovsky wrote to the Commander-in-Chief of the Air Force Air Marshal Pavel Zhigarev:

> In the USA, in 1956, the F-104A daytime air combat fighter was adopted with a maximum speed of 2,400km/h and a maximum flight altitude of 20km. The F-102 interceptor fighter is being mass-produced with a maximum speed of 1,600km/h, a maximum flight altitude of about 18km, armed with a Falcon guided missile. Our Su-7, MiG-21, and MiG-23 [the experimental E-2A, which was not adopted, and not the later aircraft of the same designation] fighters, which are being introduced into mass production, have a maximum speed of 1,750–2,000km/h, and the MiG-19P interceptor fighter is 1,420km/h, the maximum flight altitude of these fighters is 17–19km, followed by bringing them to 19–21km, armament – guns with a firing range of up to 2km.

Thus, the MiG-19 was considered outdated and unpromising soon after the start of mass production. But it turned out that it was that type that had the main responsibility of intercepting the U-2.

As for the objectives of the first operation using a high-altitude reconnaissance aircraft, they were fully achieved. During five sorties, nine airfields of Soviet bomber aviation were photographed. However, none of them turned out to have M-4 bombers. Photographs of aircraft factory No. 23 in Fili, where they were produced, showed that the company had very limited production facilities. The Americans even established that only the M-4 fuselages were manufactured there, after which they were transported by barges to Ramenskoye, where the wings were mounted. As a result, the CIA concluded that 'the Soviet Union could not have far surpassed the United States in terms of the number of strategic bombers'.

In fact, the Americans even underestimated the weakness of Soviet strategic aviation. The M-4 bomber was developed by Stalin's personal order. The leader ignored the opinion of designer Andrei Tupolev, who considered it impossible at that time to create an aircraft capable of reaching America. The project was eventually taken over by designer Vladimir Myasishchev, who followed the same path as Clarence Johnson with his U-2. Myasishchev discarded all existing norms and standards, setting the main goal of achieving the required range at any cost. The M-4 received a bicycle chassis, an aerodynamically clean wing and a lightweight body. In order to reduce the weight, a large-panel assembly was used in the structure. As a result, it was possible to achieve a design flight range of 10,000km (a combat radius of 5,000km), but many penalties had to be paid for this. Firstly, the production of the aircraft turned out to be extremely complex, expensive and, in fact, piece by piece. Secondly, the bicycle chassis made it extremely difficult to land the aircraft and almost impossible to modernise the bomb bays and use the external suspension of bombs. In general, it turned out to be a kind of analogue of the same U-2, only completely useless.

During the entire production period, aircraft factory No. 23 built thirty-two M-4 bombers, three of which crashed with their crews shortly after entering service. All aircraft joined the 201st Heavy Bombardment Aviation Division (201st TBAD) under the command of Major General S.K. Biryukov, the location of which was a specially modernised airfield in Engels (the U-2 had not yet reached it in 1956). At the same time, the aircraft turned out to be extremely unreliable and in just the first three years of operation with this unit there were many accidents and at least six crashes. Later, all the surviving M-4s were converted into M-4-II air tankers. Produced in parallel with the M-4, the Tu-16A jet bomber had a range of only 3,000km, so it could not strike at the territory of the United States (not counting Alaska).

Based on the information gathered, in early November, the CIA compiled a fairly accurate report about the state of Soviet strategic aviation. It said that the M-4 flights on parades and in front of foreign observers were a show-off and an attempt to intimidate potential opponents with 'huge and countless armadas of intercontinental bombers'. In reality, the Soviets had no more than twenty to thirty Bisons, and their production capacity was limited. The U-2 tests also provided other valuable data on the state of the Soviet military-industrial complex. Eisenhower was pleased, but decided not to bring this information to the attention of Congress. This was partly due to him being afraid of questions in the spirit of 'How did you get all this?'

But in the USSR itself, on the contrary, the government was very unhappy. On 9 July, the American ambassador in Moscow was handed an official protest note. It reported that on 4 July, an intruder aircraft penetrated the airspace of the

USSR to a depth of 320km, and was over Russian territory for an hour and a half, flying over Minsk, Vilnius, Kaunas and Kaliningrad. On 5 July, a 'twin-engine medium bomber of the US Air Force' again intentionally violated the air borders of the Soviet Union and flew to a depth of 150km. According to the established norms, which allowed up to ten days for the preparation of response notes, on 19 July, the United States officially replied that no military aircraft could fly over the USSR, therefore the statement of the Soviet government was erroneous. There was no response at all to protests received from Poland and Czechoslovakia. The protest note did not scare the Americans, but provided them with new intelligence information. It was clear that the Russians could not trace the entire flight path of the U-2 and did not even notice that they were flying over Moscow, Leningrad and Ivanovo. And most importantly, the Russians had no idea what this mysterious intruder looked like. Consequently, it could be assumed that no interceptor was able to get close enough to the aircraft to even take a good look at it.

Meanwhile, on Khrushchev's orders, several joint meetings were held with designers and the military. The Air Defence Command expressed confidence that the intruder was an upgraded version of the RB-57. In this regard, there was a fear that it could not only fly at high altitude, but also drop small nuclear bombs (the Russians took into account that the RB-57 was based on the B-57 bomber). Khrushchev himself shared this point of view. He believed that the flights were not carried out for reconnaissance, but for political purposes – to show the Soviets the invulnerability of American aviation and intimidate the Soviet leadership. The version closest to the truth was put forward by designer Andrei Tupolev, who in the later years of Stalinism became one of the Kremlin's main advisers on aviation. He stated that the RB-57 would not have been able to reach such an altitude and fly at it for a long time. According to Tupolev, compiled on the basis of surveys of pilots, the target was most likely similar to the ANT-25. He was referring to the large, single-engine aircraft on which the legendary Soviet pilot Valery Chkalov flew over the North Pole to the United States in 1937. Tupolev believed that the Americans were using a lightweight, single-engine aircraft with very long wings. He also suggested that there were no weapons on the plane, and the crew probably consisted of one or two people at most.

The result of the meetings was a series of resolutions and secret instructions, all marked 'urgent'. First of all, they concerned the early adoption of the S-75 anti-aircraft missile system, the T-3 interceptor fighter (later renamed the Su-9), the modernisation of existing and the development of new ones capable of accurately determining the parameters of targets at high altitudes. Khrushchev promised that a pilot who shot down a high-altitude intruder would be immediately (regardless of his past record and rank) presented with the title of Hero of the Soviet Union, and financially he would receive whatever he wanted. In the realities of that time, this meant a new apartment out of turn, a new GAZ-21 Volga car and a ticket to an elite sanatorium. In addition, the pilots were guaranteed an early increase in military rank up to two levels at once.

However, 'Khrushchev's Falcons' had to wait quite a long time for a new chance, and it would fall to the wrong pilots, who tried to intercept the U-2 over the western part of the Soviet Union.

Nuclear Halloween

In January 1956, the CIA began recruiting a second group of pilots for the Aquaton programme. Among the recruits was former F-84 fighter pilot Francis Gary Powers. He later recalled that during the recruitment process, he was told that volunteers were being recruited for a special government assignment, which would be risky and very dangerous. At the same time, it would be necessary to go far beyond the United States for eighteen months. Powers could only discuss the proposal with his wife. The pilot was intrigued, gave preliminary consent, and then learned that he would carry out secret missions over the USSR. According to the instructions, candidates were given twenty-four hours to make a final decision. As a result, Powers agreed, after which he underwent a series of interviews, including with psychologists, as well as a medical examination and a lie detector test.

On 13 May, Powers was officially retired, and then signed a contract with the CIA as a civilian. At the end of May, the group arrived at Area 51. After a course in theory and studying technology, test flights began. In the first of them, Powers got a little nervous and forgot to remove the landing gear after take-off. However, this did not prevent him from gaining an altitude of 22,000m and only realising his mistake when landing! But not all pilots studied well. On 31 August, during a night training flight in a U-2A (registration number 56-6687), Frank Greys was killed when he lost his bearings and collided with a telephone pole.

At the end of August, the training course was completed and preparations began for the transfer of a new detachment to the Incirlik air base in Turkey. It was located 8km from Adana near the Mediterranean coast. The construction of the base was planned back in 1943, but it was actually started only in the spring of 1951. In December 1954, the American government signed an agreement with Turkey on the joint use of Incirlik, and in February of the following year the facility was named Adana air base. It was renamed Incirlik only in 1958. During the Cold War and later, this air base played a crucial role, as it was located near the southern borders of the Soviet Union and the Middle East.

On 1 May 1956, the Americans reached an agreement with Turkish Prime Minister Ali Adnan Ertekin Menderes to base secret reconnaissance aircraft there. At the same time, he knew that flights over the Soviet Union would be carried out from Turkish territory. The United States also received the consent of another important Asian ally, Pakistan, to use airfields in Peshawar and Lahore. By early September, five U-2s had already been delivered to Incirlik, which were placed in carefully guarded hangars. As a cover legend, Detachment B was named the 2nd (temporary) Meteorological Reconnaissance Squadron (2.WRS(P)). However, the first targets of the 'meteorologists', to the considerable surprise of the pilots, was not the USSR at all, but Israel and the Middle East.

On 26 July 1956, Egyptian President Gamal Abdel Nasser, having previously secured Khrushchev's full support, suddenly announced the nationalisation of the Suez Canal. This caused a huge international scandal and a harsh reaction from France and Great Britain. Their governments declared the decision on nationalisation illegal and promised to take tough measures to protect their national interests. In August, a transfer of additional troops and aircraft to the eastern Mediterranean began. At the same time, Britain and France acted without the knowledge of their main NATO ally, the United States. However, the CIA reported to President Eisenhower in mid-August that its allies were preparing a military operation against Egypt. The same information was received from numerous sources in London, Paris and Tel Aviv.

As a result, a worried Eisenhower authorised an aerial reconnaissance operation against United Kingdom and French forces and Israel. On 27 August, Detachment A in Wiesbaden received a secret order for Mission 1104 and Mission 1105. On 29 August, two U-2 missions were completed, and the next day two more. After taking off from Wiesbaden, the reconnaissance planes passed over Malta, Cyprus, Egypt, Jordan, Lebanon and Syria. On the way back, the planes landed at Incirlik, and from there, after refuelling, they returned to Germany. The aerial photographs obtained made it possible to establish that British troops were concentrating on Malta and Cyprus.

As a result, an Emergency Committee was established in Washington on 12 September, which included representatives of the CIA, the State Department, the National Security Council, the army, navy and the USAF. This level of seriousness was due to Eisenhower's concern over a possible escalation of an already tense international situation. He believed that by all possible means it was necessary to avoid provoking the Soviet leadership and Khrushchev personally to retaliatory actions that could lead to a nuclear war. The president understood that any military operation against Egypt was very risky and believed that the problem of the Suez Canal was simply not worth it (sooner or later it would have to be returned to its owners anyway).

In the first half of September, Detachment A performed eight more flights over the Middle East. At the same time, the unit suffered its first loss. On 17 September, U-2 No. 346 56-6679 crashed over the territory of Germany. The plane crashed into a forest, and the pilot was killed. At the same time, information about the crash of a mysterious, unmarked plane was leaked to the West German press. On 11 September, the first flight to the Suez Canal area was made by Detachment B from Incirlik. On 27 September, Francis Gary Powers went on a mission for the first time. He conducted aerial photography of the Mediterranean Sea in the Malta area. Several groups of French and British warships were captured in the photographs.

During October, U-2s completed nine sorties, the targets of which were Egypt, Israel, Malta and even the French port of Toulon. A lot of intelligence information was received about the concentration of French and British troops, their numbers and types of weapons. It turned out that the Israelis had at least sixty Mirage aircraft, as well as a significant number of Vautour II bombers.

The crisis was growing, and on 23 October a new, dangerous event suddenly occurred. The anti-Soviet revolution began in Hungary. The government of Imre Nagy came to power, which announced a change of political course and reforms in the country. Allen Dulles immediately suggested that Eisenhower authorise U-2 flights over Hungary and provide support to the opposition. But the White House seriously feared that, afraid of losing control over Eastern Europe and Egypt at the same time, Khrushchev might lose his head and go to extreme measures, the extent of which they were afraid to even think about.

Meanwhile, on 28 October, after another U-2 flight over Cyprus, RAF Canberra bombers were seen at Akrotiri airfield. Comparing data from different sources, the CIA concluded that the invasion of Egypt was about to begin. At a meeting at the State Department, CIA Deputy Director Robert Amory said: 'I am sure that the Israelis will start attacking shortly after midnight tomorrow ... I guarantee that the war will start tomorrow or the next day.'

On the afternoon of 29 October, a U-2 piloted by Powers made another flight over Egypt. When he flew over the Sinai Peninsula at an altitude of 23km, Powers saw through the visor that something was happening below. Black clouds of smoke rose over the desert, and in places the flashes of gunfire were clearly visible ...

Israel launched a military operation between 14.15 and 14.35. Two pairs of piston-engined P-51 Mustang fighters were flying at low level over the desert, but not at all in order to launch the first airstrike on Egypt. Their target was aerial telephone lines connecting units of the 3rd Egyptian Infantry

Division and the Palestinian 8th Division with other units and headquarters. The Mustangs cut down the wires with their propellers, paralysing communication. Then sixteen C-47 transport aircraft, accompanied by ten Gloster Meteors, swept at low level towards the Mitla Pass, located 20km east of the canal. At 17.00, a landing party consisting of two battalions of Colonel Ariel Sharon's 202nd Parachute Brigade was dropped there. They had to hold the pass until the approach of Israeli tanks and trucks with infantry. At 22.30 on 30 October, after making a 105-mile dash through the desert, this group reached its goal.

At about the same time, the Egyptian government received a joint Anglo-French ultimatum demanding that all its troops withdraw 10 miles west of the Suez Canal. The ultimatum expired at 04.30 the next day. Of course, Nasser rejected all the demands and did not give an answer. Israeli troops faced fierce resistance and were bombed by Egyptian aircraft, constantly looking at the sky, not understanding why there were no British and French planes in it. They were not informed that the Allies had decided to postpone the attack until dark for military and political reasons.

Even before the expiration of the twelve-hour ultimatum, the war at sea began. The Egyptian destroyer *Ibrahim al-Awal* (a former British escort destroyer of the Hunt-class built in 1940) opened fire with its 4.5-in guns. After that, it was attacked by a French destroyer and Israeli aircraft, and then boarded. On the evening of 31 October, RAF Canberra B.2s and Valiant bombers took off from Cyprus and carried out the first major air attacks against the Egyptian airfields of Almaza,

Abu Suweir, Inhas and Kabrit, which lasted until dawn. As a result of these strikes, more than 100 aircraft were destroyed.

Early on the morning of 1 November, a U-2 from Detachment B took off from Incirlik and headed towards Egypt. The CIA needed a complete picture of what was happening, so the aircraft circled over the war zone for two hours. The photos showed Almaza airfield before the bombing and ten minutes after it. The total result of the attacks on airfields was as follows: 260 Egyptian aircraft were destroyed. However, the Arabs were still able to evacuate most of their new Soviet-made aircraft (MiG-15 fighters) to Syria and Saudi Arabia, and Il-28 jet bombers were transferred inland to Luxor air base.

After that, British and French aircraft launched air attacks against other Egyptian targets; the cities of Cairo, Alexandria, Suez, and Port Said. However, the operation, code-named Musketeer, did not go exactly according to plan. On the night of 30 October–1 November, the British cruiser *Newfoundland* and the destroyer *Diana* sank the Egyptian corvette *Damietta* (a former English River-type corvette of the first series) at the southern end of the Suez Canal. On 3 November, four Israeli aircraft mistakenly attacked the British frigate *Crane* in the Gulf of Suez. The ship was damaged and also shot down one of the attackers. In addition, British bombers attacked the Egyptian ship *Akka* in the Suez Canal. It was 105m long and was filled with cement and debris specifically to block the canal. The British also bombed the El Ferdan Bridge, the wreckage of which collapsed into the river. As a result, the main objective of the operation – to keep the waterway to the Red Sea open – failed at the very beginning of the military campaign. In total, from

31 October to 5 November, Anglo–French aircraft carried out more than 2,000 sorties. The neighbourhoods of Port Said were the most severely affected, and tens of thousands of residents of the impoverished country were left homeless. On the evening of 5 November, British and French paratroopers landed in the Port Said area. At the same time, Soviet troops began to storm Budapest.

In early November 1956, given that crises had arisen simultaneously in Hungary and Egypt, the world was on the verge of a major war for the first time since the Korean War. On 31 October, Khrushchev said at a meeting of the Central Committee of the CPSU: 'If we leave Hungary, it will cheer up the Americans, the British and the French imperialists. They will understand our weakness and will attack.' It was decided to create a Revolutionary Workers' and Peasants Government headed by János Kádár and conduct a military operation to overthrow the government of Imre Nagy. At the same time, the Soviet Union openly supported Egypt and even threatened to use a nuclear bomb against Israel. On 5 November, the head of the Soviet government, Nikolai Bulganin, warned the governments of Britain, France and Israel that the Soviet Union had ballistic missiles equipped with nuclear warheads and could punish the aggressors.

However, the most sensational event took place on 5 November. On this day, Bulganin officially proposed to Eisenhower that the US and USSR should form a military alliance against Great Britain and France. Bulganin's message said:

The Soviet Union and the United States of America are permanent members of the UN Security Council and two great powers possessing all modern types of weapons, including nuclear weapons and thermonuclear weapons. We have a special responsibility to stop the war and restore peace and tranquility in the Middle East region ... Mr. President, in these terrible hours, when the most exalted principles of morality, foundations and goals of the United Nations are being tested, the Soviet Government appeals to the Government of the United States of America with a proposal for close cooperation to stop aggression and stop further bloodshed. The United States has a strong navy in the Mediterranean Sea area, and the Soviet Union also has a strong navy and powerful aviation. The joint use of these assets by the United States and the Soviet Union, according to the UN decision, would be a reliable means to prevent aggression against Egypt.

Bulganin argued that if action was not taken, the actions of Britain and France would lead to the Third World War. Therefore, he proposed to Eisenhower to achieve a UN resolution condemning aggression, after which he would launch a joint Soviet–American military operation in the Mediterranean Sea.

This unexpected diplomatic step on the part of the USSR actually showed Khrushchev's true intentions and desires. The new Soviet leader believed that Western Europe had fallen into decline, and the main goals of Great Britain and France were to preserve the remnants of their colonial empires. After learning that Eisenhower condemned the attack on Egypt, Khrushchev decided that a split in NATO was beginning. At that time, the

North Atlantic Treaty Organisation had existed for only seven years and still did not look like a stable union. According to Khrushchev, Britain and France, by their actions, undermined the authority of NATO, disgraced the UN and damaged their relations with the United States. In this situation, he saw a chance for an alliance between the Soviet Union and the United States. It was these two superpowers, in his opinion, that were supposed to define the new world order.

Khrushchev's position was also supported by the absence of US intervention in the Hungarian events. The fact that the Americans did not openly support the rebels also indicated a split in NATO. A propaganda campaign against Great Britain and France was launched in the USSR. Thousands of rallies were held in factories, universities and schools. The population was being prepared for the worst. The Soviet newspaper *Pravda* wrote:

Why are the British and French shooting at Egyptian peasants? Who gave the right to attack peaceful people? England and France do not need free navigation on the canal, but profits from it. The imperialists forget that the Egyptian people paid with hundreds of lives of their sons who built this canal. Hands off Egypt!

The *Gorkovskaya Pravda* newspaper reported:

Yesterday at the Metalist plant in the city of Gorky was held a factory-wide rally under the slogan 'Hands off Egypt'. Locksmith A.V. Frolov took to the podium. With a feeling of deep indignation, he spoke about the aggressive actions of the interventionists, about the enormous destruction they had caused in this peaceful country. Comrade Frolov made a proposal: to express united solidarity to the people of Egypt, to provide them with financial assistance. Following the locksmith Frolov, other metal workers spoke at the rally. All of them with great unanimity supported the statement of their workmate and confirmed their determination to work two hours over the shift schedule and contribute the money they earned to the fund to help the people of Egypt.

Funds were collected in many collectives, schools and kindergartens. The students deducted part of their scholarship to give it to their Arab brothers.

While the Soviet people were indignant about the shooting of Egyptian peasants, their own army stormed Budapest. The newspapers opened a permanent column called 'On the situation in Hungary', in which they covered the events taking place there every day. On 2 November, it was reported:

The last days in the capital of Hungary and the province have been marked by outrages and rampant counterrevolutionary gangs. The premises of many public and party organisations were destroyed, mass massacres and murders of public figures were committed. Planes leave almost continuously from Austrian airfields to Budapest. Hundreds of Hungarian soldiers from the West, former officers of Horthy's army, hundreds of

Hungarian officers and soldiers who served in Hitler's army are being transported to Hungary.

All this caused the just indignation of the people. For example, a rally of wire shop workers was held at the Krasnaya Etna plant. The people who spoke expressed indignation at the 'revival of fascism' in Hungary and the atrocities of 'counter-revolutionary gangs'. As a result, the participants adopted a resolution to send to the Soviet government calling for support for the 'people's government' of János Kádár. And the 'will of the workers' was fulfilled.

On 7 November, the column 'On the situation in Hungary' reported:

The joyful news has been received that the Hungarian people have created a Revolutionary Workers' and Peasants' government headed by Janos Kadar, and with the support of Soviet troops stationed in Hungary they have overthrown the reactionary government of Imre Nagy, who betrayed the Hungarian people and the Hungarian nation. The Hungarian people defeated the plans of the counter-revolution and took control of the situation in Hungary. Our Hungarian brothers, caught in the grip of counterrevolutionary terror, have been released. Hungary has once again received a guarantee for the further development of socialism, national independence and people's democracy. The Hungarian people achieved victory with the help of the Soviet Union. The position of the Soviet Union in relation to the Hungarian events is the absolutely correct position of proletarian internationalism. The Soviet Union respects the territorial integrity and sovereignty of the Hungarian People's Republic and does not interfere in the internal affairs of Hungary. However, the Soviet government and the Soviet people cannot calmly watch as the Hungarian people became slaves to fascism.

Many American politicians put serious pressure on Eisenhower. They believed that the events in Hungary could be the beginning of the end of the Soviet system. In this regard, they asked him to authorise the delivery of weapons and ammunition to the rebels, as well as U-2 flights over the country in order to objectively assess the situation. However, the president categorically forbade both, being convinced that it was unthinkable to create an extra reason for a large-scale war at such a crisis moment.

Extraordinary classes on civil defence were held in Soviet factories and plants. Bomb shelters were constantly kept open. All troops in the territory of the Soviet Union and the Warsaw Pact countries were constantly in a state of combat readiness. The crews of the bombers with nuclear bombs on board were waiting for further instructions. But on 6 November, two key events occurred at once that influenced the further course of world history. Firstly, at a time when fierce fighting was taking place in the Port Said and Budapest areas, presidential elections were taking place in the United States, in which Eisenhower won a landslide victory and was re-elected for a second term. Secondly, in the UK, which was not in the best economic situation, a financial crisis broke out, which led to a sharp devaluation of the pound sterling. At the same time, there was a split in the government into opponents and supporters of the war. On the same day, the British, fearing economic disaster, officially turned to the United States for help. But Eisenhower bluntly told Prime Minister Eden that he would give money only if the fighting in Egypt stopped by midnight on 6 November. Eden considered these demands humiliating for Britain, but had to agree out of fear of an even more disastrous financial collapse.

From 7 November to 18 December, U-2s from Detachment B made fourteen flights over the Middle East. The data obtained showed that the truce was generally being implemented, and the Soviet Union did not transfer its bombers to air bases in Syria (the Americans were seriously afraid of this). In December, having failed to achieve their goals, the British, French and Israelis were forced to withdraw their troops from Egypt. It seemed to Khrushchev that he had held his ground everywhere, and Eisenhower was pleased that nuclear war had been avoided again. After that, relations between the two countries thawed. After all, for the first time since the Second World War, they took a common position at the UN on the Suez crisis. Interestingly, in the United States itself, the events in Suez were called the 'Halloween Attack', since the fighting began on 30 October, the day when this peculiar holiday is celebrated in the country.

However, all this did not prevent the newly re-elected President Eisenhower from authorising new U-2 flights over the USSR on 15 November.

Chapter 4

The Dark Territory

In Search of Rockets

On 20 November, Francis Powers from Detachment B took off from Incirlik. Half an hour after the launch, the pilot pressed the button on the radio transmitter – it was a signal that everything was going according to plan. The base responded with a special short signal, which meant that Powers should then act in accordance with the task. At first, the U–2 flew east, passing over the northern part of Iraq and Iran, after which it turned towards Armenia. The aircraft made several zigzags over the Soviet territory, photographing the Sangachaly air base and the Baku area. After that, Powers noticed some failures in some of his electrical equipment and decided to return to base. Mission 4016 was not fully completed, while no actions of the Soviet air defence were recorded. On 10 December, two flights took place at once (Mission 4018 and Mission 2029), the targets of which were military facilities in the Warsaw Pact countries: Yugoslavia, Albania and Bulgaria. One U–2 took off from Incirlik and the second from Giebelstadt in Germany. The second was flown by Carmen Vito from Detachment A. During the flight over the Balkans, several fighters tried to intercept the aircraft, but none of them could gain the necessary altitude.

Meanwhile, with Eisenhower's approval, on 11 December, three new RB-57D high-altitude reconnaissance aircraft of the USAF made reconnaissance flights over Soviet territory in the Vladivostok area. According to technical data, this modification of the B-57 bomber was similar to the U-2: the speed was 800km/h, the maximum flight altitude was 19,500m. The military convinced the president that the new Canberra had similar characteristics to the U-2 and that the Russians would not only be unable to intercept, but even track it. The first part of the statement turned out to be correct: the MiG-17s scrambled to intercept could not gain the necessary height. However, the Russians did identify the flight routes of the violators and their type – 'B-57'. After that, on 15 December, the American ambassador in Moscow received a note of protest from the USSR.

On 18 December, an angry Eisenhower banned further planned reconnaissance flights over the USSR. In the near future, U-2s were supposed to be limited to sorties along the Soviet borders using equipment for radio interception and radar tracking. But the president did not accept the proposals of his colleagues to repent and admit guilt. On 11 January, an American response note stated that 'only routine training flights authorised by the USAF command were conducted in the area of the Sea of Japan'.

After that, a six-month period of U-2 flights along the southern borders of the Soviet Union began. The first of them (Mission 4019) took place on 22 December 1956. The plane from Detachment B flew along the border from the Black Sea to the Caspian Sea, and then along the border with Afghanistan. The next, Mission 4020, was completed on 18 March 1957. At the same time, there were problems with the compass and the pilot made a mistake when calculating the course. Due to cloudy weather, the pilot realised that he was flying over Soviet territory only when he saw several MiG-19 fighters through his visor.

According to Soviet information, the intruder crossed the border three times. The first time the plane entered Russian airspace in the Hasan Kuli area (it was across the border for about five minutes), the second time in the Astana area (about eight minutes) and the third was south-west of Imishli. In the latter case, the U-2 was over Armenia and Georgia for almost an hour, after which it left for Turkey in the Batumi area. Eleven fighters from the Baku Air Defence District and the Transcaucasian Military District were scrambled to intercept. The target was at an unattainable altitude for almost the entire route, but shortly before crossing the Turkish border it dropped to 11,000m. At that moment, there was one MiG-17PF nearby, which took off from Meria airfield. The pilot, Senior Lieutenant Mikhail Georgiev, reported back to base that he saw a target on his radar sight but it was already flying over Turkey at that moment. Therefore, there was no order to intercept and destroy.

Meanwhile, at the end of 1956, the training of the third group of U-2 pilots was completed at Area 51. Detachment C was formed from them. There was one technical loss during the training programme. On 19 December, during a training flight over Arizona, U-2A No. 357 56-6690, pilot Bob Ericson, suffered an oxygen system failure at an altitude of 10,500m. The pilot ejected and landed safely, and the plane crashed into the territory of the Navajo Indian Reservation. In January of the following year, the pilots arrived in strict secrecy at Atsugi air base near Tokyo in Japan. The Americans did not inform the local government about the upcoming operations and the true purpose of the arriving aircraft. For six months, the pilots flew training flights over the Sea of Japan.

American intelligence knew that most of the plants associated with the creation and production of nuclear and missile weapons were located not in the densely populated western part of the USSR, but in the sparsely populated Asian part of the country. This area was bounded on the west by the Caspian Sea and the Volga, and on the east by Lake Baikal and the Lena River. This huge region, 3,000km long, was a dark territory. It was mostly covered with monotonous steppes and deserts with an underdeveloped railway network and a small number of cities. Foreigners hardly ever visited these spaces. The 'dark territory' was very far from the allied countries of the United States. For example, there were 2,400km from Turkey to the area of Lake Balkhash, where, according to the CIA, Soviet nuclear tests were conducted (the exact sector was not known). Chita, the nearest major industrial centre, is about 2,000km from Japan. From the south and south-east, Soviet Central Asia was reliably covered by the boundless expanses of China and Mongolia. And only the territory of Pakistan was relatively close to Kazakhstan and Western Siberia.

Back in October 1954, the USAF signed a contract with General Electric for the construction of a powerful long-range radar station on the territory of Turkey. The world's most powerful (at that time) AN/FPS-17 radar, code-named 'XW-1', was designed to track Soviet missile launches. It was equipped with a huge antenna with a radius of 53m and could record take-offs and initial flight parameters of missiles at a distance of up to 4,000km. The radar station was located in a deserted mountainous area in the vicinity of Diyarbakir in the east of the country. The facility was commissioned on 1 June 1955 and two weeks later recorded the launch of a rocket from the Kapustin Yar test site in the Astrakhan region.

On the morning of 2 February 1956, AN/FPS-17 recorded another launch of a ballistic missile towards the Aral Sea, however, the fact that a nuclear explosion occurred after falling on a target was not recorded. In fact, on this day, in an atmosphere of strict secrecy, the Soviets conducted Operation Baikal. Launched from launch pad No. 4, the R-5M ballistic missile with a nuclear warhead flew 1,190km and fell ten and a half minutes later in the Aral Karakum desert (150km north-east of the city of Aralsk). The power of the nuclear explosion was 0.5 kilotons.

On 15 May 1957, AN/FPS-17 recorded another take-off of a non-conventional ballistic missile that landed near the Kamchatka Peninsula. It became clear that the Soviet Union had created the first intercontinental ballistic missile with a range of 4,000km. In NATO, it was designated SS-6 'Sapwood' but it was named the R-7 rocket by the Soviets. After studying the flight path, American experts came to the conclusion that the launch was carried out from somewhere in the central part of Kazakhstan and the Soviets had used a new proving ground on the Kamchatka Peninsula as a target.

On 7 June, a U-2 from Detachment G took off from Eielson Air Force Base in Alaska. The aircraft was supposed to fly over the Kamchatka Peninsula in order to identify the crash site of Soviet ballistic missiles. However, on approach to the target area, the pilot found that it was covered with clouds. A repeat mission (Mission 6005) took place on 19 June. This time the weather was clear, and the U-2 photographed most of Kamchatka. The new Klyuchi missile site had been discovered and photographed. Now the CIA knew where the ballistic missiles were falling, but still did not know where they were coming from.

There were even more mysteries surrounding the Soviet nuclear programme. In the Soviet Union itself, the location of nuclear explosions was carefully hidden from the very beginning. After the first nuclear bomb was detonated at the Semipalatinsk test site on 29 August 1949, the Soviet media did not inform their population. The Soviets admitted to the test only after President Truman officially stated that 'a nuclear explosion occurred in the USSR in one of the last weeks'. On 27 September, a month after the explosion, Russian newspapers published a TASS report, but it did not say anything about the test. Russian newspapers wrote:

As you know, large-scale construction works are under way in the Soviet Union: construction of hydroelectric power plants, mines, water channels, roads, which necessitate large-scale blasting operations using the latest technical means. Since these explosions occurred and occur quite often in different parts of the country, it is possible that this could attract attention outside the Soviet Union. As for the production of atomic energy, TASS considers it necessary to recall that on November 6, 1947, the Minister of Foreign Affairs of the USSR Vyacheslav Molotov made a statement regarding the secret of the atomic bomb, saying that this secret had long since ceased to exist. This statement meant that the Soviet Union had long ago discovered the secret of atomic weapons.

This rather vague and confusing message hinted that there had been no nuclear tests recently, it was just that something had exploded so violently at a construction site that it could be heard in America, and it also hinted that the Soviets had had an atomic bomb for a long time. With this confusion, Stalin sought to fog up the Soviet atomic programme, which lagged far behind the American one, and hide the true state of affairs in an industry that was still being created.

Based on acoustic tracking data collected over several years, the Americans established that the Soviet nuclear test site was located in Kazakhstan somewhere near the city of Semipalatinsk. This small town was located on the western bank of the Irtysh River. The epicentres of the explosions were determined with an error of 300–400km, so the exact location of the landfill and its size remained unknown. In addition, American intelligence established that to the north of Tomsk (1,000km north-east of Semipalatinsk), somewhere in the area of the Tomsk-2 railway station, there was a secret site associated with the production of nuclear weapons.

Back in early 1951, the CIA learned that a large secret facility was being built in the Krasnoyarsk region, located on the Yenisei River. In reality, it was a mining and chemical plant located in the secret city of Zheleznogorsk. The construction of the largest weapons-grade plutonium production plant in the USSR began in 1950 and ended in 1958. The complex was built inside a mountain range located on the right bank of the Yenisei River north-east of Krasnoyarsk. The mining and chemical plant was hidden at a depth of 200–300m, the underground halls had a height of up to 55m and were designed for a direct hit by a nuclear bomb. The heat produced by the reactor was used to warm buildings in Zheleznogorsk.

In addition, American intelligence received data on a uranium production plant located north-east of Novosibirsk, and on uranium enrichment plants in the Ferghana Valley and south of Alma-Ata. Having summarised all available information about the Soviet nuclear industry, the CIA began to prepare flight plans and routes over the 'dark territories' of Soviet Asia. The operation was code-named Soft Touch.

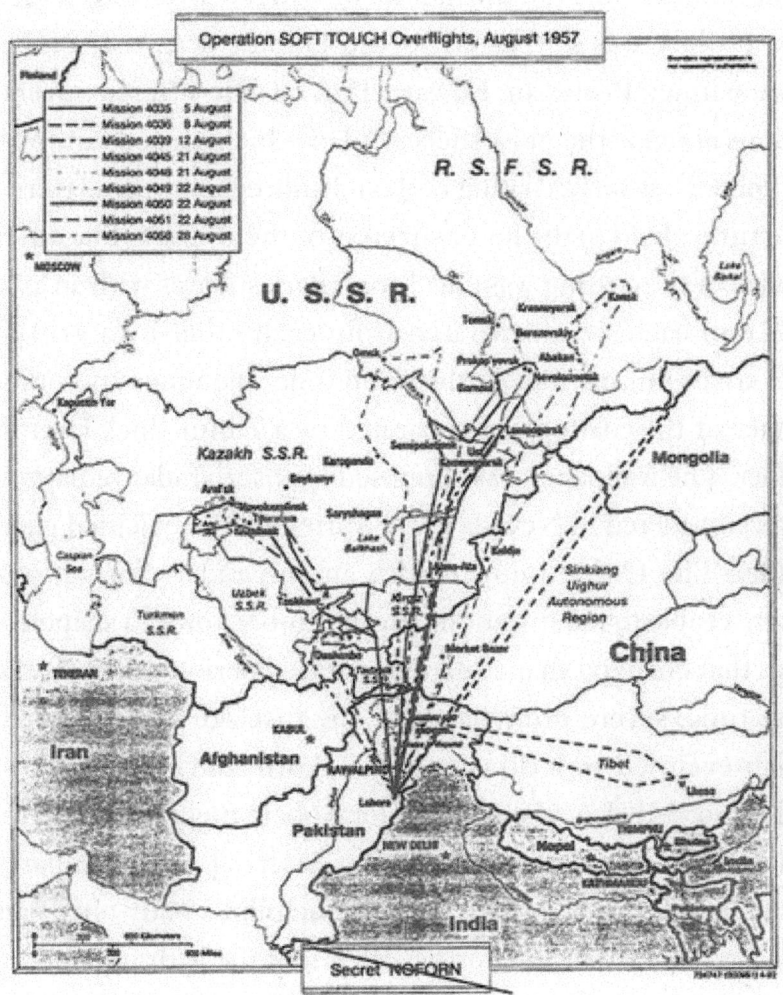

The scheme of the Soft Touch operation.

The First Flight of the Stealth

Meanwhile, an anti-radar coating for the U-2 was being tested in Nevada. The idea to make the aircraft, if not invisible, then at least barely noticeable to imperfect Soviet radar stations arose in the summer of 1956 during the first flights over the USSR. The project was entrusted to the famous scientist, Nobel Prize winner Professor Edward Purcell. He offered several options at once, the most successful of which turned out to be 'wallpaper'. It was a coating of flexible fibreglass with a layered structure, glued to the lower surfaces of the aircraft. The outer surface of the coating was checkered: dark squares with an area of 21mm each were separated from each other by a grid of steel strips 4mm wide. At the same time, the inner and outer surface of the coating was separated by a 7-mm-thick layer of rubber. The wallpaper was supposed to absorb radar radiation. Tests conducted in Nevada in the spring of 1957 yielded good results. The U-2, equipped with an anti-radar coating, was poorly visible to radar stations (the monitor showed a shapeless mark that changed shape and disappeared periodically). At the same time, severe overheating of the fuselage was recorded, which even led to a disaster. On 2 April, during a flight in U-2A No. 341, Lockheed test pilot Robert Sieker lost control and crashed in a remote area of the desert. The search party was able to locate the crash site and the pilot's body only four days later. The investigation revealed that the hydraulic pump had failed due to overheating, which led to engine failure. Due to the pressure drop inside the cabin, Sieker's spacesuit began to inflate, he lost consciousness, then regained consciousness at low altitude and ejected. The pilot hit the tailplane and died. The disaster also refuted the assumption that after falling from such a great height, the U-2 would be totally destroyed and no one would be able to determine its true purpose. The aircraft was severely deformed but the camera equipment and radar were only slightly damaged. Despite these troubles, the tests were recognised as successful, and in fact they became the beginning of Lockheed's work on stealth technology. On 6 May, the results were reported to Eisenhower. Despite some doubts about the invisibility, he still gave permission for Operation Soft Touch.

But However, before sending the 'invisible' U-2 over the USSR, they decided to test it in semi-combat conditions. On 21 July, a modified reconnaissance aircraft from Detachment B flew over Syria, Lebanon and Egypt. And on 31 July, the same aircraft, piloted by James Cherbonneaux, flew over the Black Sea. For several hours, the U-2, equipped with equipment for recording radar signals, flew along the coast of Crimea and the Caucasus. Returning to base, Cherbonneaux said that the

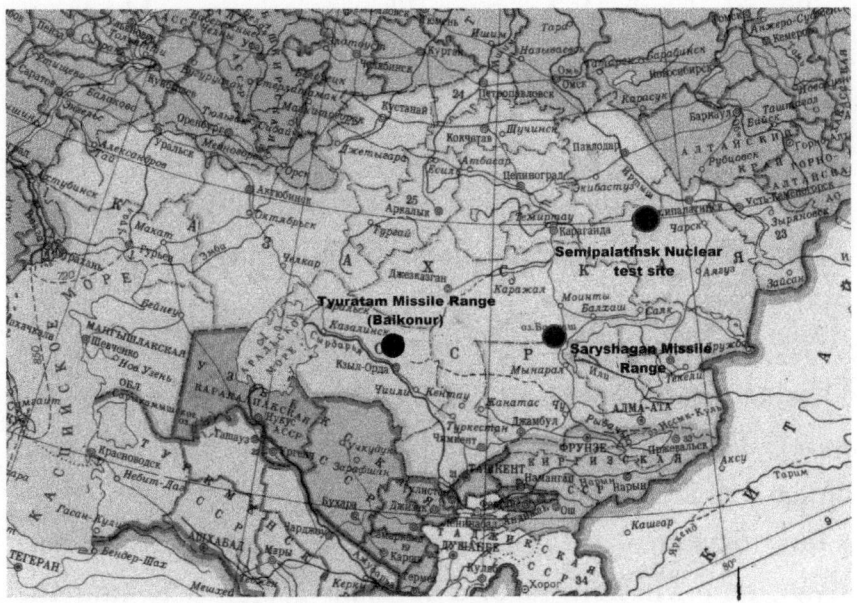

The location of the main secret objects on the map of the Kazakh SSR.

Russians quickly discovered him and monitored the flight, as radar radiation from Soviet sites was recorded dozens of times. According to Soviet information, their air defence recorded an unidentified target located 100–130km from the coast. However, the Russians could not accurately determine the altitude of the aircraft and identify it.

The Americans believed that the Soviet air defence in the 'dark territory' was much weaker than in the western part of the USSR and was significantly sparser, so the wallpaper would definitely work there. In addition, by this point, the U-2s were equipped with advanced 'B'-type cameras. Their HR73B1 lens consisted of ten lenses with a focal resolution of 36in and a aperture of ten units, and could cover the entire surface bounded by the horizon. At the same time, the resolution was 100 strokes per millimetre, compared with 60 strokes per millimetre for the A-2 camera. The equipment could operate in two modes, taking both vertical and angular photographs. In the vertical image taken from a height of 21,000m, objects up to 70cm long could be clearly seen. In the images taken at a high angle, the lenses covered an area with a diameter of 185km. At that time, it was the best photographic equipment in the world.

By early August, eight pilots and ground staff from Detachment B were flown to the Peshawar air base in Pakistan in a C-124. On 4 August, the first test flight was performed along the Soviet border over the northwestern regions of China to Mongolia. The next day, the U-2, piloted by Eugene Evan, flew Mission 4035. The main goal was to find the alleged launch site of Russian ballistic missiles. The Americans logically assumed that this facility should be located near a railway, which would have delivered the missiles themselves, as well as fuel and other cargo. In addition, there should be a river or a large body of water nearby, since rocket launches required a large amount of water for technical purposes and the daily life of the test site. Therefore, the flight route was along the Tashkent–Aralsk railway, which runs east of the Aral Sea and along the Syr Darya River.

The Soviet air defences did not record the reconnaissance flight, so the Americans decided that this was proof of the effectiveness of anti-radar coverage. In fact, there were simply no powerful radars in the territory over which Eugene Evan was flying. The study of the obtained photographs as a whole showed nothing interesting, except endless desert and steppe landscapes with underdeveloped roads. In just one of the photos taken at an angle, a strange structure was discovered, located 25km from the railway. The decryption team concluded that this was probably the launch pad for the rockets. Since the object was relatively close to the air base in Peshawar (about 1,500km), it was decided to postpone further study until a later date, when more distant goals would be achieved.

The next flight took place on 11 August, but it turned out to be fruitless due to camera failure. Then, on 20 August, a U-2 flown by Sammy Snyder set off on Mission 4045. After passing along the Soviet–Chinese border over Lake Balkhash, the reconnaissance aircraft headed north-east. Snyder flew near Semipalatinsk, but did not find the nuclear test site. Next, he took aerial photographs of Biysk and Novokuznetsk, after which he headed for Krasnoyarsk. However, in the area of

Abakan, a band of continuous clouds began, which stretched along the Yenisei riverbed. As a result, it was not possible to photograph the target (although the U-2 flew directly over it), and Snyder headed west towards Tomsk. There, 2,800km from its base, the U-2 photographed a huge nuclear complex, which, according to American information, included a uranium enrichment plant, a nuclear reactor, a plutonium production plant, as well as a large village with many administrative, scientific and residential buildings.

The complex was the secret city of Seversk. Back in March 1949, the Soviet government adopted a resolution on the establishment of a plant for the production of highly enriched uranium-235 and plutonium-239 near Tomsk. Initially, it had the code name 'Mailbox No. 5' (the name was known to the CIA), and in 1954 it was renamed Seversk (aka Tomsk-7). The nuclear reactor photographed by Snyder's U-2 was the industrial nuclear power plant NPP-1 (aka Siberian NPP) with a capacity of 100 megawatts, commissioned in 1958.

On the way back, Snyder flew over a city that had not been mapped before – Berezovsky (actually Berezniki). A uranium mining plant was also discovered there.

On 21 August, the next flight, Mission 4050, took place. Pilot James Cherbonneaux headed north-east, and then due north to Semipalatinsk. After seventy-five minutes, when the city lost in the endless steppe was not far away, he saw clear, ring-like contours. Soon, Cherbonneaux saw a metal tower, apparently with an atomic bomb mounted on it. The pilot experienced rather unpleasant emotions, as he was afraid that an explosion could happen any minute right under him!

And this fear was not unfounded. On 22 August – the next day – a thermonuclear explosion with a capacity of 520 kilotons was produced at the experimental field, which was recorded by American tracking stations (the Americans identified it as a nuclear explosion with a capacity of 0.5 megatons). However, the bomb itself was dropped from an aircraft and exploded at an altitude of 1,880m. As for the bomb on the tower, it is likely Cherbonneaux saw one of the control towers designed to measure the parameters of the explosion. In fact, the last ground-based nuclear test (the RDS-9 bomb) at the Semipalatinsk test site had occurred on 19 October 1954 and ended unsuccessfully (there was no explosion, and plutonium was simply scattered around the test site). In future only aerial (atmospheric) tests of nuclear bombs dropped from aircraft were carried out at this test site. In 1957 the Soviets began to conduct most of its tests in the Arctic Ocean, in the Novaya Zemlya archipelago.

After Semipalatinsk, Cherbonneaux flew to Omsk, on the right bank of the Irtysh. He photographed all the facilities in the city, including aviation plant No. 166. In the 1950s, it was engaged in the production of Il-28 jet bombers (758 examples were produced) and the first Tu-104 jet passenger aircraft. At the moment when the facility (now the Polet plant) was photographed by the reconnaissance aircraft, its conversion to the production of ballistic missiles had already begun.

On the way back, in the area of Lake Issyk Kul, the U-2 experienced engine issues, but in front of him the pilot saw the peaks of the two highest mountains of the Pamirs: Kongur (7,579m above sea level) and Stalin Peak (7,495m). The first was located on the territory of China, and the second was on the territory of the USSR. During Operation Soft Touch, these two mountain peaks were the 'gates' of the dark territory. Upon returning from the mission, the Kongur on the left pointed the course towards Pakistan, the only friendly country for Americans in this vast and wild region of the globe. Another landmark in this lifeless mountain desert was the pyramidal peak of Khan Tengri, located 500km north-east of Kongur and the highest point of the Tien Shan mountain range.

After a nine-hour flight, the U-2 landed safely in Peshawar. At the same time, no Soviet air defence activity was recorded along the entire route. Prior to this flight, American intelligence believed that the centre of atomic testing was located 120km east of Semipalatinsk. Therefore, it was not detected during previous missions. In fact, the landfill was located 130km west of this city on the left bank of the Irtysh (at the junction of the Semipalatinsk, Karaganda and Pavlodar regions).

The flight of James Cherbonneaux was the last in the framework of the operation. However, on 21 August, the AN/FPS-17 tracking radar in Turkey recorded the launch of a ballistic missile from the area east of the Aral Sea. It was flying towards Kamchatka. The training warhead separated from the second stage and burned up in the atmosphere, but the Soviet government declared the test a success. 'A few days ago, an ultra-long-range multistage ballistic missile was launched. The test was successful. It fully confirmed the correctness of the calculations and the chosen design,' TASS reported five days later. After that, the CIA immediately turned to Eisenhower with a request to authorise another flight to the 'Tyuratam' test site. The Americans gave this conditional name to an unknown site from which Soviet ballistic missiles were launched. Given the huge response and concern in American society caused by the TASS report, the president gave permission.

On 28 August, a U-2 (Mission 4058) took off from the air base in Incirlik. Since the estimated location of the target was already known, the aircraft was equipped with an old set of A-2 photo cameras that shot vertically downwards. After passing over the Caspian and Black Seas, the aircraft reached the target area. As a result, detailed and high-quality photographs were obtained of the Scientific Research Test Site No. 5 of the Ministry of Defence of the USSR, which later became known as Baikonur. The launch pad was a giant metal platform hanging over a large pit that absorbed the flames from the rocket engine nozzles. A railway line led to the site, along which the missiles themselves were delivered. The photos obtained of 'Tyuratam' allowed the CIA to make a large-scale mock-up of this complex. The test site was built specifically for testing R-7 ballistic missiles. They were designed to deliver thermonuclear charges, and at the same time served as prototypes for space rockets.

On 10 September, another mission was completed – over the Kapustin Yar missile range. At the same time, a rocket was photographed, which was on the launch pad and was already preparing for launch. And on 15–16 September a U-2 from Detachment C in Japan flew over Kamchatka, that is, the area where ballistic missiles launched from Central Asia fell.

The flights carried out from 4 August to 10 September 1957, including as part of Operation Soft Touch, yielded more results than the CIA had expected. Even Allen Dulles, upon learning that a huge nuclear complex (Seversk) was photographed in the Tomsk region, surrounded by huge impassable swamps, was very surprised. He was even more amazed when he saw the images and the analysts' report. The complex on the right bank of the Tom River covered an area of 40 sq km, had its own thermal power plant, and food processing plant located next to uranium enrichment facilities. Analysts concluded that the production capacity of the zone was about 17% of all similar enterprises in the United States.

Thanks to the U-2 flights, in just five weeks, the huge 'dark territory' in Soviet Central Asia and Siberia became much brighter for the Americans. Dozens of large and hundreds of small military installations were plotted on maps and diagrams. The CIA had obtained a fairly detailed diagram of the Soviet nuclear industry and missile programme. From now on, it was known exactly where the missile launches were made and where the nuclear tests were conducted. The only unfulfilled requirement was the aerial photography of Krasnoyarsk.

Dulles' Plane Lands in Armenia

While the U-2s were flying over Central Asia, the CIA became aware that in October 1957, major manoeuvres of the Soviet Northern Fleet were to take place in the Barents Sea. As a result, it was decided to conduct two missions – one for radio interception and radar tracking of ships, the second for aerial photography of shipyards in Murmansk and Severomorsk. Since one U-2 could not carry a set of cameras and electronic tracking equipment at the same time, two flights were required. At the end of September, Eisenhower authorised both.

On 11 October, U-2B No. 351 from Detachment A took off on Mission 2073 from Giebelstadt airfield in Germany. On the eve of the operation, the aircraft was seriously modernised. In addition to the 'wallpaper', the U-2 was equipped with the latest radar reconnaissance system, consisting of eleven receivers that recorded radio waves in the range from 150 to 4,000MHz. In addition, tanks of 400 litres of fuel each were suspended under the wings. The estimated flight range of such a U-2 reached 7,400km (a combat radius of 3,700km). The aircraft took off at 05.25 and three hours later reached Tromsø on the northeastern tip of Norway. After that, it began to fly in zigzags over the Barents Sea. Despite its 'invisible' coating, the flight over neutral waters was recorded by radar stations of the Russian Northern Air Defence Corps, as well a MiG-17F fighter from the Northern Fleet Air Force. After spending almost ten hours in the air, the U-2 returned safely to base at 15.18.

The next day, the electronic equipment system was removed from U-2B No. 351, and replaced with a set of A-2 cameras. On 13 October, at 06.35, it set off on Mission 2040, a flight over the northeastern part of the USSR. It was assigned to an experienced pilot, Harvey Stockman. Unlike the previous mission, which passed without any problems, this time the aircraft was plagued by continuous troubles. At first, the air conditioning system in the cabin failed, it heated up and the windows fogged up. The pilot had to break radio silence by informing the base about the issue. After receiving instructions from the ground, Stockman managed to adjust the operation of the air conditioner, but soon the engine began to overheat and there was a resulting loss of altitude. However, the pilot managed to cope with this problem as well. Stockman drew attention to the fuel overspending and decided to shorten the route a little. Four hours and fifteen minutes after take-off, the U-2 reached cape North Cape, after which it turned towards the Barents Sea. It reached a point 230km north of the city of Gavrilovo on the Kola Peninsula, after which it abruptly changed course to the south-west. Soon, the aircraft entered Soviet airspace. At an altitude of 21,400m, it passed over Severomorsk, then over Murmansk. The pilot saw all the facilities of the port and the naval bases surrounding it, as well as fifteen to twenty warships and several airfields. The route then passed over Monchegorsk and Pechenga. In the Pechenga area, Stockman saw contrails and then a Soviet MiG-19 fighter. At the same time, engine overheating started again. Nevertheless, the flight continued and in the area of Bolshoy Island, the U-2 left Russian airspace and landed successfully at 15.52. The duration of the flight with extra fuel tanks was nine hours seventeen minutes.

On this occasion, the anti-radar coverage did not work. Soviet radar stations recorded the flight of the intruder when he was moving along the territorial waters, and at 12.50 he crossed the border over the Kola Peninsula and flew deeper into the territory of the USSR. Within an hour, the unidentified aircraft flew 700km along the route: Kharlovka–Severomorsk–Murmansk–Kirovsk–Monchegorsk–Pechenga–Bolschoy Ainov Island. At 13.44 the target left for the territory of

Norway. Seventeen Russian fighters were scrambled to intercept, with two pilots reaching an altitude of 16,000m and visually observing the target, which was at an altitude of 20,000m. Trying to catch up with the intruder, the pilots reached 17,000m (at that moment one of the interceptors was spotted by Stockman), but they could not attack.

After returning to base, the Russian pilots compiled a detailed description of the target. They said the unknown reconnaissance aircraft had very light (silver or white) colouring and long straight wings without engines. At the same time, the target moved slowly (at subsonic speed) and made smooth turns.

After comparing various data and information available at that time (including those in the American and West German press, foreign aviation magazines), Soviet experts came to the conclusion that the mysterious intruder was the 'research' aircraft of the Lockheed company, the U-2. The exact purpose and true parameters of the aircraft were unknown, but some foreign experts suggested that the type was designed for high-altitude reconnaissance flights. This is how the Soviet air defence command first learned what it was dealing with, although there was still no complete certainty about it.

Meanwhile, in September 1957, the CIA decided to disband Detachment A. Firstly, the risk of flights over the western borders of the USSR was recognised as too great, given that the Soviet air defence in this area was the most powerful. Secondly, most of the Russian military and strategic facilities were located in the southern and eastern parts of the vast country. Thirdly, the U-2 flights over Europe had too many witnesses. They were seen by pilots of NATO aircraft, crews of passenger airliners and numerous civilians.

Already on 15 November, all personnel and aircraft of Detachment A were transferred to the United States, and the pilots were sent to other units. For example, Harvey Stockman returned to service in the USAF. In just a year and a half, twenty-three U-2 flights had been carried out from the territory of Germany, including six over the USSR, five over Eastern Europe, and the rest over the Mediterranean Sea.

After that, there was a long break in the secret missions of U-2. President Eisenhower believed that the goals for which the Aquaton project was once conceived had been generally achieved. In addition, the Russians failed either to shoot down the U-2s, nor to collect serious evidence of the violation of their airspace by the Americans. The president considered it a great stroke of luck. At the same time, the international situation remained extremely tense, and an economic downturn began in America itself, complemented by mass protests among the Black population. Being completely preoccupied with internal problems and fearing complications in foreign policy, the president did not authorise new flights for a long time, despite pressure from the State Department and the CIA. It was only at the end of January 1958 that, believing the advice of experts that 'reconnaissance flights have become common practice and no serious reaction should be expected from the Soviets', Eisenhower authorised new missions.

On 28 January, a U-2 from Detachment B flew over Albania (this was the sixth flight over this country). And on 1 March, an example from Detachment C flew over the Far East (Mission

6011). After taking off from Atsugi air base, the aircraft entered Soviet airspace over Sakhalin, after which it passed over Sovetskaya Gavan harbour, Komsomolsk-on-Amur, Svobodny and Khabarovsk. At the same time, aerial photography of the Trans-Siberian railway and several mysterious military facilities was carried out (one of them, in Malaya Sazanka, now Orlynyi, 100km south of Blagoveshchensk, was identified as a 'plant for installing detonators on nuclear charges'). Pilot Tom Krall saw numerous contrails left by Soviet fighters, and realised that the 'wallpaper' clearly did not work. In fact, more than fifty Russian interceptors were scrambled to intercept the aircraft! On the last leg of the flight, the U-2 had engine issues, and it eventually stalled. However, he still returned safely to the base.

A serious reaction followed nevertheless. On 6 March, the American ambassador in Moscow was handed a protest note, which did not provide any details about the violator's flight. However, Eisenhower considered the mission a failure and immediately ordered CIA Director Allen Dulles to cancel all further flights. In a response, the American note said that the United States had no idea what kind of aircraft the Russians were talking about, but would 'take decisive measures' to prevent such possible cases. On 21 April, the Soviets repeated their protest, which described in detail the entire flight route of the reconnaissance aircraft. According to Soviet information, the target, discovered at 03.18 300km south of Vladivostok at an altitude of about 13,000m, was heading north-east in a climb. At 04.05, the intruder entered the airspace of the USSR at an average speed of 500km/h and passed along the route Velikaya Kema–Sovetskaya Gavan–Komsomolsk-on-Amur–Svobodny–Khabarovsk. Then, after staying over Soviet territory for four hours and seven minutes, the aircraft entered the area of neutral waters of the Sea of Japan. The total length of the spy plane's route over the territory of the USSR was 3,200km.

Such a detailed assessment showed that the 'wallpaper' was ineffective in conditions of radar-saturated air defence. This further convinced the US president of the danger of playing with fire. Eisenhower told Dulles that such a U-2 flight could well provoke the outbreak of the Third Word War. He believed Soviets may mistake the intruder for a reconnaissance aircraft sent before the attack and launch a pre-emptive nuclear strike.

During this period, the CIA got into another unpleasant situation. On 27 June, a USAF C-118 Liftmaster transport aircraft (a military version of the Douglas DC-6 civilian transport aircraft, registration number 51-3822), during a flight from Wiesbaden air base to Peshawar via Cyprus and Iran, accidentally invaded the airspace of the Soviet Union near Armenia. Presumably, the pilots confused Lake Sevan with the Turkish Lake Van. There it was suddenly attacked by a pair of Soviet MiG-17PF fighters, piloted by Captain G.F. Svetlichnikov and Captain B.F. Zakharov. There were nine people on board the C-118, including six crew members and three CIA officers. Five of them (Colonel Dale Brennon, Robert Crans, Benny Schupp, Earl Riemer, and Peter Szabo) parachuted out over Soviet territory. Pilot Major Luther Lyles was able to extinguish the flames and make an emergency landing at the Gindarkh

Soviet military airfield (30km south of Yerevan). During the landing, the C–118 was severely damaged, broke apart and burnt out, but the pilot and first navigator, Captain Jane N. Kay; second navigator, First Lieutenant James N. Luther; and Sergeant James Gee were not injured. The incident was settled fairly quickly, and on 7 July, all nine Americans were transferred across the border with Turkey through diplomatic channels. At the same time, there is a version that this was the personal plane of the Director of the CIA (DCI) Allen Dulles. Most likely, the episode was another reason for Eisenhower to postpone the U-2 flights over the USSR.

At the end of 1958, relations between the USSR and the United States deteriorated again. In November, Khrushchev unexpectedly issued an ultimatum in which he demanded that the Allied forces leave West Berlin within six months. In addition, he demanded that the United States, Great Britain and France conclude a peace treaty with both German states. In fact, this meant diplomatic recognition of the GDR and legal recognition of the status quo. In case of refusal, the Soviet leader threatened to conclude a peace treaty with East Germany unilaterally and transfer control of all communications with West Berlin to the Germans. Khrushchev's main goal was to obtain guarantees that West Germany would not start a war and try to annex the GDR. The Allies did not give an immediate response, while simultaneously beginning preparations for a military operation in case of a blockade of West Berlin. It was only on 16 February 1959 that the US government gave an official response to the Soviets. It said that the United States and its allies were ready to use 'all appropriate means' to protect their interests in West Berlin.

Khrushchev was very angry at this ambiguous answer. While Eisenhower considered West Berlin only a symbol of resistance to the Soviet takeover of Europe, the Soviet leadership quite logically believed that it was just a springboard for an attack on the GDR, and that all the arguments about 'interests' were just excuses. On 2 March, Soviet Foreign Minister Andrei Gromyko met with US Ambassador Plenipotentiary Llewellyn E. 'Tommy' Thompson and handed him a response note. On the same day, the embassies of France and Great Britain in Moscow received similar notes. The document provided a response to American threats and reported that the Soviet Union was not afraid to use 'all means' and gave a similar rebuff. 'Now more than ever, it is necessary to take urgent effective measures in order to prevent a dangerous course of events. Therefore, the Soviet government is returning to its previous proposal for a meeting of state leaders at the highest level,' the document said. Khrushchev proposed to organise a meeting of the leaders of the USSR, the USA, Great Britain, France, and also invite representatives of Czechoslovakia, Poland, Germany and the GDR.

Interestingly, the Soviet note was drafted at a time when British Prime Minister Maurice Harold Macmillan and Foreign Minister John Selwyn Brooke Selwyn-Lloyd were in Moscow. They arrived in the Soviet capital on 26 February and stayed there for ten days. It was a very long and eventful visit. Khrushchev and Macmillan discussed many different issues and topics, including trade, housing, and cultural exchange between the two countries. They talked a lot about the need to completely stop nuclear tests in the atmosphere, in water and on the surface of the Earth. Of course, the Berlin crisis was also discussed. Macmillan agreed that this problem should not be solved militarily, but only through negotiations. He assured Khrushchev that the presence of a military contingent in West Berlin had political, but not military purposes. At the end of the visit, a Soviet–British communique was published, which stated: 'The parties recognise that the urgent settlement of problems related to Germany and Berlin should be important for maintaining and strengthening peace and security in Europe and around the world. Therefore, the parties recognise the need for negotiations between the parties concerned in the near future in order to create a basis for resolving differences in positions. The parties believe that such negotiations can lay the foundation for a solid European security system.'

The visit ended in an optimistic spirit on 3 March. When Macmillan and Selwyn-Lloyd arrived at Vnukovo airfield, a large crowd of Muscovites, including schoolchildren, gathered there. The entire Soviet government came to see off the British in full force, and Khrushchev made a long speech at the ramp. The Soviet leader was very pleased, and a series of articles were published in the newspapers, in which the results of the visit were evaluated very positively. Khrushchev believed that all the problems would be resolved. He soon cancelled his ultimatum and waited for further developments. And on 16 March, President Eisenhower publicly stated that the United States was 'ready to participate fully in all sincere efforts to negotiate'. Three days later, Khrushchev spoke at a press conference of Soviet and foreign journalists in Moscow:

> We firmly believe that concluding a peace treaty with Germany and ending the occupation of West Berlin are in the national interests of the German people, in the interests of strengthening peace and universal security. The international atmosphere must become cleaner, and we are striving for only one thing – that the dark clouds of war disappear forever from the international horizon … We would like the Governments of the West, putting aside the reckless threats of their generals and admirals against our country, to sit down with us at the negotiating table. The peoples hope and expect that prudence will prevail in the policies of the United States and other Western states – our allies in the Second World War.

He said that he considered President Eisenhower a peacemaker who was under pressure from an aggressive military and politicians. This was Khrushchev's naive conviction. Until the last moment (which happened in May 1960), he believed that reconnaissance flights over the USSR were carried out without Eisenhower's knowledge.

The Hot Shop and the Ural Secrets

January 1959 in the USSR was marked by the beginning of the so-called 'great seven years'. According to the plan announced by Khrushchev, it consisted of gradual and rapid 'steps into communism', during which the life of the people was to improve by seven-mile ('seven-year') steps. For example, grain production was promised to increase by 30% in a few years, meat by 19%, and milk by 23%. Citizens were promised a solution to the housing problem (to provide apartments for free to all those in need), the creation of comfortable public transport, and breakthroughs in cultural and consumer services. And the main New Year's gift to the Soviet people from the Communist Party was the launch of the first space rocket towards the Moon. It took place on 2 January. However, the mass media reported this success only on 5 January, when all the newspapers came out with slogans like 'Our flag is flapping between the stars' (a quote from a Vladimir Mayakovsky poem). Joyful people composed poems that were published in the press. Here is an example of one of them:

The doors of the first seven-year-old have been opened, the people led by the party to feats.

The new year has already been marked by big plans and audacity of intelligence!

He was greeted with a constant toast to our party and the triumph of victories,

And the New Year soared into the sky to the stars, rushing like an unprecedented star between the planets!

The take-off of a space rocket is getting higher against the background of our Russian poplars and willows,

Towards the Sun, to wake up the sunrises, so that the coat of arms of the Soviet country could be seen everywhere!

In addition, people wrote enthusiastic letters to the newspapers. For example, Alexey Zharikov, the head of the office of the Communist Party in the carriage depot of the Gorky-Passazhyrski railway station, wrote: 'After learning about the launch of a space rocket towards the Moon, I shared the good news with the workers of the technical inspection point. They greeted my story with stormy applause.' The inspector of the wagons Desyatskov wrote: 'No one, not even our enemies, is now trying to challenge the power of Soviet science, stubbornly paving new and new ways to conquer the universe and reveal its secrets. We must be worthy of our great era, and multiply our labour successes day by day.'

In fact, the Soviet leadership lied to its people (this was the reason for the delay in reporting the launch of the rocket). In fact, the Vostok–L launch vehicle was supposed to deliver the Luna 1 automatic probe to the Moon. However, due to gross errors in calculations, it missed the target badly and flew 6,000km wide of its target. Therefore, after the fact, the probe was renamed into a 'rocket launched towards the Moon', and then into the 'first artificial planet' (Luna 1 entered the heliocentric orbit of the Moon and has been orbiting the Sun ever since, its 'year' lasting 450 days).

But however, from a propaganda point of view, the missile hit the target exactly! Another round of panic began in the United States, and newspapers, columnists and congressmen attacked the presidential administration. Eisenhower was accused of underestimating the Soviet threat and lagging behind Russia in the missile race. On 12 February, the president, Secretary of Defence McElroy, his deputy and Chairman of the Joint

Chiefs of Staff General Nathan Twining, held a meeting at which the military tried to convince the president to launch new U-2 flights over the USSR. However, he hesitated for a long time, assessing the risks and possible consequences. Despite the hysteria in the press, it was only in early summer that Eisenhower authorised reconnaissance flights along the southern Soviet border.

The first flight as part of Operation Hot Shop to monitor rocket launches took place on 9 June. Knowing that launches were always carried out at night, by the specified time, a U-2 was airborne from Incirlik in advance. It was travelling into the airspace over Iran and circled at an altitude of 21,000m in the area south of Ashgabat. With the help of the equipment installed on board, the reconnaissance aircraft could record all telemetry data and radio signals transmitted over the air during launch. The U-2 recorded the flight of the rocket during the first ninety seconds after launch, and the pilots could visually observe it from a distance of about 12,000km. 'It was a spectacular sight. The launching rocket illuminated everything for hundreds of miles,' Francis Powers later recalled, who flew on similar missions several times. Often, the U-2 flew in tandem with another aircraft, mainly an EB-47E electronic reconnaissance platform. The Americans actually learned about the telemetry of the launched rocket even earlier than the Soviet ground-based tracking stations. It turned out to be a kind of information ladder. The EB-47E received signals from missiles reaching the altitude at which the aircraft was located, the U-2 collected flight data starting from the moment of separation of the first stage of the rocket, and American ground stations tracked the last quarter of the path of the R-7 flight. Soon, thanks to natural phenomena, it was possible to obtain telemetry of the rocket flight up to the separation of the warhead from the last stage. The last task of the CIA – to calculate the weight of the missile and warhead – was helped ... by Khrushchev himself. He wanted to impress the whole world with his achievements and sent a copy of the Luna 1 along with the third stage of the rocket on a world tour. During this event, the Americans pulled off a daring operation. Taking advantage of the fact that the container holding the exhibit was not guarded around the clock, the agents entered it during the night, disassembled it, photographed it, recorded all the designations and records, and then put it back together.

Having received detailed information about Soviet missiles, in the following months Eisenhower and Dulles were concerned about another question: what was their number and how many would the USSR will be able to put into combat duty in the near future? Under pressure from the military and the CIA, on 8 July, the president authorised a flight over Soviet territory, dubbed Operation Touchdown, aka Mission 4121. The aim was aerial photography of the Tyuratam landfill (Baikonur) and nuclear power plants in the Sverdlovsk region. The CIA learned about these facilities by examining a photograph of one of the premises of the Sverdlovsk power plant, printed in the popular Soviet magazine *Ogonyok*. The picture showed a diagram of large electrical substations and power transmission lines in the Urals with retouched names. Comparing it with many other sources, including articles in Soviet newspapers about successes in the energy sector, CIA experts concluded that the largest consumers of electricity in the Sverdlovsk region were presumably the diffusion plant in Verkh-Neyvinsky, the plutonium rector in Kyshtym and an unknown nuclear facility near Nizhnyaya Tura. It remained only to verify these assumptions with the help of aerial photography.

On the morning of 9 July 1959, a U-2 flew from Incirlik piloted by Marty Knutson. After passing over Iran, he turned north and entered Soviet airspace near Ashgabat. Flying west of the Aral Sea, Knutson photographed several sites in the Urals, including Nizhnyaya Tura, located 220km north of Sverdlovsk. Then the U-2 turned south and flew over many sites in Central Asia, including Baikonur. After that, the reconnaissance aircraft passed through the 'gate' between the mountains Stalin Peak and Kongur and landed at the reserve airfield in Peshawar. The Americans received high-quality photographs of the diffusion plant in Verkh-Neyvinsky and a secret facility in Nizhnyaya Tura, which experts identified as a place of production and storage of nuclear material.

And they were right. The secret city of Sverdlovsk-45 (now the closed city of Lesnoy) was photographed in the area of Nizhnyaya Tura. There was a so-called 'Facility No. 813', also known as the Electrochempribor plant. Of course, no 'chemistry' or 'devices' were produced there, but charges for RDS-2 and RDS-3 nuclear bombs and 501 type nuclear ammunition were manufactured. In the area of Verkh-Neyvinsky, 67km north of Sverdlovsk, there was another secret city that did not appear on maps – Sverdlovsk-44. The Ural Electrochemical Combine, the first enterprise in the USSR for the gas diffusion separation of uranium isotopes and the production of highly enriched uranium for nuclear munitions, was hidden there. In addition, the CIA specialists saw the condition of the launch complex in Baikonur, from which all space rockets were launched, and found out that another launch pad for ballistic missile tests was being built to the east of it.

The Reverse Side of the Moon

After that, there was another pause in the reconnaissance flights. The fact is that in 1959 there was a sudden warming of Soviet–American relations. Anti-American rhetoric practically disappeared from the Soviet media, and angry and accusatory publications with cartoons about the United States gradually disappeared from the pages of newspapers. The real sensation was the article 'The Soviet Exhibition in New York', published in Russian newspapers in early June. The exposition opened in the Colosseum Exhibition Centre and occupied a huge area of 14,600 sq m. Numerous exhibits demonstrated the peaceful orientation of the Soviet regime and showed its best achievements. Visitors were presented with a 6m operating model of the nuclear icebreaker *Lenin*, as well as a mock-up of its nuclear reactor, a giant mock-up of an airfield with moving aircraft models, and exact copies of three artificial Earth satellites. In addition, the exhibition featured working models of a metallurgical plant, an offshore oil platform, coal combines, machine tools with software control, tractors, agricultural implements and much more. A huge mock-up of a new residential neighbourhood located in the south-east of Moscow and a diorama of a Ukrainian collective farm demonstrated the good living conditions of Soviet citizens. 'We hope that the Soviet exhibition in New York will help our peoples get to know each other better and strengthen mutual understanding between the two great countries. This is the lofty goal of the Soviet–American agreement in the field of science, technology and culture,' the Soviet press wrote.

At the end of July, Vice President Richard Nixon arrived in Moscow on a visit. This event became a real sensation both for the population of the Soviet Union and for Americans. The formal reason for the visit was the opening of the exhibition 'Industrial Products of the USA' in Sokolniki Park. The exhibition was organised by the United States Information Agency. The exhibition featured samples of American art, fashion, cars, samples of residential buildings and supermarkets, lawn mowers, dishwashers, cosmetics, clothes and Pepsi drinks. Information booths reported that it was enough for an American worker to work for one week to buy a month's supply of food for the family, and the average monthly salary of a worker in the United States was more than $300. The exhibition aroused great interest. In six weeks of operation, it was visited by 3 million people! The Russians were shocked by what they saw. Most of the items shown seemed to them to be fiction, which they had never seen. Soviet newspapers wrote about the exhibition with restraint, emphasizing that all this was just advertising, 'window dressing' and 'facade', behind which social inequality, unemployment and poverty were hidden.

On 24 July 1959, Nixon and Khrushchev visited the exhibition. During this event, the Soviet leader actually voiced his foreign policy doctrine, which repeated the theses of the Suez crisis. Khrushchev actually proposed to create a bipolar world in which the USSR and the United States would play a dominant role. And also, to organise an honest and open competition in the socio-economic sphere in order to prove whose system was better and set an example to everyone else. Khrushchev told Nixon:

We want to live in peace and friendship with the Americans, because we are the two most powerful powers, and if we live in friendship, then other countries will also live together. But if there is a country that is too prone to war, we will slightly box its ears and say: 'Don't you dare! You can't fight now. These are the times of nuclear weapons, some fool can start a war, and then even wise people will not be able to stop it.' Therefore, we are guided by this idea in our foreign and domestic policy.

In addition, the Soviet leader called Nixon a 'lawyer for capitalism' and himself a 'lawyer for communism'. This conversation later went down in history as the 'kitchen debate'.

Nixon personally presented Khrushchev with Eisenhower's invitation to visit the United States. This event in the USSR was perceived as an unambiguously friendly act and a signal for a further reset of relations between the two countries. Recall that the idea that the United States and the USSR were two leading powers that should live in peace and determine the world order seized Khrushchev during the Suez crisis of 1956. After that, for the Soviet leader, it became a fundamental doctrine in foreign policy. It was this idea that Khrushchev voiced to Nixon during the kitchen debate.

The Soviet leader arrived in America on 15 September. Three days before this event, Soviet rocket scientists achieved an unexpected success – the Luna 2 probe reached the surface of the Moon. Therefore, Khrushchev was in a good mood, bragging about his missiles. After meeting with Eisenhower and the senators, he voiced several proposals at once: to conclude a global Soviet–American treaty, announce to the whole world the beginning of general disarmament and ban nuclear tests. In addition, Khrushchev proposed to conclude an agreement on the status of West Berlin. Eisenhower was generally positive about the Soviet proposals, but asked for time to think about it. The twelve-day visit was very emotional, and in the end Khrushchev and Eisenhower agreed to hold a summit meeting in Europe in the spring of 1960. It was also decided to discuss the issue of the status of West Berlin, as well as diplomatic recognition of the GDR. In addition, the delighted Khrushchev invited the president to pay a return visit to the Soviet Union. Soviet newspapers reported in detail about the visit and its results. People took it with great enthusiasm. It seemed to the Russians that at last the main world leaders would come to an agreement among themselves, and the threat of global war would go away. The future of Soviet–American relations seemed joyful and happy.

Proof of this was the design of a giant dam across the Bering Strait, which was published at the end of 1959. A fantastic engineering structure 75km long was supposed to connect North America with Asia and change the climate of the Arctic. The dam was supposed to block the way to the Arctic Ocean of cold and not very salty waters from the Pacific Ocean, while increasing the influx of warm waters of the Gulf Stream. In this case, the temperature of the Arctic Ocean should have increased gradually, and the ice cover with an area of 13 million sq km should have melted. This was supposed to reduce the reflection of sunlight from the Earth's surface, lead to an increase in air temperature in the northern part of Eurasia, increase air humidity, reduce droughts, and increase the flow of Siberian rivers. Alaska and Canada would turn into a warm, blooming land. A railway and a highway from the USSR to the USA were going to be laid along the upper edge of the dam.

Here is how the project parameters were described in the Russian press:

The construction of such a dam will cost 70 billion rubles. The dam will be constructed of precast reinforced concrete. The length of the dam is 74 kilometres, the height is 50–60 metres. The dam can be assembled from separate sections. The construction of such a powerful structure will require a lot of electricity. But this problem cannot be considered difficult, since there are oil, coal and gas fields nearby. In extreme cases, electricity can be transmitted via wires from Siberia and Canada ...

US scientists are going to make their final judgment on this issue only after a thorough study of it. The Governor of Alaska, in a letter to the US Secretary of State, K. Herter, suggested that the State Department 'consider the question of what benefits from an international point of view a joint study would bring'. The statement of Senator Ernst Gruning, a Democrat from Alaska, is also given about the need to organise a meeting of scientists from both countries, the USSR and the USA, in the near future.

It is now obvious that from a scientific point of view, the dam project was utopian. It completely ignored the consequences of melting ice and rising sea levels, and other global environmental risks were not taken into account. But this project is a clear example of the emotional background that developed in the Soviet Union in the late 1950s. The Russians sincerely believed in an early end to the arms race, general disarmament and a reduction in military spending. They believed that the USSR and the USA would jointly ensure peace on the planet, and the released resources would be used to build roads, power plants, dams, and improve the climate on the planet.

Now the main enemy of the Soviet system was the Federal Republic of Germany. In the summer of 1959, a large-scale visit to the USSR took place by the party and government delegation of the German Democratic Republic (GDR), headed by Walter Ulbricht, first secretary of the Central Committee of the Socialist United Party of Germany, and Otto Grotewohl, chairman of the Council of Ministers of the

GDR. They visited not only Moscow, but also other major cities including Gorky (now Nizhny Novgorod). Ulbricht and his colleagues arrived in this city by plane and were met by crowds of pioneers, who handed them bouquets of flowers. Then the deputy chairman of the Democratic Peasant Party of Germany, Paul Scholz, made a speech. He told Soviet children that a prosperous and beautiful life was being created in East Germany, the main enemy of which was militarism being revived in West Germany.

After that, the German delegation went to the Gorky Automobile Plant (GAZ). There, the Germans inspected the production process and talked with the workers. Then there was a mass rally, for which the work of the plant was practically stopped. In conclusion, the Germans presented the car manufacturer with a mock-up of the new Trabant car, the hope of the East German automotive industry. At the end of the visit, Ulbricht and Grotewohl, together with members of the Soviet government, took a river trip on the ship *Dobrynya Nikitich* along the Volga. This cruise ship was built in 1957 in the GDR at the VEB Mathias-Thesen-Werft Wismar shipyard. In total, in 1954–61, the Germans built forty-nine such three-deck motor ships for the USSR, which still (in 2024) form the basis of the Russian cruise fleet on the Volga and other rivers. This trip aboard a German ship with a Soviet flag was symbolic of the spirit of the great friendship between the GDR and the USSR. During this period, dozens of articles were published in Soviet newspapers about life in the 'good' GDR, which was called an exemplary country of people's democracy.

In the autumn of 1959, the Soviet missile programme achieved new successes. On 4 October, the Vostok-L rocket with the Luna 3 automatic interplanetary spacecraft was launched from the Baikonur missile range. It was equipped with a camera loaded with American film, resistant to radiation and temperature changes. No such film was produced in the USSR and it was taken from the American WS-119L reconnaissance probes that flew over the territory of the USSR as part of the secret Project Genetrix. These vehicles were regularly shot down by the Russian air defences, but they did not have any identification marks or markings. The film obtained in this way was planned to be used to photograph the far side of the Moon.

For a long time (almost from time immemorial), various conjectures and legends have been associated with the 'dark side'. The fact that only one half of our natural satellite is always visible from Earth was noticed in ancient times, which gave rise to numerous theories about civilisation, vegetation and other secrets hidden on the other side. The flight of Luna 3 was supposed to finally dispel these myths. Interestingly, neither the name of the spacecraft nor the true purpose of the flight was reported in the newspapers (in case of mission failure), and the project itself was referred to in a streamlined way as the 'third Soviet space rocket'. Only when the device began to successfully approach the Moon, and all on-board systems were working normally, did newspapers publish a message that 'an automatic interplanetary station, approaching the Moon strictly at the appointed time at a given minimum distance, will fly around it, passing behind the invisible part of the lunar disk, and then turn back towards Earth'.

On 7 October, Luna 3 circled the Moon and successfully photographed its dark side. The image was transmitted using an analogue method by a travelling beam camera. On the ground side, the images were received in several ways: from shooting a running beam camera on film, photographing from a skiatron screen, recording on magnetic tape and direct image output on thermochemical paper. Recordings on magnetic tape could not be reproduced, while images on thermal paper and skiatrons only allowed those back home to evaluate the plot of the image. The only successful method of registration turned out to be the one using a travelling beam camera. On 18 October, when the station approached the Earth again, seventeen images with interference, but with visible relief details, were obtained from it, but on 22 October communication with Luna 3 stopped. Academician Mstislav Keldysh, one of the project managers, was dissatisfied with the quality of the photographs, and on 27 October they were published in heavily retouched form in all Soviet newspapers. From them people were convinced that the reverse side of the Moon did not differ from the visible one as it featured the same numerous craters from the fall of asteroids and 'seas'.

In January 1960, the Supreme Soviet of the USSR approved a law 'on a new significant reduction of the Armed Forces of the USSR' without discussion. After that, 1.3 million soldiers and officers were dismissed from the army and navy. This was almost a third of the total number of all military personnel in the USSR at that time and significantly reduced military spending.

Unfortunately, further events in world politics also became the 'other side of the Moon', and the improvement of relations between the USSR and the United States became another illusion.

System 75

During his visit to the United States, the Soviet leader never mentioned the flights of reconnaissance aircraft. Khrushchev pretended not to be bothered by this problem. Surprised, Eisenhower's entourage made the optimistic conclusion that he had come to terms with U-2 flights as a means of preserving peace. In fact, Khrushchev was completely convinced that Eisenhower was a real peacemaker and a naive person. He was convinced that the US military was blatantly deceiving its president, and that the flights of reconnaissance aircraft were conducted secretly, with Eisenhower knowing nothing about them. However, at the same time, the Soviets were actively preparing to eliminate this threat. Back in March 1958, immediately after the U-2 flight over the Far East, the Central Office of the Communist Party held a discussion on the state of the air defence forces and about equipping them with new equipment. The leadership of the Ministry of Defence and the State Committees on Aviation Technology and Radio Electronics participated in it. The military admitted honestly that the equipment in service was not able to shoot down a plane flying at an altitude of 20,000m. Then Khrushchev demanded the speeding up of work on new weapons, primarily new-generation, anti-aircraft missile systems.

The decision to create a mobile anti-aircraft missile system, System 75, was taken by the Soviet government on 20 November 1953. Initially, the complex was planned as multi-channel (with the possibility of simultaneous firing at several targets at once) and self-guided. However, due to the necessary haste, these 'excesses' were soon abandoned. The anti-aircraft missile system was created as single channel, with the ability to hit a target from any angle with a radio command missile guidance. The complex included a guidance station with a radar station (with linear space scanning) and six rotating launchers, one missile on each. The latest mathematical guidance model, the half-straightening method, was applied to the S-75. Based on the data on the flight of the target received from the radar, the missile was directed not at the actual position of the target, but to an intermediate point. It was located between the current position of the target and the estimated rendezvous point. This made it possible to minimise errors associated with the inaccuracy of determining the rendezvous point and to change the course of the rocket during flight.

Design Bureau No. 1 Almaz was engaged in the development of the guidance station, transponder and radio control equipment. The chief designer was engineer Boris Bunkin. Work on the rocket was carried out by a separate design bureau, No. 2 Torch, and the engine was designed in another design bureau, NII-88. The radio fuse was developed at the Scientific Research Institute No. 504, and the high-explosive warhead of the rocket was developed at the Scientific Research Institute No. 6 of the Ministry of Rural Engineering. The launchers were manufactured by the Central Design Bureau No. 34, and the ground equipment was manufactured by the State Special Design Bureau. All these organisations were strictly classified, with their location and activity profile known only to a narrow circle of people. All the people who worked there had to observe the strictest secrecy. Even close relatives (wives and husbands) were not supposed to know anything. All staff telephone conversations were tapped by the KGB, and they were monitored around the clock.

The adoption of the S-75 anti-aircraft missile system was carried out in two stages. On 11 December 1957, a simplified version was adopted under the designation SA-75 'Dvina' with a V-750 missile. And in May 1959, the air defence forces received the S-75 'Desna' complex with a V-750VN missile and a radar station operating in the 6cm range.

The V-750VN rocket was a two-stage surface-to-air missile with a solid-fuel launch accelerator and a liquid-propellant main engine. The guidance station aimed three such missiles at one target at the same time. Tracking of the target was carried out in automatic or manual mode, or automatically by angular coordinates and manually by range. After launch, the rocket fell into a sector of space scanned by radar. In it, it was picked up by the operator and linked to the coordinates of the target on the radar screen, at an altitude of 3km to 22km and at a range of 7km to 29km. By 1960, the Soviets had managed to deploy sixty regiments of S-75 anti-aircraft missile systems. This was still a very small number to cover the vast territory of the Soviet Union. However, for the United States, the risks of losing a U-2 were constantly increasing.

'Cruciform, With Large Wings'

Back in November 1956, the CIA, in strict secrecy, introduced the U-2 to representatives of the Royal Air Force. Despite the complication of relations with the Allies caused by the Suez crisis, the Americans offered the British a joint reconnaissance flights project. It was supposed to prepare a group of British pilots who would go on missions with the personal approval of the British prime minister. After long negotiations, Harold Macmillan agreed. At the end of 1957, four pilots were selected to participate in the programme: Christopher Walker, Michael Bradley, David Downling and John MacArthur. All of them had long experience, but had no families and were under 30 years old. As a cover story, the British pilots were officially transferred to the meteorological service, and in the spring of 1958 they arrived at Laughlin Air Force Base, located in the prairies of Texas.

After theoretical, technical training and medical examinations, training flights began on 3 June. At first everything went fine, but on 8 July, during a high-altitude flight, U-2 No. 380 56-6713 crashed while being flown by Walker and he was killed. The cause was determined as a loss of control due to a malfunction of the oxygen system, or failure of the autopilot. Lieutenant Robert Robinson, a pilot of Canberra reconnaissance aircraft, was sent to Laughlin to replace Walker. On 29 September, he had his first training flight in the U-2. In January 1959, the British pilots arrived in Turkey, where they completed several missions over the Middle East, as well as along the southern borders of the USSR. At the same time, it took almost a whole year before

Above and below: U-2 during test trials in Nevada.

Tu-4 bombers (a copy of the American B-29) at the air base.

Tu-16 bomber air base near Novgorod.

The P-20 Periskop radar station is in position.

Above: MiG-19 fighter.

Below: Tupolev ANT-25.

U-2A in flight.

Aerial view of the secret city of Seversk (Tomsk-7).

Aerial view of the Tyuratam missile range.

Above: The first prototype of the S-75 anti-aircraft missile system.

Left: The warhead of the B-750 anti-aircraft missile in the museum of the Federal State Unitary Enterprise Sverdlov Plant (Dzerzhinsk). (Photo by the author)

Above: The building that first housed Design Bureau-11 (KB-11). (Photo from the Nuclear Weapons Museum (Sarov))

Right: Mysterious Sarov dungeons. (Photo by the author)

Above: A secret residential village in the forest. (Photo from the Nuclear Weapons Museum (Sarov))

Below: The creators of Soviet nuclear weapons Igor Kurchatov and Andrei Sakharov in the secret city of Kremlev. (Photo from the Nuclear Weapons Museum (Sarov))

Above: Street of the secret city. (Photo from the Nuclear Weapons Museum (Sarov))

Below: Aerial view of the explosive test site in Kremlev.

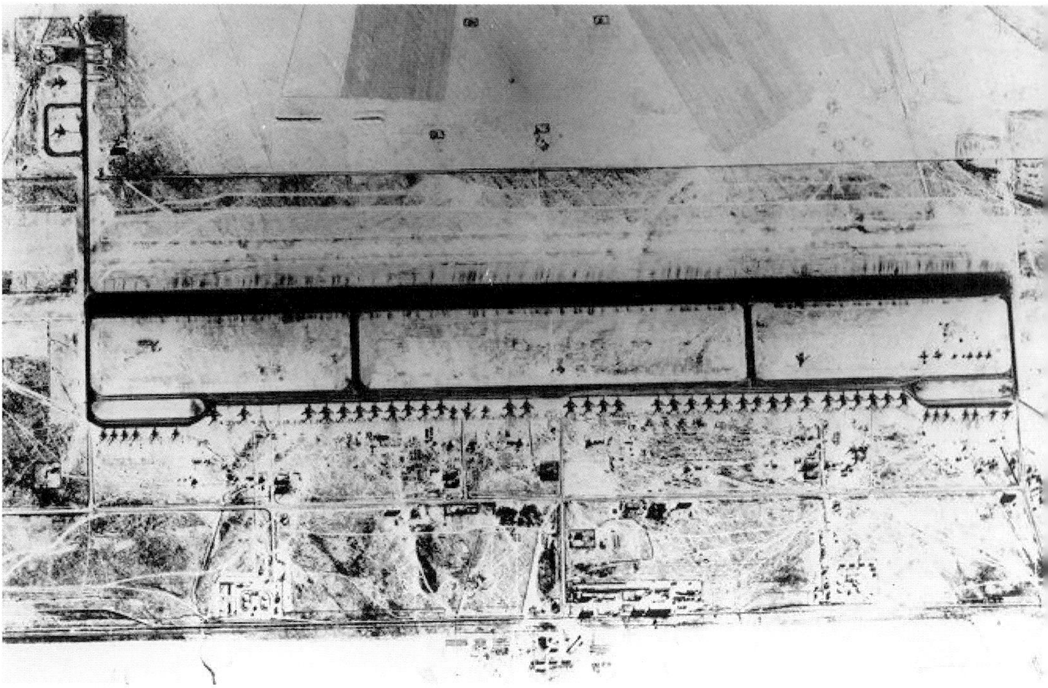

Above: Aerial view of the Semipalatinsk air base.

Left: U-2C is coming in for landing.

U-2C in flight.

The remains of the U-2 aircraft.

Major Mikhail Voronov and his subordinates.

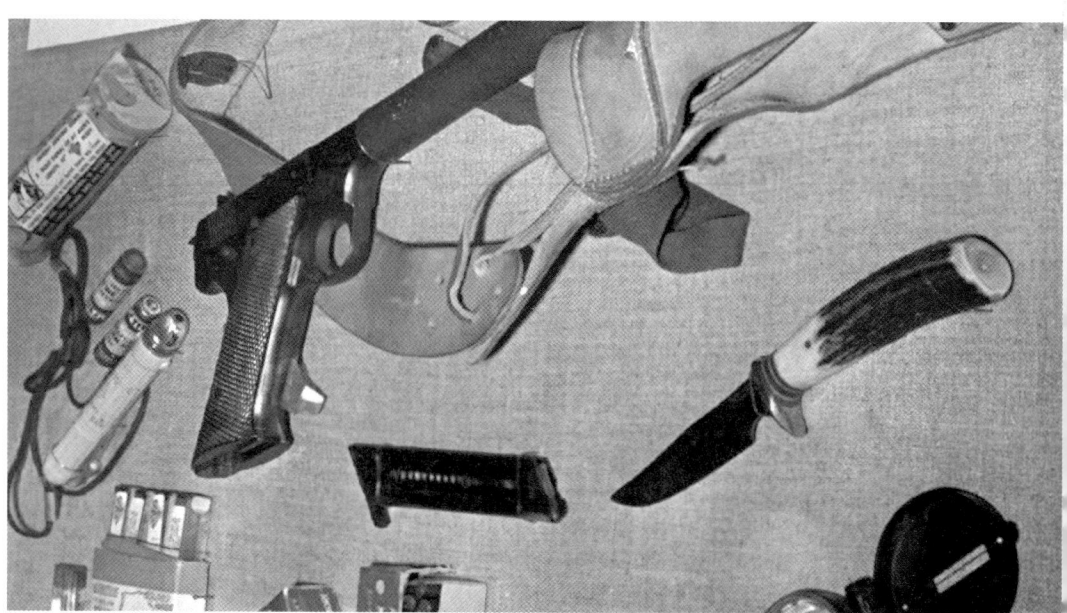

Khrushchev shows photos of items confiscated from Powers.

Powers' pistol and ammunition for it.

Летчик сбитого самолета США
Фрэнсис Гарри Пауэрс.

Right: Photo of Powers published in Soviet newspapers.

Below: Powers examines the remains of his aircraft and equipment.

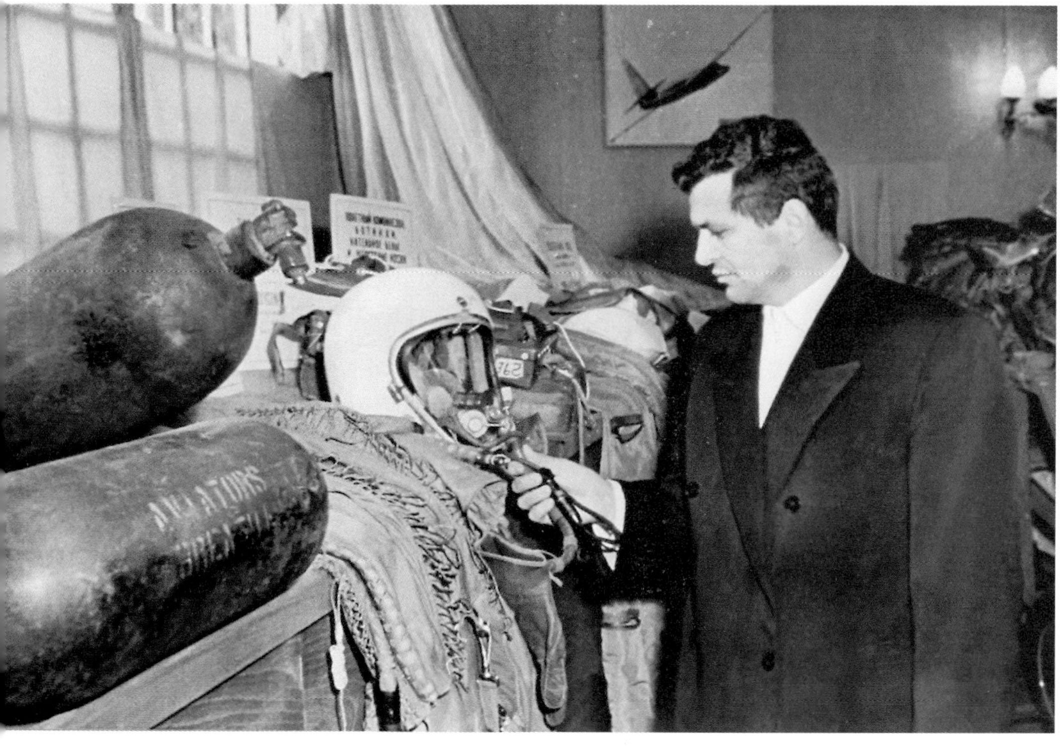

Above: U-2 equipment elements.

Below: Vladimir Central Prison.

Above: U-2 66-703 from the USAF.

Below: Aerial view of Soviet ballistic missiles in Cuba on 14 October 1962.

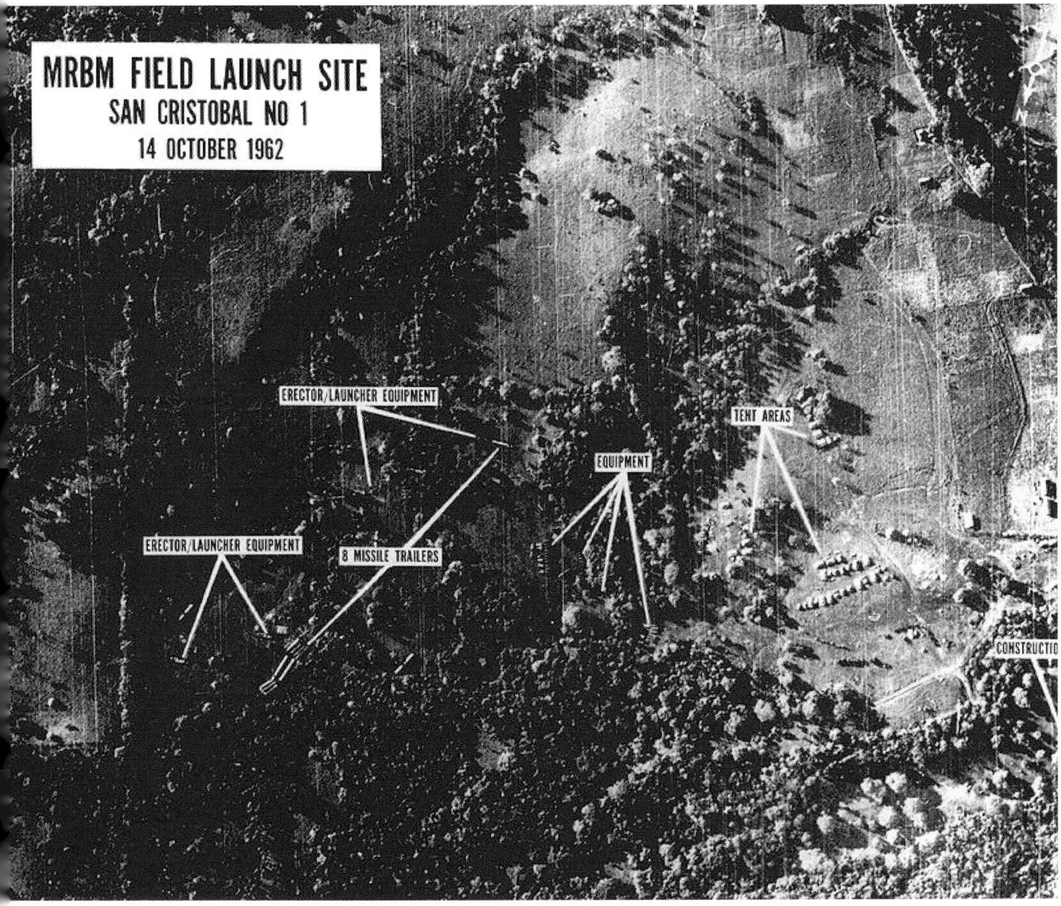

MRBM FIELD LAUNCH SITE
SAN CRISTOBAL NO 1
14 OCTOBER 1962

ERECTOR/LAUNCHER EQUIPMENT

EQUIPMENT

TENT AREAS

ERECTOR/LAUNCHER EQUIPMENT

8 MISSILE TRAILERS

CONSTRUCTIO

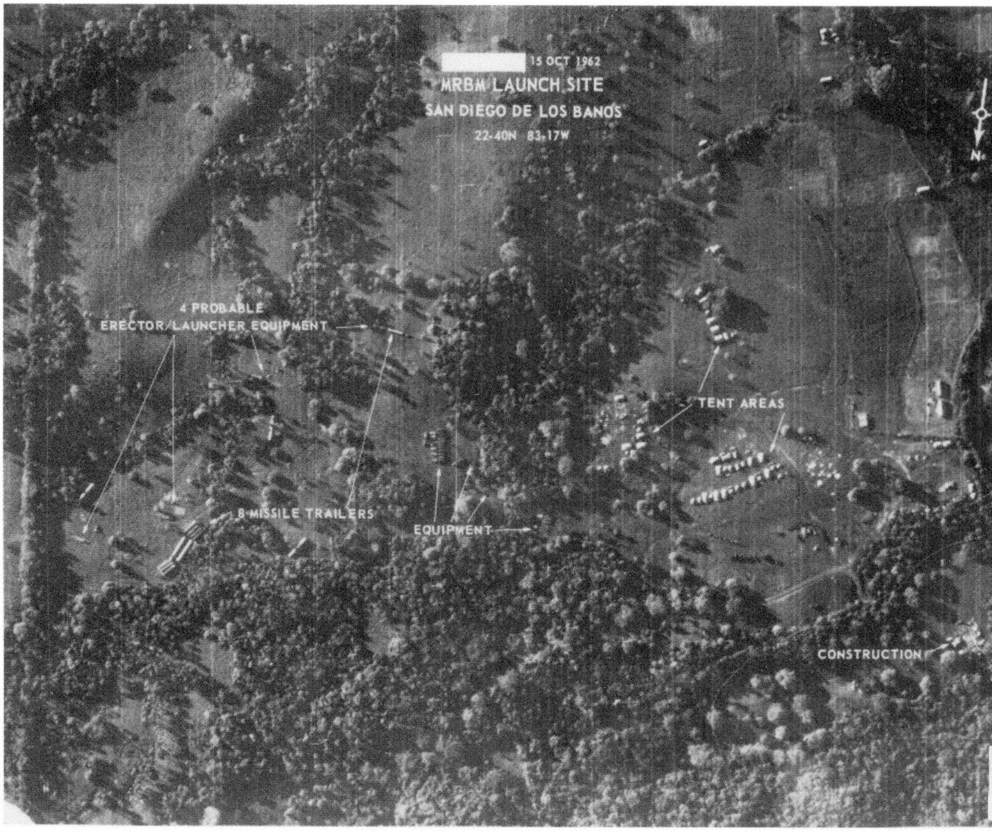

Above: An aerial view of the same sector, taken on 15 October 1962.

Below: Movement of a military convoy.

Macmillan authorised a flight over the territory of the USSR. It was designated as Mission 8005.

On 6 December 1959, Robert Robinson took off in U-2 No. 351. After entering Soviet airspace in the Dushanbe area, the aircraft flew on a straight course to the north-west (across Uzbekistan and over the Aral Sea). West of Orenburg, the U-2 turned right and went straight to the city of Kuybyshev (now Samara). This was the main purpose of the mission. Robinson flew directly over the city on a northwesterly course, photographed large aviation enterprises, then made a turn over the bend of the Volga and turned to the south-west. After that, the U-2 turned to the south-west and soon passed over Saratov and Engels, photographing the airfield, which was home to about thirty M-4 bombers from the 201st TBAD. After that, the plane reached Volgograd and turned towards the Kapustin Yar missile range. This was the last target, after which the aircraft set a southwesterly course, left Soviet airspace over the Caucasus in a straight line and headed for Incirlik.

Before Robinson's flight, Soviet air defences in Central Asia practically did not notice the U-2 flights. In addition, there seemed to be no American bases near the southern borders of the USSR, and there seemed to be nowhere for the aircraft to fly from. However, now the flight of the intruder had been recorded. Yuri Votintsev, then commander of the Tashkent Air Defence Corps, recalled:

The modern P-30 radar station, the only one we had at that time, detected an aerial target at an altitude of 20,000 metres. She did not respond to inquiries. It was assumed that the target had invaded the airspace of the USSR. An experienced pilot, the squadron commander, took off to intercept it in a MiG-19 aircraft. He managed to accelerate the MiG and, due to a dynamic jump, reached a height of about 17,500 metres. The pilot reported that he saw an aircraft above him by 3,000 to 4,000 metres. But at an altitude of 17,500 metres, the MiG-19 lasted a few seconds and began to descend. The pilot lost sight of the target. The locators soon lost it, or rather the only one that saw it was the P-30. When the pilot landed, he reported the results of his observation. He drew the plane he saw. Cruciform, with large wings. This was reported to Moscow, to the Main Headquarters of the country's Air Defence Forces. From there, Colonel-General Yevgeny Savitsky, commander of the fighter aviation, soon arrived with a group of specialists. The Muscovites had a long conversation with the pilot, analyzed the received data. The result of the commission's work puzzled the entire regiment – the observations of the pilot, who was climbing to intercept the 'invisible', were questioned. Savitsky said: the pilot invented that he observed the target during ascent. Allegedly, he wanted to distinguish himself, to earn a reward. It seemed that the commission had a firm belief that there are no such aircraft that could stay at an altitude of 20,000 metres for several hours in nature ...

However, the fact remains that at the end of 1959, the Soviet air defence could already detect U-2s flying from Pakistan, which further increased the risk and raised the stakes. Was this risk worth the results achieved? It had been known for a long time that there were large aircraft factories in Kuybyshev (Samara). The Americans had photographs taken by German reconnaissance aircraft in 1942. What was useful for national security from the new photographs taken from the U-2? The Americans learned that the aircraft factories had not moved anywhere and remained in their place. They saw that the Russians had built several more buildings there. Was it impossible to do without these details?

Nuclear Moria

At the beginning of 1960, sharp debates again unfolded in Congress over the Soviet missile breakthrough and the inadequate defence policy of the administration of President Dwight Eisenhower. The issue of the US lagging behind in the development of ballistic and space missiles was discussed. The CIA and its chief Allen Dulles were also severely criticised by congressmen as complacent, as well as by many media outlets. Dulles was often asked sharp questions, which he could not answer in full, so as not to reveal the secret of U-2. He had to speak in the spirit of 'I know you're wrong, but I won't tell you why'. Meanwhile, horrifying articles were published in the press about the consequences of a possible sudden missile attack by the Soviets. In this regard, the president was once again put under pressure, offering to conduct a new series of flights over the USSR. However, Eisenhower still hesitated. Prime Minister Maurice Harold Macmillan did not object and authorised the second flight of a British pilot over the

USSR. The so-called 'suspicious areas' in the southern part of the USSR and the Volga region were selected as targets, where, according to CIA analysts, SS-6 (R-7) intercontinental missiles could be deployed. Those targeted were considered areas to which the access of civilians, according to intelligence, was limited. At the same time, experts believed that missiles, due to their bulkiness, could only be placed near railway lines, since it was impossible to deliver them in any other way. As a result, a number of areas were selected to be checked during the flight, designated Mission 8009. However, the Russian Los Alamos, the main and top-secret nuclear centre of the Russians, was the main goal.

On 11 February 1943, a resolution was adopted by the Soviet State Defence Committee to begin work on the creation of a nuclear bomb. The overall leadership was entrusted to one of Joseph Stalin's closest aides, Lavrentiy Beria. He appointed Igor Kurchatov as the head of the Soviet nuclear project. Beria personally oversaw all operations to steal American nuclear secrets. On 9 April 1946, Stalin signed a secret government decree on the creation of a secret laboratory code-named Design Bureau-11 (KB-11). Pavel Zernov, former deputy people's commissar (minister) of the tank industry, was appointed the first director of the KB-11, and Yulii Khariton was appointed chief designer.

In April 1946, the small village of Sarov was chosen as the site of the country's main secret facility. Khariton recalled:

It was clear that to create a nuclear bomb, enormous pressures would be required to compress fissile materials

No. Pages : _77_
COPY NO.: _13_

TOP SECRET

Joint Mission Coverage Summary

MISSION B 8009
5 FEBRUARY 1960

ARMY

NAVY

CIA

PIC/JMCS-5/60
MARCH 1960

TOP SECRET

CIA report on Mission 8009

and that such pressures in the right volumes could be created by exploding large quantities of explosives. Moscow was an unsuitable place for such work. It was not so easy to find a site isolated from the population, near Moscow, suitable for such work. We visited many factories that produced ammunition during the war. And so, after a long search, on 2 April 1946, Pavel Zernov and I arrived in the small village of Sarov, where St Seraphim once lived and prayed. There was a small factory here, where shells for Katyusha multiple rocket launchers and other ammunition were made during the war. There were impenetrable forests all around. This created the conditions for carrying out the necessary explosions, as there was a lot of space and it was well isolated from populated areas. Thus, by the will of fate, the holy city became the birthplace of Soviet nuclear weapons.

Interestingly, the secret facility is located above the real 'Russian Moria'. It was an analogue of the huge underground city from the book *The Lord of the Rings*. Inside the mountain, on the surface of which there was an ancient monastery, the monks there dug deep caves. They had underground temples, living quarters, cells, refectories and spacious storage areas for monastic relics and treasures. The author of the book managed to visit these mysterious labyrinths and found that this whole underground city is very similar to Moria!

The KB-11 facility was built by a special construction organisation, the Construction Department No. 880 of the NKVD of the USSR. In February 1947, the design bureau was classified as a special regime enterprise with the transformation of its territory into a closed zone. The village of Sarov was withdrawn from the administrative subordination of the Mordovian Autonomous Republic and excluded from all accounting materials and maps. In the spring of that year, the activities of research laboratories and divisions of KB-11 began, in parallel with the first production workshops of experimental plants No. 1 and No. 2. In addition to Kurchatov and Khariton, the famous Soviet scientists Yakov Zeldovich, Igor Tamm and Andrei Sakharov worked there.

In 1949, the construction of the USSR's first factory for the industrial production of nuclear bombs began. By the end of 1951, twenty-nine had been manufactured there. The bombs were stored in a special underground reinforced concrete warehouse, and transportation was carried out along a classified railway line, which also did not exist on maps.

Given the specifics and importance of the facility, only the best university graduates, the most talented specialists and highly qualified workers were invited to work there. The most capable students were carefully selected at educational institutions and they were offered interesting jobs and good conditions (high salaries and housing). For example, in 1950, the future academician Andrei Sakharov was hired as head of the laboratory with a salary of 6,000 rubles and an allowance of 75%. For comparison, the Soviet GAZ M20 Pobeda car cost 16,000 rubles in dealerships. No employer in the USSR could offer such conditions in those years. At the same time, the training of specialists began inside the facility. In 1952, the Evening Institute, a branch of the Moscow Institute of

Engineering and Physics (MIFI), opened in the former monastery.

In order to maintain secrecy and mislead foreign intelligence agencies, the Soviets changed the site's name several times. Up to 1954 it was called Object 550, Base 112, Shatki 1, Moscow Centre 300 and the Volga Office of the Glavstroy of the USSR. In 1954–60, it was the city of Kremlev; in 1960–66, Arzamas-75; and in 1966–94, Arzamas-16. All residents were under the control of the KGB and all correspondence, telephone conversations and even personal lives were strictly controlled. For a long time it was possible to leave the city only by a special train to Moscow, and it was connected to the city of Gorky by a secret bus route that had no number.

A fragment of a map of the Gorky region. The secret city of Arzamas-16 (Sarov) is not marked.

By the end of 1959, the CIA had a generally complete understanding of Soviet nuclear facilities, which were quickly mapped and became potential targets in case of a war. However, at the same time, experts concluded that some important and possibly central link was missing in the entire scheme. Namely, a scientific, think tank centre in which the Russians developed nuclear and thermonuclear munitions themselves and, probably, produced experimental samples. It was eventually possible to calculate its location using communications intelligence (COMINT). In general terms, this is the collection of intelligence by intercepting signals, whether they are messages between people or electronic signals. Since secret and confidential information was always encrypted, such intelligence involved the use of cryptanalysis to decrypt messages. In other words, the CIA conducted a systematic analysis of intercepted traffic (radiograms, telephone messages, encoded signals), analyzing who was transmitting signals to whom and in what quantity. Later, the entire data set was used to re-combine the information.

In October 1959, CIA experts concluded that 'suspicious communication activity' was being observed in the southern part of the Gorky region, near the city of Arzamas. A significant part of the signals and messages related to this area turned out to be of the same type when compared (for example, 'we need another 300 tons of sand', 'give another 200 tons of sand', 'the sand is running out', 'sand will be allocated to you urgently', etc.), which indicated the use of encryption. At the same time, the type of messages changed radically at certain intervals (sand was often mentioned first, then coal, then cement, etc.), and this in turn indicated that the ciphers changed from time to time. In addition, the intercepted and decrypted messages very often mentioned the name 'Arzamas', as well as 'Arzamas-75'. At the same time, the number of mentions of this word almost corresponded to such a large metropolis as the city of Gorky; that is, it was clearly out of the general communication traffic. From all this, an obvious conclusion followed: somewhere in the Arzamas area there was an important classified facility.

After analyzing the entire array of available information about this region, CIA specialists drew attention to two interesting reports. One, dated back to 1951, reported a large number of prisoners working at a certain 'very important construction site'. Another reported the dissatisfaction of

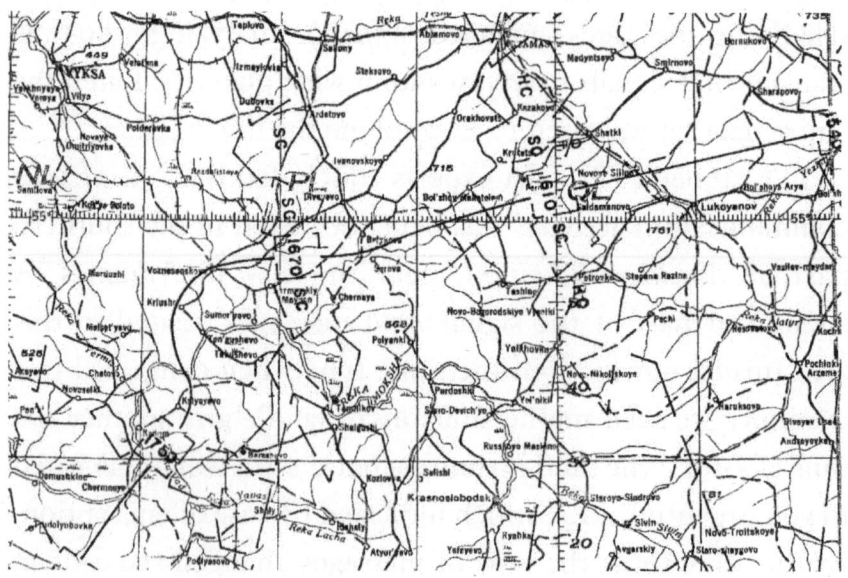

The flight path of the U-2 over the secret city of Kremlev (Sarov).

religious people, who for some reason stopped being allowed into holy places. And both mentioned the same name – Sarov! Later, the experience of studying the 'dark territory' in Siberia helped, on the basis of which the CIA roughly understood the principle of the establishment of closed cities and the appearance of their encoded names (as a rule, the name of another city located nearby). In early 1960, Allen Dulles was already almost certain that he had managed to find the 'Russian Los Alamos'. All that remained was to photograph the set target area.

Mission No. 8009 was named 'Knife Edge'. And it was a very accurate name. The Americans and the British guessed that the Soviet Union was taking emergency measures to intercept the offending aircraft. Considering that the reconnaissance aircraft had to fly over the central regions of the country, not far from Moscow, the mission really looked like a knife-edge passage!

On the morning of 10 February 1960, a U-2 piloted by Englishman John MacArthur, took off from Peshawar airfield in Pakistan and headed north-west. Following an almost straight course, the plane flew 2,500km over the territory of the USSR and reached the first goal, Kazan. The U-2 made a circle around the city, photographing an aircraft factory and an airfield with a new Tu-98 strategic bomber standing on it. Despite the excellent and clear weather, the Soviet air defences did not react in any way. Therefore, MacArthur flew over the Volga and headed for the next objective – Sarov (in the CIA documents it is designated as 'Sarova'). Near the village of Sumerlya, the U-2 entered the airspace of the Gorky region, then proceeded directly over Gagino, just north of Lukoyanov, photographed Arzamas with a side camera, and then went out exactly on target.

According to the archive of weather reports, that day in the Gorky region there was frosty (up to -18°C) and completely clear weather. MacArthur clearly saw a secret zone spread out in the middle of a snow-covered taiga forest, including residential settlements and mysterious concrete objects. South of the city of Kulebaki, the plane turned smoothly to the left, then flew over Michurinsk, Voronezh, Kharkov, Dnipropetrovsk, Zaporizhzhya, Melitopol, Sevastopol and safely left the airspace of the USSR over the Black Sea. After spending about nine hours in the air, the aircraft landed in Turkey. As it is now known, the U-2 flew just 100km from the positions of the S-75 anti-aircraft missile systems, which were located near the city of Gorky.

After careful decryption of the images obtained (for example, the mysterious circle in the forest was identified as an 'explosive test cell', an explosive test camera), the CIA made an unambiguous conclusion: this was the 'Russian Los Alamos'. In addition, experts identified an alleged nuclear bomb storage base, designating this facility as the 'Sarova/Shatki weapon site'. From then on, the location of the secret city was no secret to the Americans, and the renaming of the city to Arzamas-16, which took place in the same year, no longer made sense.

This U-2 flight was another extremely risky mission; an American military plane flew over the heart of the Soviet Union and over the most classified Russian military facility. From the point of view of international legal norms, this was the grossest act of aggression, which could become a formal reason for war. Was this journey on a knife's edge justified in terms of the results achieved? Moreover, very soon the location of the target could in any case be determined using space satellite reconnaissance.

Eisenhower, thanking fate for the fact that U-2 was not detected and intercepted again, reasonably considered this as proof of the absence of the missiles themselves. However, alarmists in the CIA and the State Department, on the contrary, concluded that they flew to the wrong places. Yielding to pressure, in mid-February, Eisenhower authorised another flight, setting a deadline of 30 March. However, in the negotiations between the Americans and Pakistan (the flight was planned mainly over Kazakhstan and Central Asia) on the use of the airfield in Peshawar, some difficulties arose, as a result of which Mission 4155, code-named Square Deal, could not be carried out on schedule.

Finally, on 9 April 1960, a U-2 flew from Peshawar under the control of pilot Bob Ericson. After passing through the 'gate' between the Stalin and Mount Kongur peaks, brightly illuminated by the newly risen rays of the sun, at 04.05 Moscow time, the reconnaissance aircraft entered Soviet airspace. Initially, its course ran due north to Lake Balkhash. Having rounded it from the west, the plane turned to the north-east – to the Semipalatinsk nuclear test site. Ericson then turned around and headed for the Saryshagan missile range, located west of Balkhash. Over this object, which was the main objective of the mission, the U-2 made three passes, passing three times on a parallel course over one target area.

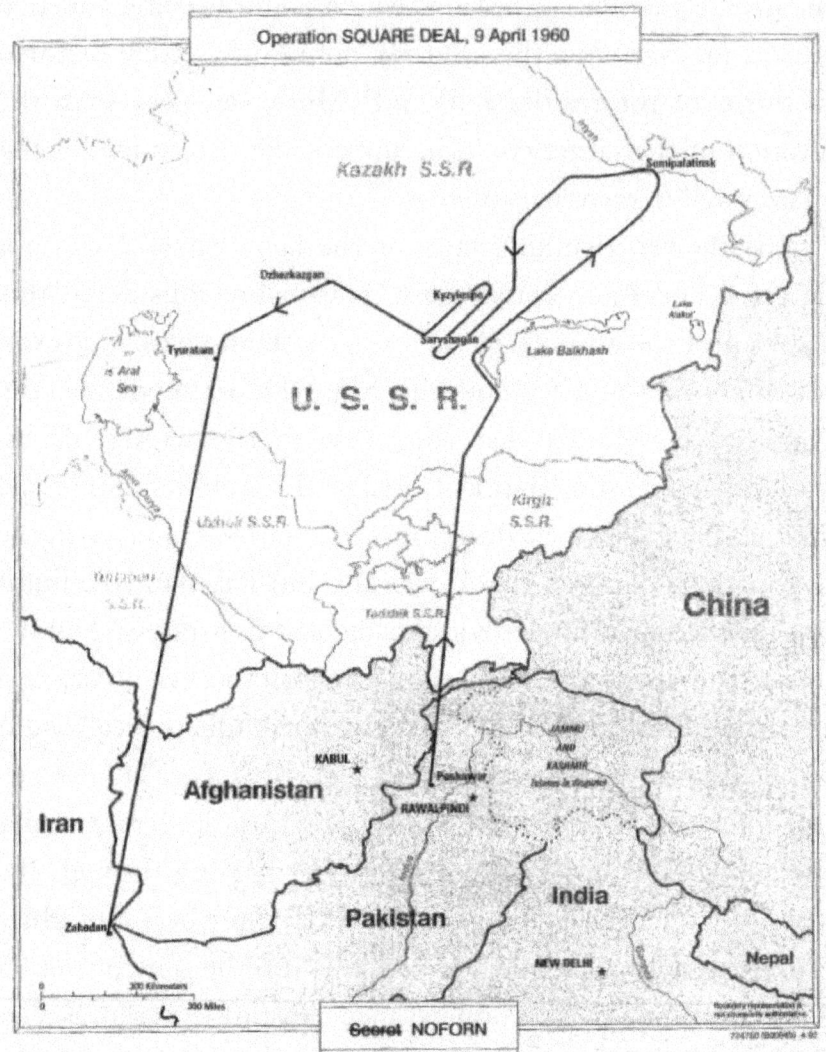

Flight diagram of the U-2 on 9 April 1960.

At the same time, Ericson did not notice any visible activity in the vast yellow-brown spaces located under the fuselage of the aircraft. It seemed to the pilot that no one was watching him. However, Ericson was wrong …

Already at 04.47, a Soviet radar station located in the area of Lake Issyk Kul, at an altitude of 4,500m above sea level, detected the passage of the intruder in a northerly direction. Four MiG-19s were scrambled to intercept, but none of the pilots could detect the target.

By this time, S-75 anti-aircraft missile launchers had already been deployed in the Semipalatinsk area, but most of them were not on combat duty yet. Besides, it was not possible to track the flight route of the intruder throughout. Also, at the Saryshagan training ground just the day before, the fighters of anti-aircraft missile systems conducted exercises, after which the missiles were removed from the launchers. While they were being re-installed, the U-2 managed to pass over this object three times and then fly off a safe distance.

An even more ridiculous situation arose in the 179th Guards Fighter Aviation Regiment (179 GIAP), which recently received the latest Su-9 high-altitude interceptors. At the regiment's command post stationed at Krasnovodsk airfield (in northern Kazakhstan), a message was received that an unknown aircraft had passed at high altitude in the area of Lake Balkhash and was moving towards Semipalatinsk. However, the command to take off the interceptors was not given. Boris Staroverov, one of the Su-9 pilots, recalled:

Time passed, but there was no team to take off. Of course, we were worried, the spy plane was already near Semipalatinsk ... we were tormented by two questions. First: why is it taking so long to give the command, the intruder will slip away! And the second one: How will we fly to Semipalatinsk? We don't have enough fuel for the return trip. So, we need an airfield for landing. We knew that there was a top-secret facility in the Semipalatinsk area, and an airfield nearby. It was called the 'Moscow-400'. However, it was not indicated in the instructions for flight operations, where alternate airfields are indicated. Therefore, it is difficult to find a runway without knowing the frequencies of the controller's radio. And to fly to nowhere in a high-speed fighter ... Somewhere, an hour after the announcement of readiness, the chief of aviation of our air defence army, General Yakov Pazychko, arrived in the regiment. 'Cowards! Fly out immediately,' he immediately shouted. 'Fly along the Irtysh River, you will find an airfield there, and from there you will be guided to the target.' We objected: 'Who will guide us? We have no connection with that airfield. And if they do, what should we do after carrying out the attack – eject?'

As a result, instead of the interceptors taking off, while every minute counted, the regiment sent a message upstairs that the Su-9 aircraft was ready for take-off, could intercept the intruder and asked for the coordinates of the 'reserve airfield' (bombers were based there, conducting nuclear bomb tests). However, from above, instead of an order, they sent ... a request. The command asked if the pilots had permits to land at a secret airfield? Of course, there were no permits, and for the next hour and a half the pilots sat in pressure helmets and altitude-compensating suits, waiting for the signal. During this time, the request for the use of a secret airfield was worked out in the government of the USSR, the headquarters of the air defence forces, the air force and even the KGB!

It was only around 07.00 that pilots Vladimir Nazarov and Boris Staroverov received the order to take off. Moreover, the exact location of the target was already unknown at that moment. A pair of Su-9s flew to the area of the Semipalatinsk nuclear test site, but did not find the target. At that time, the U-2 was making circles 800km to the south-west – over Saryshagan! After conducting a detailed aerial survey of the landfill, U-2 set a northwesterly course, reached Dzhezkazgan, and from there returned to the south-west – to Baikonur. Along the way, it photographed the railway lines with the surrounding areas. After passing over the main missile range, the U-2 headed south and flew through the territory of Uzbekistan and Turkmenistan to Iran. After six hours of flight, Ericson landed successfully at the airfield in Zahedan.

The photographs obtained gave the CIA a large amount of information. A huge complex for testing anti-missiles, that is, air defence missiles for intercepting enemy ballistic missiles, was discovered at the Saryshagan test site. And at Baikonur, the third launch complex under construction was photographed, designed for testing second-generation intercontinental ballistic (strategic) missiles R-12 (SS-7 according to the NATO classification). In addition, the cameras recorded huge new radar stations designed to track the telemetry of ballistic and space missiles, as well as new air defence radars. Also, the positions of new anti-aircraft missiles were found everywhere, which the Americans designated SA-2 (actually S-75).

It became clear that air defence was strengthening rapidly, and the Soviet missile programme was developing and expanding.

But in the Soviet Union there was no joy. When Khrushchev found out about the intruder's unpunished flight over a number of secret facilities, he became furious. Indeed, at one time, in order to hide large-scale construction work in Central Asia, a whole disinformation campaign was undertaken, which included extensive media and cultural coverage of virgin land development and other cover-up programmes. A special commission was immediately formed to clarify the question of why the spy plane could not be shot down. It quickly identified serious shortcomings in the work of the air defence and military air forces. According to the results of the inspection, the commander of the Turkestan Air Defence Corps, Major General Yuri Votintsev, was warned about incomplete official compliance, and the commander of the troops of the Turkestan Military District, Army General Ivan Fedyuninsky, received a severe reprimand.

Other middle and junior commanders, including pilots, radar operators, were also scolded. At the same time, the type of the missed intruder and the parameters of its flight could not be reliably determined. And the assumption of some experts that the reconnaissance aircraft was constantly at an altitude of 20km and above was considered delusional. So, at a special meeting of the Politburo of the Central Committee of the CPSU, Chairman of the State Committee on Aviation Technology Petr Dementiev and General Aircraft Designer Artyom Mikoyan stated (based on their Soviet experience) that there were no planes in the world that could fly at an altitude of

20,000m for six hours and forty-eight minutes. 'It is possible that this aircraft periodically gained such a height, but then it certainly descended. This means that with the air defence means that were available in the south of the country, it had to be destroyed,' the experts said.

The only thing that could be determined for sure was the speed of the intruder, which did not exceed 800km/h. This fact infuriated Khrushchev even more. 'Shame on you! The country has provided air defence with everything necessary, but you can't shoot down a subsonic plane!' he shouted at his subordinates. In response, the military complained about the interference created in the sky by other aircraft: civilian, passenger and military (for example, making scheduled and training flights near the areas over which the intruder was flying). In this regard, a plan for a complete cleansing of the sky was hastily developed. Henceforth, by a special signal 'Carpet' (Kover), absolutely all aircraft and helicopters not involved in the destruction of the target and regardless of affiliation, were to immediately land at their nearest airfield. As for the protests, after conferring with his comrades, Khrushchev decided not to do anything. As he himself explained later during the historic meeting of the Supreme Soviet of the USSR on 5 May 1969: 'We decided not to take any special measures, not to write protest notes and memos, because we knew from previous experience that this actually does not give anything. The aggressors, considering themselves stronger, acted on the principle that the weak complain about the strong, the strong do not pay attention to this and continue their brazen actions.'

Chapter 5

From Sunny Peshawar to Vladimir Central

Secrets of the Russian North

Only by a happy coincidence, Mission 4155 did not end in failure. The game was getting riskier and the stakes were getting higher. However, the CIA continued to hastily develop plans for new flights deep into the USSR.

American intelligence had received information that the deployment of R–7 strategic ballistic missiles had begun in the northern regions of the Soviet Union. To confirm this data, it was necessary to obtain at least one image of the launch pad in order to further map areas for new missions. In addition, the CIA wanted to get pictures of the nuclear test site on Novaya Zemlya. A mission plan called 'Time Step' was drawn up. According to this, the U–2 was supposed to take off from the USAF air base in Tule (Greenland), then pass south of Svalbard and reach Novaya Zemlya, flying over it from north to south. Then the route ran over railway lines from the Polar Urals to Kotlas. On the way back, the U–2 was supposed to pass over Murmansk and land at Bodø or Andøya on the northeastern coast of Norway. The last time aerial reconnaissance was conducted over these areas, including Salekhard and the Northern Urals, was in 1942, when German Bv-138 seaplanes carried out such missions.

In fact, the American intelligence data was accurate. Back on 11 January 1957, a secret resolution of the Central Committee of the CPSU was adopted on the creation of a military facility with the conditional name 'Angara'. It was created as the first military missile unit armed with intercontinental strategic missiles. The choice of location was determined by the tactical and technical characteristics of the R–7 missile: the reach of the territories of potential opponents, the possibility of conducting and monitoring test launches in the Kamchatka region and the need for special secrecy. Therefore, a deserted wooded area between Vologda and Arkhangelsk was identified for the construction of the launch sites. In February 1959, the Angara facility was renamed the 3rd Artillery Training Range. At the same time, the CIA calculated the location of the target quite accurately. By analogy with Tyuratam (Baikonur), it was believed that such an object should be located in a desert area, but close to a major railway. And so, it was in reality. The rocket test site (now the Plesetsk spaceport) was located east of the Moscow–Arkhangelsk railway and 368km from Kotlas. Thus, the flight route within the framework of operation Time Step was diligently located directly above the desired object.

In parallel, an alternative flight route was developed, called the 'Grand Slam' mission, which became the most daring in the entire history of secret flights over the USSR. If earlier U-2 and other aircraft entered the country's airspace, took aerial photographs of certain areas, and then returned in approximately the same direction, now the raid was supposed to be straight through. After taking off from Peshawar, the U-2

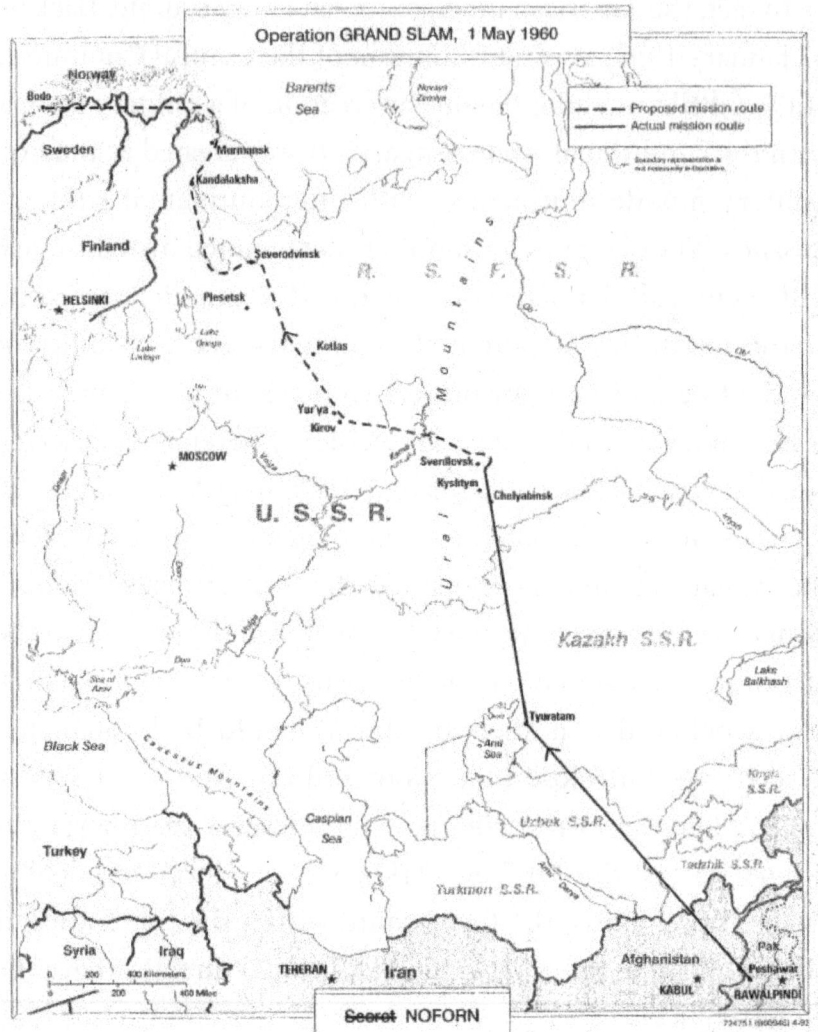

The scheme of Operation 'Grand Slam'.

was supposed to fly over Baikonur, then the iron valleys north
of Aralsk, Chelyabinsk and Sverdlovsk. Then the route turned
north-west through Perm, Kirov and Kotlas. At the final stage
of the flight, the U-2 was supposed to fly over the shipyards in
Severodvinsk, and then over Murmansk. The final point of the

route, which had a total length of 6,000km (including 4,600km in Soviet airspace), was the Norwegian Bodø airfield. The plan was named Mission 4154.

In early April, Dulles submitted both options to Eisenhower for approval. However, the president suddenly doubted the expediency of such large-scale reconnaissance missions at an inopportune period. The fact is that a summit meeting was scheduled for mid-May in Paris, where the president of the United States, the prime minister of Great Britain, the president of France and Khrushchev were to meet. In a world constantly teetering on the brink of war, great hopes were pinned on this meeting, and large anti-war demonstrations took place in many cities, including American ones. And in June, Eisenhower was going to go to Moscow. 'If one of the planes is lost while we are engaged in negotiations, I may thereby be deprived of the opportunity to take effective action. A big scandal will break out if the plane crashes,' the president said.

And Eisenhower was absolutely right in his fears. In the Soviet Union, everyone was also very hopeful for the upcoming negotiations. The people of the huge country were tired of living in constant fear of war, missile attacks and nuclear explosions. They were tired of the constant tension, conflicts and rallies. In the late 1950s, massive housing and road construction began in Russian cities, new bus and trolleybus routes were built regularly, and new shops and cinemas were opened. The standard of living began to grow rapidly. People wanted a peaceful life. Khrushchev hoped that the emerging friendship with the United States and Great Britain would give him the opportunity to reduce military spending and devote more money to social spending and space flights.

Dulles was the main proponent of continued flights. The CIA director's main argument was those very R-7 missiles. He suggested to Eisenhower that if they had more accurate information about the potential of the Russians, it would be easier to negotiate. The second argument was the possible success of these very negotiations. Dulles feared that if substantial agreements were reached with the Soviets, it would become impractical to undertake further flights. It is obvious that Dulles' position at that moment was adventurous and irresponsible. The Americans could have obtained information about the Soviet missile programme from other sources. And the value of some additional photos did not outweigh the likely risks. In addition, the flight route within the framework of the 'Grand Slam' mission was extremely risky. The U-2 was supposed to enter the airspace of the USSR on a course that had long been known to the Russians. This gave them a high chance of tracking and intercepting the target.

In the end, Eisenhower still agreed, but on the condition that the missions would not be conducted after 1 May. 'There should be no incidents two weeks before the summit,' he told Dulles. As subsequent events have shown, this decision turned out to be fatal for world history.

Both proposed routes required the use of the airfield at Bodø, for which the appropriate permission was obtained from Norwegian intelligence and military command. But since the base was used for NATO military manoeuvres then taking place in the Barents Sea area, Richard Bissell informed the White House that none of the missions could be completed earlier than 19 April. After the manoeuvres ended, bad weather over the Soviet Union prevented it. Meanwhile, CIA planners focused on the Grand Slam option as the most likely route for the proposed mission, as it seemed to offer the best chance of photographing suspicious areas where Soviet intercontinental missiles may be based. Experts concluded that Operation Time Step, with a departure from Greenland, was likely to take place in bad weather conditions (which would affect both navigation and photography), since the entire flight route passed above the 60° north latitude.

In addition, this path was considered riskier. In his letter to Bissell, one of the developers of the plan from the USAF, Colonel Berk, pointed out that Time Step was the worst option, since there was a 90% probability the U-2 would be detected and tracked, which would cause a strong air defence reaction. He wrote:

> This flight plan will allow the Russians to prepare the SA-2 positions in advance and pre-send fighter jets equipped with missiles to the Murmansk area (exit point), thereby increasing the likelihood of a successful interception. In addition, we must assume that even if the Soviets are unable to stop the flight, they will have enough evidence to allow them to document a diplomatic protest if they want to do so.

In fact, the Grand Slam mission, on the contrary, was a riskier and more dangerous undertaking!

One of the most experienced pilots, Francis Powers, was chosen to perform such an important task. In 1956–59 he had already completed 27 flights in the U-2, flying more than 500 hours. Powers had made one flight over the USSR, several missions over Egypt, six along the Soviet border, and one over China. At the same time, he had the most extensive experience of long-term flights over record distances.

On 27 April, two C-130 transport planes delivered fuel and ground personnel, as well as pilots Francis Powers and John Shinn (reserve), to the Peshawar air base. On the night of 28 April, the U-2C was delivered as well. The CIA feared that the Pakistanis would guess the true purpose of the aircraft, and earlier it was reported that foreign intelligence had become aware of the deployment of reconnaissance aircraft in Incirlik. Therefore, additional precautions were taken before Mission 4154. According to the instructions received, the U-2 was supposed to stay in Peshawar for no more than six hours and only at night. If for some reason the flight was postponed, the plane should be transported back to Incirlik.

And so it happened. Initially, the operation was scheduled for the morning of 28 April, but due to weather conditions over the Soviet Union, it had to be postponed. As a result, the mission was scheduled for the deadline set by Eisenhower – 1 May 1960. If there had been bad weather over Eastern Europe on this day, the wheel of history would have turned differently! Powers started preparing for departure twice, but it was cancelled. Before dawn on 29 April, the U-2C flew back to Turkey again. As a result, according to the regulations, that aircraft had to be put on maintenance, and on the night of 30 April to 1 May, another U–2C (factory number No. 360, registration number 56-6693) was flown to Pakistan by Bob Ericson. This plane had a bad reputation. The previous autumn it had made an emergency landing in the Fujisawa area of Japan and attracted the attention of the Japanese public and journalists. Although it was repaired and now had a more powerful J-75 engine, the pilots did not fully trust this aircraft and even nicknamed it 'Hangar Queen'. U–2C No. 360 was an upgraded version of the aircraft, equipped with a 'B'-type camera, an electronic reconnaissance module System-Vl and an electronic jamming device System-IXB. It was capable of detecting radar radiation and automatically sending a generated signal with false coordinates of the aircraft.

Americans, of course, knew that 1 May in the Soviet Union marks the second most important public holiday after 7 November (the anniversary of the October Revolution). They knew that a traditional military parade would be held in Moscow, during which the USSR would once again demonstrate to the world the power of its army and the latest achievements of the military industry. It was clear that flying a spy plane on such a day would be another brazen challenge to the command of the Soviet Army and Khrushchev personally. And if successful, a real spit in his face! But the Americans (at least some of them) for some reason naively believed that during the holiday the air defence system would not be in full combat readiness. The CIA lacked data on the true state of the Soviet air defences and the breakthrough in development that it had made recently.

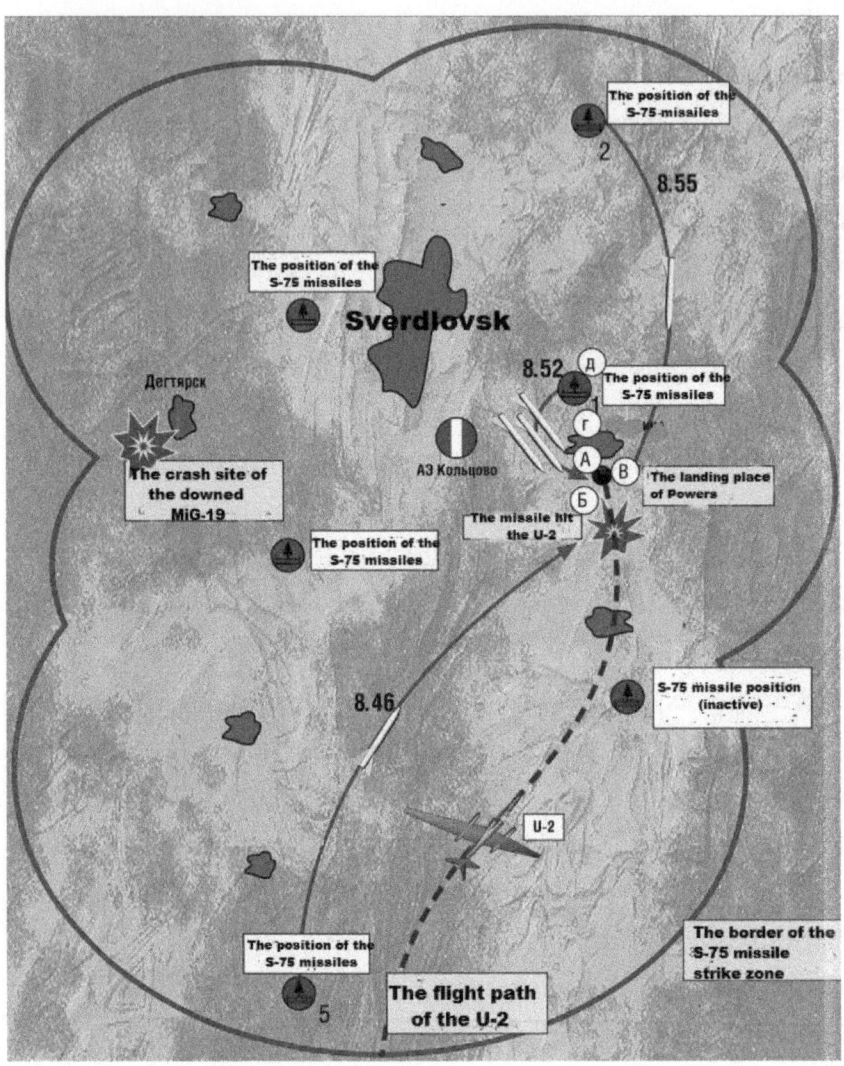

The scheme of destruction of the U-2 aircraft.

Nevertheless, the Americans calculated the risks. They assumed that after passing the Tyuratam missile range and the Aral Sea, the Russians would be able to calculate the further direction of flight – the Urals. This would allow them to put the S-75 missile divisions probably located there on alert in a timely manner. At the same time, the length of the route did not give the pilot the opportunity to manoeuvre, fuel was scarce, and the possibility was even considered that on the last leg of the route the U-2 would have to plan for landing with the engine turned off. Therefore, the commander of Detachment B, Colonel William Shelton, just in case, approved a back-up route – from Plesetsk or Severodvinsk directly over the territory of Finland and Sweden – directly to Norway. Landing on the territory of Finland or Sweden was allowed, but only as a last resort. Shelton told Powers that he should make it to Norway if possible.

By the way, Francis Powers, as an experienced reconnaissance pilot, understood that the upcoming mission would be very risky. That is why he took a silver dollar with him for the first time. In a special case inside the coin, a very thin needle was hidden that was lubricated with the deadly poison of the Conus geographus mollusc. A prick from it would cause a person to die within two minutes. The needle was hidden in a channel that was drilled into the dollar, protruding slightly from it. The channel was closed with a plug, at one end of which there was a thread, and at the other an eyelet. It was enough to unscrew the plug and prick with the revealed tip, and death would happen immediately. This rather exotic invention, which fully corresponded to the spirit of the entire Aquaton project, was invented to replace cyanide capsules.

The Dragon's Order

On the night of 1 May, immediately after receiving a weather report that indicated relatively clear weather over the Urals and the northern regions of the USSR, the final start time was set at 06.00. Then there were some more unforeseen delays. Finally, at 06.26, the U-2 took to the air. First, it headed for Afghanistan, simultaneously gaining a set altitude, and from there turned towards the Soviet Union. According to Soviet information, the plane crossed the border at 05.36 (Moscow time) in the sector south-east of Kirovobad, and was detected by radar over Afghanistan. According to the recollections of Powers himself, during the first leg of the flight, the earth was completely covered by clouds, and the first light appeared only when he was already south-east of the Aral Sea. From a height of 20km, the pilot saw almost the entire panorama of the Central Asian part of the Soviet empire, which he had to fly through in nine hours. After correcting the course, Powers saw contrails below and realised that his flight was no longer a secret. He failed to photograph Baikonur, as there was a huge cloud above it. The U-2 slightly changed the direction of flight and at 07.09 (Moscow time) flew 75km east of the spaceport. So, the aircraft passed very close to the area of action of the anti-aircraft missile regiment equipped with the S-75. Now the U-2 had set a course for the Urals ...

At 80km, over Chelyabinsk, Powers suddenly had control problems. The autopilot began to malfunction, and the nose of the aircraft turned up. The pilot restarted the device several times, but the failures did not stop. As a result, Powers simply turned off the autopilot and switched completely to manual control. During this period, the U-2 deviated somewhat from its planned course and passed 60km west of one of the anti-aircraft missile regiments located in the Chelyabinsk region. After that, Powers photographed the secret city of Chelyabinsk-40 (now Ozersk) located between Chelyabinsk and Sverdlovsk. The Mayak plant, which was engaged in the production of weapons-grade plutonium, was located there. Two and a half years earlier, there had been a major accident that involved the release of radioactive waste.

After Chelyabinsk-40, the U-2 headed for Sverdlovsk. Seeing the peaceful sky and sunny morning around him, the pilot did not even suspect what kind of movement he had created down there...

At about 06.00 Moscow time, an alarm was announced in all radar, anti-aircraft missile, and fighter units from Central Asia and Kazakhstan to Siberia and the Far North. Soon, the Commander-in-Chief of the Air Defence Forces Marshal Sergei Biryuzov, the Chief of the General Staff of the Air Defence Colonel-General Pyotr Demidov, the Commander of the Fighter Aviation of the Air Defence Lieutenant General Yevgeny Savitsky, the Commander of the Anti-Aircraft Missile Forces Colonel-General Konstantin Kazakov and other responsible persons arrived at the Central Command Post of the USSR Air Defence Forces. The appearance of the intruder aircraft was reported to the Minister of Defence of the USSR Marshal Rodion Malinovsky, and Nikita Khrushchev, who were going to the parade. The Soviet leader took this news as another direct challenge from the Americans and ordered that the spy plane be shot down at all costs, as well as asking that he be kept constantly informed of events. Following this, General Savitsky, who had the code call sign

'Dragon',[1] ordered his subordinates to attack the intruder with all available fighters on duty, and if necessary, to ram. At the same time, a Carpet signal was given to all aviation units, as well as the civil airline Aeroflot. Without exception, all planes and helicopters that were in the air at that moment were ordered to land immediately at the nearest airfield. A pair of MiG-15bis from the 412th IAP from the 101st Fighter Aviation Division took off first to intercept. However, these outdated aircraft could not cope with the task due to the high altitude of the target.

At about 07.35 (Moscow time), the U-2 reached the territory of the Urals and entered the area of operation of the 4th Ural Separate Air Defence Army. Not long before that, General Savitsky called the army command post and clarified which fighters were available. It turned out that at the Koltsovo civil airfield in Sverdlovsk there were two of the newest Su-9 high-altitude interceptors and their pilots, captains Anatoly Sakovich and Igor Mentyukov. An order was immediately received: urgently prepare both fighters for take-off and interception of the target. When Savitsky was told that the planes lacked high-altitude equipment for pilots and missile weapons, he gave the order to ram the target. If successful, it meant certain death for the pilots!

It should be noted that these fighters were not on combat duty, they were actually there purely by accident. At the end of April, Mentyukov, who served at the Sevasleika air base in the Gorky region, had received a task – to take the Su-9 from

---

[1] Savitsky used it while flying a fighter during the Second World War.

Novosibirsk to the Baranovichi air base, where the 61st IAP was located. On 27 April, Mentyukov and his partner Sakovich arrived at Novosibirsk Aviation Plant No. 153, accepted a pair of new Su-9s there and flew west. On 30 April, the interceptors landed at Koltsovo, where they stayed overnight due to bad weather.

At 07.40, Captain Sakovich's Su-9 took off. It was aimed at a sector 150km south of Troitsk (450km from Koltsovo). However, due to erroneous guidance service data indicating a target altitude of 10,000m, the fighter flew to 12,000m and did not find the target.

By 08.00, the Soviet air defence command, having studied the information received, concluded that the U-2 would probably fly over Sverdlovsk, then to the White Sea and land in Norway. In general, the CIA's plan was revealed quite quickly. At 08.28, when the U-2 was already on the approach to Sverdlovsk, the second Su-9 took off from Koltsovo airfield. Igor Mentyukov recalled:

On the morning of 1 May, after 6 am, we were picked up, I received the command on the phone: 'Readiness number one'. I thought the weather had improved; we were in a hurry. I took off, and they're sending me to Chelyabinsk. The question immediately arose: why was I sent to the east? A little later, the anxiety intensified. It was not the airfield command post that contacted me, but the commander of the Air Defence Army aviation, Major General Yuri Vovk.

'I am the Falcon, 732nd, can you hear me? Listen to me carefully. The goal is real, high-altitude. Ram it.

The order of Moscow. The order was given by the "Dragon"!'

There were minutes of reflection. This means that it is a serious case if the order is transmitted by the 'Dragon' himself.

I answer: 'I am ready for a suicide attack. The only request is to take care of the family and mother … Everything will be done.'

I fly in the direction of Chelyabinsk for 17 minutes, but no one gets in touch. I've already thought about it: they sent it and forgot. But then I heard in my headphones: 'Can you hear me?' 'It's fine,' I reply. 'Follow this course.' A little bit later: 'Did the fuel run out in the outboard fuel tanks?' I say, 'No.' However, the command immediately followed: 'Drop the outboard fuel tanks, you will go to ram!'. Dropped the outboard fuel tanks. I get the command: 'Hit your afterburners'. I turned on the afterburner mode of the engine, turned the plane 120 degrees and accelerated it to a speed of M = 1.9, or maybe to M = 2.0. They began to take me to a 20-kilometre altitude.

A few minutes have passed, they tell me: '25 kilometres to the target.' I turned on the scope, and the whole screen is in interference. That's the problem. It worked fine after the start, but nothing is visible here … I say: 'The sight is clogged with interference; I use visual detection.' But there are problems here too. The speed of the target is 750–780km/h, and I have a speed of more than twice the speed of sound. In short, I don't see the goal. When I was about 12 kilometres away from the target, I was informed that she had started a U-turn. Later I found out that at that moment the target disappeared from the radar screen. I'm making a U-turn behind the offending aircraft. I am informed that I am chasing a target at a distance of 8 kilometres, skipping past it.

General Vovk shouts at me: 'Turn off the afterburner, slow down!'

'I can't turn it off.' I also got mad, realising that the command post did not know how to use and aim the Su-9 at the target.

'Turn it off, this is an order,' the general relayed once again. I swore and turned it off.

And then a new order: 'Get out of the zone, they're shooting at you!'

In this case, the targeting was also inaccurate. Captain Mentyukov's Su-9 gained an altitude of 20,750m and turned out to be almost at the same height as Powers, flying at an altitude of 21,500m. But he was 10–12km to the right. At the same time, while the Soviet pilot did not visually observe the target, Powers did not see the Su-9 either.

Meanwhile, the U-2 entered the area of destruction of the 5th and 6th Divisions of the 37th Anti-Aircraft Missile Brigade. At 08.43, the first B-750IR missile was fired at it, and then, after a short period, the second and third missiles. However, at that moment, the target began to turn left, and all the missiles exploded away from it. Mentyukov also saw rocket explosions:

By that time, flashes of explosions appeared in the air, one flash slightly ahead of the course, the second on the right. Anti-aircraft missile launchers were working …

I turn around, leave the affected area, and then ask about the location of the target. They tell me from the command post: 'The target is behind.' I'm making a new U-turn, but I feel like I'm falling. I was flying without afterburner; I didn't notice how the speed dropped to 300km/h. I fell to a height of 15,000 metres. And from the command post they shout: 'Hit your afterburners.' Evil has taken me again, I'm screaming: 'You need to know how and at what speeds it turns on.' I accelerated the plane to 450km/h, I try to turn on the afterburner, although it turns on at 550km/h. At this time, the emergency fuel residue light turns on. It becomes clear: the targeting failed. They give instructions – fly to Koltsovo.

Meanwhile, the U-2 entered the affected area of the 57th Anti-Aircraft Missile Brigade located in the Sverdlovsk region. Due to the fact that the radar signal was weak and periodically interrupted, it was not possible to catch the target immediately, but when it had already begun to move away in a northerly direction. At 08.52, the calculation of the 2nd Division (commander Major Mikhail Voronov) fired a missile at an already receding target ...

Being 60km south-east of Sverdlovsk, Powers first turned left, and then set a course on which he was going to pass over the northwestern outskirts of the city. The city, spread out on the Ural Mountains, was already clearly visible ahead. The pilot observed low peaks and passes still covered with snow, while the surrounding area was already covered in greenery. Flying up to Sverdlovsk, Powers began to fill out the flight log, when suddenly a bright orange flash lit up everything around and even the inside of the cabin. A second later, the pilot heard a loud bang from somewhere behind. Frightened, he began frantically checking the aircraft's systems. At first, Powers thought that everything was working fine. But then, to his utter horror, the U-2 began to slowly dip to the right. The pilot turned the steering wheel and managed to level the the wings. Powers mentally mapped out a course in his head that he would have to use to reach friendly territory in case the plane was damaged. And it was very far away!

Then it turned out that things were even worse. The nose of the U-2 began to drop, and even taking moving the controls, Powers failed to align it. In all likelihood, the right stabilizer had been damaged by rocket fragments, and then it completely fell off.

Descending rapidly, the plane went into a tailspin, falling tail first. Centrifugal force threw Powers against the dashboard, then the cabin depressurized, the flight suit began to inflate,

A cartoon in one of the Soviet newspapers.

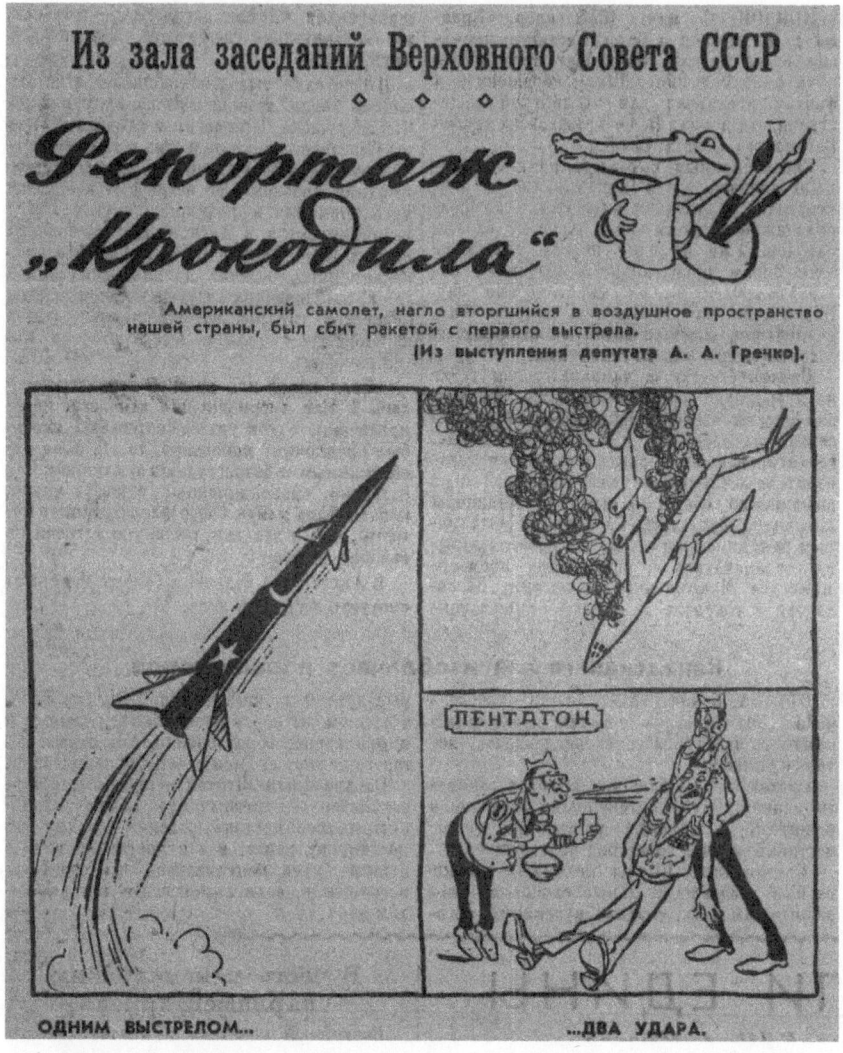

A cartoon in one of the Soviet newspapers.

and he could not reach the ejector seat lever. The pilot was able to partially move the canopy and unfasten his straps, after which he was thrown out of the cockpit, but only halfway as he was restrained by his oxygen hoses. At the same time, the glass of his helmet was immediately covered with frost, and the pilot could not reach the button for destroying the equipment compartment either (or maybe he did not want to, for fear of exploding with it). Powers finally freed himself by ripping out the oxygen hoses. The parachute opened automatically at an altitude of 4,500m, when it was already close to the ground …

'He's in a Space suit, and Here We Are With Moonshine'

Neither the headquarters of the 57th Anti-Aircraft Missile Brigade nor the command post of the 4th Separate Air Defence Army realised that the target had been hit (and it just couldn't be believed!). The radars gave a fuzzy picture, which made it impossible to determine the situation. As a result, another B-750BH was fired at the target, the result of the explosion of which could not be traced either. Then a report came to the brigade's command post: 'The target increased jamming and was lost.' At 08.43, by order of the deputy commander of the 4th Separate Air Defence Army, General Vovk, a pair of MiG-19 fighters flown by Captain Boris Ayvazyan and Senior Lieutenant Sergei Safronov from the 365th IAP were scrambled from Koltsovo. The pilots were tasked with attacking the target if it dropped or lost altitude for some reason. At the same time, Vovk apparently got nervous, so he forgot to report this to his commander. At 08.53, a navigator of the army fighter aviation, Colonel Pavel Tereshchenko, found a pair of MiG-19s on the radar screen and ordered them to follow the anti-aircraft missile explosions at an altitude of 11,000m. Then, as later indicated in the results of the investigation of the Ministry of Defence, Tereshchenko withdrew from their management.

Meanwhile, the 9th Separate Radio Engineering Battalion under the command of Lieutenant Colonel Ivan Repin continued to stubbornly report to the main command post about the flight of the target at an altitude of 19,000m, while instead of the U-2, Russian MiG-19s flying at an altitude of 11,000m were in the sky. Soon, the fighters, having used up most of their fuel, turned towards their airfield and headed straight through the zone of destruction of the 4th Division of the 57th Anti-Aircraft Missile Brigade. The equipment for identifying friend or foe aircraft on the P-12 radar station attached to it turned out to be faulty. As a result, Major A.V. Shugaev's division fired three missiles one after the other, one of which shot down Senior Lieutenant Safronov's MiG-19. The pilot was killed. Ayvazyan, seeing a bright flash in the sky, realised from his experience that this was not good. He immediately threw his fighter into a sharp dive, thereby dodging the next B-750BH missiles.[2] Until 09.30 Moscow time, the air defence command was not sure that the target had been hit. Only when the signal completely disappeared from the radar (and the sky at that time was literally clean) did the commander-in-chief of

---

[2] A memo to the Minister of Defence following the investigation of the incident stated: 'The reason for the death of the pilot was the poor performance of the combat crew of the main command post of the air defence army. The heads of the units did not inform the main command post about the decisions taken, and the main command post, in turn, did not inform the commanders of the units about the situation. The 57th Anti-Aircraft Missile Brigade did not know about the presence of fighters in the air. That's why Safronov's plane was shot down.'

the air defence forces, Marshal Sergei Biryuzov, finally gather his resolve and personally call Khrushchev. It happened half an hour before the start of the military parade on Kraskaya Square. Biryuzov reported excitedly: 'Nikita Sergeevich, the intruder plane has been shot down!'

In total, the troops of the 4th Ural Separate Air Defence Army carried out eight fighter sorties on 1 May and fired eight anti-aircraft missiles, including five at the target and three at Russian fighters. It should be noted that the hunt for the U-2 over the Urals also became the apotheosis of the competitive struggle between Soviet aviators and rocket scientists. Khrushchev believed that the future lay with missiles, including anti-aircraft missiles, and the aviation command was trying to defend its position. The amount of funding depended on it. Therefore, it was extremely important as to who was eventually be able to shoot down a reconnaissance aircraft first. General Savitsky was very much counting on the new Su-9 interceptors, which is why he gave the order to ram the target. But in the end, the victory still turned out to be for the rocket men.

While the battle continued in the sky over Sverdlovsk, Powers peacefully parachuted down almost in the very centre of the country, which in the West was called the 'evil empire'. He had a map showing the routes of passage to Turkey and Pakistan, but he would have had to have been a major optimist to hope that he would be able to walk several thousand kilometres unnoticed from the territory of the Urals and make his way to the border! When the ground was close, Powers saw a small village and realised that he was not descending into a deserted taiga.

On a warm May morning, peasants from the village of Kosulino celebrated Pervomay (as this holiday was called in the USSR) on the state farm field. Unlike residents of large cities, leisure in the province was less pretentious and cultured. The peasants drank moonshine (samogon, home-made vodka) and ate it with fried meat. A small fire was smoking nearby, on which a barbecue was being fried … Suddenly, someone noticed a parachutist in the sky, who smoothly descended at the other end of this field.

Four young men: Vladimir Surin, Leonid Chuzhakin, Peter Asabin and Anatoly Cheremisin, ran to meet the 'guest'. Chuzhakin later recalled: 'We ran up to Francis Powers. He was in a spacesuit, sweating all over. And we had a bottle of moonshine in our hands.' The strange attire of the pilot immediately reminded the peasants of fantastic drawings from books about astronauts. Everyone had heard that people would soon fly to near-Earth space, so the young men immediately decided that they had the first astronaut in front of them! The stranger helped Powers (to his considerable surprise, because the pilot was taught that Russians were animals and would immediately tear him apart) extinguish the parachute and remove the equipment. Soon the rest of the residents, women and children, ran up. Immediately, an offer was made to him that they get drunk (including moonshine) and feed an important guest from heaven. However, Chuzhakin showed responsibility, asked someone to quickly bring a car and delivered the 'astronaut' to the office of the collective farm. Chuzhakin did this not because he suspected why the guest did not say anything (maybe he was in shock), but simply thought 'it's necessary'. After all, he was a man who had just returned from an important government assignment. Soon, the shocked Powers, who had recently been in the cockpit of one of the most advanced aircraft in the world, found himself in a primitive and creaking Moskvich-407 car!

Regarding further events, there are several similar versions but they have one common point. The collective farm office informed their bosses about the arrival of the 'astronaut'. There, after puzzled questions in the spirit of 'what kind of astronaut?', they in turn then reported this to the military. The information then flew around the headquarters at lightning speed and reached the command post of the 4th Separate Air Defence Army. And only there did they realise that the reports were about the pilot of the downed plane.

While this process was under way, the morally broken Francis Powers did not try to escape or use his silver dollar.[3] During his first interrogation, when KGB officers and the military arrived in Kosulino by helicopter, he himself gave out this souvenir, simultaneously explaining its purpose. According to Soviet information, during the search, a pistol with a silencer, coins and two bundles of Soviet banknotes were seized from Powers. Later, other items were added to this physical evidence. Not far from the pilot's landing site, a bag was found containing a hacksaw, pliers, fishing gear, a mosquito net, trousers, a hat, socks and other things from his emergency reserve.

---

[3] Later, Surin, Chuzhakin, Asabin and Cheremisin were awarded medals 'for bravery' for the detention of a foreign spy.

At 12.00, a Tu-104 plane took off from Moscow on its way to Sverdlovsk with a commission consisting of employees of the Central Committee of the CPSU, KGB military counterintelligence, officers and generals of the General Staff of the Air Defence Forces. They were tasked with analyzing the actions of the units, and collecting and delivering all the wreckage of the reconnaissance aircraft to Moscow. The remains of the U-2 were soon discovered by a helicopter near the village of Povarnya. The wreckage was scattered over a large area, while the front part of the fuselage with the cockpit and the centre section, the engine and the tail section were relatively well preserved. But most importantly, a camera with film was found in the forest, that had received only minor damage.

At 15.00, Powers was taken by helicopter to the airfield in Koltsovo (the same one from which fighters took off to intercept him seven hours ago), and from there he was taken by Tu-104 to Moscow. The American was given a special cell in the KGB's Lubyanka building, where he was put under round-the-clock surveillance.

'Dirty Lark' and the Best Case Scenario

Even before U-2C No. 360 did not arrive at the base in Norway, the Americans realised that something had happened to it. At 03.30 Washington time (Powers was shot down at 01.55), the CIA Operations Centre received a message compiled on the basis of radio interception data. It reported that an hour and a half ago, the Russians stopped tracking the flight of the reconnaissance aircraft. The area where the U-2 supposedly disappeared from radar was even identified – south-west of Sverdlovsk. The Americans managed to decrypt the messages that 'the intruder has descended and is making a U-turn' (in fact, it was about the missile attack against MiG-19 fighters). As a result, the CIA concluded that, in all likelihood, the U-2 had engine problems, as a result of which Powers dropped to a lower altitude to restart the engine and was shot down in the Sverdlovsk region. It turned out that Senior Lieutenant Safronov did not die in vain! The fatal mistake of the air defence forces misled the Americans and forced them to act on the basis of obviously erroneous data. At the same time, the CIA was absolutely sure that Powers had died or, at the very least, committed suicide.

In this regard, an operation code-named 'Mudlark' was quickly developed and a pre-prepared cover story was put into action. As the CIA officers themselves put it, it proceeded from the best case scenario, according to which neither the pilot, nor the plane, nor the film survived the mission. 'After almost four years of successful U-2 missions, Richard Bissell and the rest of the project staff became overconfident and were not ready for the "worst case" scenario, which actually occurred in May 1960,' the CIA report on the U-2 programme said later.

On the morning of 2 May, at Incirlik air base in Turkey, a CIA officer responsible for public relations made an official statement that a non-military weather scout U-2 from the 2nd (temporary) Meteorological Reconnaissance Squadron (2.WRS(P)) went missing during a scheduled flight over Turkey. At the same time, the pilot – an employee of Lockheed, who worked for NASA – managed to report interruptions in the operation of the oxygen system. On 3 May, NASA itself duplicated this statement. However, contrary to the fears of Eisenhower and Dulles, there was no reaction from the Soviet Union. In this regard, the CIA staff, who were intensely all Soviet communications monitoring, even suggested that perhaps the U-2 had not been shot down at all, but had crashed and simply come down 'somewhere in Siberia'.

Meanwhile, the American leadership seriously feared that the incident could provoke the outbreak of the Third World War. It is no coincidence that three days later, Eisenhower authorised the start of one of the largest nuclear training alerts in the history of the country.

At 02.15 on 4 May, all 730 air defence sirens wailed in New York, heralding the beginning of a 3-day training air alert, called Alert 1960. The terrifying wail of sirens sounded in all American states at once. At the same time, all radio and television stations were interrupted. The population was ordered to take shelter in bomb shelters and the basements of houses. Any dissenters were forced there. At the same time, police cars with sirens turned on blocked passage through the streets, departures were delayed at airports, and railway trains were halted. An American journalists, who watched these events from the 102nd floor of a skyscraper, described his impressions as follows: 'I was scared. It seemed like I saw the sudden death of the city.'

The alarm did not go smoothly everywhere. For example, in Philadelphia, Boston and Texas, most citizens refused to go to the bomb shelters. Instead, anti-war activists held a series of demonstrations demanding a ban on nuclear weapons. Many Americans rationalised ignoring the alarm by the fact that in the event of a nuclear war, no bomb shelters would help anyway. Why hide, they say, so that you can live in a radiation-infected world? It's better to die right away and not suffer … Fatalism and panic accompanied the entire 'Alert 1960'. And just a few hours later, the Americans realised what had caused this alarm.

On the morning of 5 May, a meeting of the Supreme Soviet (Parliament) of the USSR began. Nikita Khrushchev, who was constantly smiling, came up to the podium and made a long report. He talked about new successes in industry and agriculture, and then smoothly moved on to foreign policy and the upcoming meeting of heads of state in Paris. At the same time, Khrushchev praised Eisenhower in every possible way, noting that he 'sincerely strives for peace'. But there were, he said, certain circles (groupings) that limited and restrained the peaceful efforts of the president. Among the representatives of such groups, the Soviet leader named only … Richard Nixon. Khrushchev even compared him to a goat who was assigned to guard cabbage. This comparison caused loud laughter in the audience. Khrushchev then made another comparison, saying that trying to conduct politics from a position of strength now looked like trying to 'revive a dead rat'.

When the hall and the journalists present in it, including foreign ones, had already had a lot of fun, Khrushchev moved on to the main sensation:

Moreover, recently we have encountered facts of direct provocative actions. Fellow deputies! On behalf of the Soviet Government, I must inform you about the aggressive actions that have taken place in recent weeks by the United States of America against the Soviet Union. What were these aggressive actions expressed in? They expressed themselves in the fact that the United States of America sent planes that crossed our state borders and invaded the borders of the Soviet Union.

He further said that in previous years there had been many similar incidents, and the Americans always responded to protests about them with formal replies. Recently, on 9 April, another such violation of Soviet airspace occurred. Khrushchev said that the reconnaissance plane came from Afghanistan and probably took off from Turkey, Iran or Pakistan. And then Khrushchev revealed another secret, explaining why the USSR did not protest after this incident, and at the same time told how he personally demanded that the air defence command resolutely stop such actions.

As if laying out one trump card after another on the table, the leader continued the story:

The American military apparently liked impunity, as it was on 9 April. And they decided to repeat the aggressive act. For this purpose, the day of 1 May, a solemn day for our people and the workers of all countries, was chosen – the International Holiday of Fraternal Solidarity of the working Class. On this day, early in the morning, at 5.36 am (Moscow time), an American plane crossed our border and continued its flight deep into the Soviet country.

The Minister of Defence immediately reported this aggressive act to the Government. The government said: the aggressor knows what he is doing when he invades someone else's territory. If he goes unpunished, he will go on new provocations. Therefore, we must act decisively – shoot down the plane! This mission was accomplished – the plane was shot down. After the first investigation, it turned out that the plane belongs to the United States of America, although it does not have identification marks, these signs were painted over.

This news had already caused the effect of an exploding political bomb. Stunned foreign correspondents were still translating Khrushchev's words, but already according to the words 'the plane was shot down', 'the United States' and the violent reaction in the hall, accompanied by shouts and exclamations in the spirit of 'this is banditry', 'shame on the aggressor', and 'they shot it down correctly', it was clear that Khrushchev said something incredible.

Having fairly fed the excited audience with sensations and threatened the Americans with missiles with thermonuclear warheads (also to cheers from the audience), Khrushchev wondered: who sent this plane into the airspace of the USSR? Eisenhower himself or some aggressive groups from the Pentagon? Then Khrushchev compared the flights of American high-altitude reconnaissance aircraft with the reconnaissance flights of the German Luftwaffe before the outbreak of the Great Patriotic War. He asked the audience, do you remember how the 'possessed Hitler' sent his planes into our airspace, we wrote protests, and how did it end? Isn't there an analogy here? 'How do we assess the invasion of an American aircraft, and not the only one, but a repeated one? How can we regard it as a harbinger of war, a harbinger of an attack, that is, a repetition of what was done by Hitler at the time?' howled Khrushchev. But at the end of the speech, he nevertheless relented, saying that he still believed in Eisenhower's peacefulness and in no way wanted to believe that he could have personally authorised such flights.

Nikita Khrushchev was still giving his speech when the sensational news flashed around all the world's news agencies. The Americans modestly responded to this accusation with another NASA press release, which reported that 'all U-2 weather scouts have been suspended from flights to check the oxygen system'. But Pandora's box was already open, and the consequences were completely unpredictable.

On the same day, 5 May, Democratic Senator Mike Mansfield addressed Congress. At first, he burst into an angry speech about the fact that the communists were just waiting for an excuse to take advantage of 'our weakness' and strike at Western democracy. And here we ourselves give the Bolsheviks an obvious pretext for aggression and aggravation of the international situation! 'The government should answer what kind of plane it was, what was it doing near the border with the Soviet Union, and why did the president know nothing about it before receiving the message from Moscow?' Mansfield asked reasonably. White House Press Secretary James Hagerty stated with an honest face that he did not know anything at all about the incident with the plane mentioned in Khrushchev's report. Later, Hagerty held a second press conference, at which he informed the media that 'on the instructions of the president, a full investigation of the circumstances of the plane incident is being conducted, the results of which will be published'.

Meanwhile, on the evening of 5 May, the US ambassador to the USSR, Llewellyn E. 'Tommy' Thompson, accidentally overheard at a banquet how Deputy Foreign Russian Minister Yakov Malik blabbed to the Swiss ambassador that, 'We are still interrogating the pilot.' Thompson, white with horror, immediately referred to feeling unwell ('the champagne hit my head') and ran to call the State Department via a closed communication channel. But they did not believe in these panic reports.

Meanwhile, the White House's attempts to hide the details about the downed U-2 led to an unexpected reaction. American society and the media, electrified by anti-Soviet propaganda, decided that the USSR had committed an act of aggression against the United States, but for some reason the president did not react to this incident in any way. On the morning of 6 May, dozens of American newspapers published headlines such as 'The Russians shot down our plane!' and 'The Soviet Union attacked us!' Similar cries were heard on the air of numerous radio stations, as well as on television. Many journalists, senators and congressmen, especially from the Democratic Party, screamed that the president should respond immediately and directly to Khrushchev's accusations. Others, with faces red with excitement, called for the immediate torpedoing of the upcoming summit meeting in response to this, 'another Soviet provocation'. Meanwhile, the State Department continued to adhere to the old best case scenario and officially stated that 'there was no attempt at a deliberate invasion of the Soviet Union's airspace'. And he even called 'monstrous' any suggestion that the United States was trying to mislead the world community about the goals of the mission.

Despite the anti-communist hysteria, America still remained a democratic country. Therefore, there were those who immediately blamed the incident on Eisenhower and the government, which was constantly hiding something from the people. One of the TV companies released a sensational story that a military aircraft in service with the USAF was probably shot down in the sky over the USSR. The *Wall Street Journal* newspaper wrote:

> These aircraft are taking part in nuclear tests at the Nevada test site and are capable of rising to a great height. They are used to monitor missile test flights and other reconnaissance purposes. The American plane shot down over Soviet territory is a new victim of the constant practice of looking over the border for intelligence purposes.

James Reston, a well-known columnist for *The New York Times* newspaper, wrote:

> It is the United States that has military and aviation bases on the border with the Soviet Union and China, and

not vice versa. These are unpleasant facts that are rarely mentioned in this part of the world … It is unclear why it was necessary to send planes a few days before the summit meeting with Khrushchev to collect meteorological information and study wind shear on the Soviet–Turkish border … The events taking place near the southern border of the Soviet Union are not some kinds of child's play, and countries, as well as individuals, should ask themselves how they would feel if we switched places. Suppose the Soviets had a base in Mexico from which planes would fly daily along the Texas border – bombers, sometimes weather observation planes, sometimes planes equipped with cameras for reconnaissance. Let's assume that they would occasionally accidentally fly over the territory of the United States. How would Washington react to this?

The CIA, apparently, was quite surprised by such awareness of journalists about their top-secret programmes. The Canadian newspaper *Globe and Mail*, with reference to its Washington correspondent, accurately described not only the aircraft, but also the purpose of the mission carried out by Francis Powers:

> Aircraft flying at high altitudes are used by the United States in a determined attempt to establish the exact location of Soviet missile bases. The United States sends single-engine reconnaissance aircraft (similar to the plane shot down by the Russians) that fly at extremely high

altitudes, carrying special radar and infrared equipment with which they take pictures of Soviet territory ... It is extremely important for the United States to establish the exact location of Russian missile launch bases, because otherwise it will be impossible to target Soviet weapons if such a need arises.

As you know now, Khrushchev paused, keeping both his own and the world community in the dark. He wanted the Americans to put all their playing cards on the table first, and only then he would throw his trump ace on the table. And this plan worked completely. On 7 May, Khrushchev again came to a meeting of the Supreme Council (considering himself an adherent of Leninist principles, he sought to turn this body from formally representative into a real organ of democracy), where he stated that the pilot of the downed spy plane was alive and had confessed that he worked for the CIA, and the equipment of his aircraft that had been found clearly indicated the espionage nature of his mission. Moreover, Khrushchev accurately described all the preparations for the mission: 'If someone believes that the pilot lost consciousness due to lack of oxygen and the plane continued to fly on autopilot, then let him believe that on autopilot you can fly from Turkey to Pakistan, land at Peshawar airport, stay there for three days, take off on the morning of 1 May, and then fly two thousand kilometres over our territory in four hours.'

And again this news (and especially the details) again produced the effect of an exploded (not yet nuclear) bomb all over the world.

Just a couple of hours after the Soviet leader's speech, the United Press International agency reported:

> President Eisenhower and other American officials today carefully studied the statement of Soviet Prime Minister Nikita Khrushchev that the pilot of the American plane shot down over Russia confessed that he had a spy mission. The president, who is spending Sunday rest at his farm in Gettysburg (in Pennsylvania), was informed about Khrushchev's statement by White House press secretary Hagerty. When asked about Eisenhower's reaction, Hagerty told reporters that all comments would come from the State Department. The State Department said it was preparing a statement. Neither the State Department nor NASA has responded yet.

The Washington newspaper *Sunday Dispatch* asked bluntly: 'Many Americans are asking the question: what kind of idiot sent a plane into the airspace over the Soviet Union on the eve of a meeting of heads of government?'

Meanwhile, the White House was not so much shocked by Khrushchev's statement itself, as by the fact that Francis Powers not only remained alive and did not kill himself, but also had confessed to the Russians that he was a CIA agent and talked about the details of his top-secret mission and the specifics of U-2 flights, including the locations!

After a pause, on 9 May, Secretary of State Christian Herter made his third official statement regarding the incident with the reconnaissance aircraft. It was the most sensational yet and caused a violent reaction both in the United States and around the world (especially in the USSR, where the State Department was still waiting for repentance). Herter stated that the reconnaissance flights were carried out in the interests of the national security of the United States, which simply had no other choice. Allegedly, back in 1955, the American government proposed to conclude an agreement on open skies so that all interested parties could openly monitor each other's military preparations. But since the USSR categorically refused to do this, the Americans had to act secretly. Even more sensational was Herter's admission that Eisenhower, from the very beginning of his reign, had ordered the collection of military information about other states by all possible means, including '… by infiltrating aircraft into the airspace of foreign states …' Herter added: 'No special permission from the president is required for each individual flight. A general directive put into effect several years ago is enough.' In general, military secrets were surrendered during these days, as if simultaneously laid out on the playing cards table after a long and hard game.

A day earlier, on 8 May, a USAF representative in Japan officially confirmed that several U–2 aircraft were based in that country. Moreover, he admitted that they had been at Atsugi air base, 45 miles from Tokyo, 'for at least the last two years'. In Japan itself, this caused a huge resonance and scandal. It turned out that the Americans lied to their allies that the unusual aircraft were designed for research of the upper atmosphere, but in reality, the Japanese territory was actually used for military operations on the territory of the USSR and China. Mass demonstrations were held in Tokyo, Osaka and other cities demanding that U-2 be removed from the country and that dangerous missions be stopped. Citizens who remembered Hiroshima well feared that if war broke out, their small island state would be caught between a rock and an anvil and would be destroyed in no time.

The German government at first categorically denied the fact that the U-2s had ever used German air bases to fly over Eastern Europe. However, on 11 May, the *Frankfurter Rundschau* newspaper published sensational material on this topic, in which, in particular, it was reported:

As we learned from reliable sources, contrary to the statements of the Federal Minister of Defence that reconnaissance flights over the Warsaw Bloc countries are not carried out from airfields in West Germany, in fact such long-range flights start and they land on the territory of the Federal Republic. The Frankfurt airfield is also used for this purpose. At the same time, every time such aircraft, including the U-2 type, land, special security measures are taken at the airfield. In such cases, all German personnel are excluded, who usually work closely with the Americans.

Then Chancellor Konrad Adenauer, to a direct question from ubiquitous journalists about his attitude to secret flights, replied ambiguously: 'Thank God that the Americans are doing this ...'

In general, this time became a real El Dorado of sensations for journalists all over the world!

'So, to Study the Air Flow...'

On 6 May, the Soviet newspaper *Pravda* published a cartoon entitled 'Don't go into your heaven!' and an uncomplicated poem by an unidentified author:

> A winged predator full of arrogance,
> Circled in the Soviet sky.
> I had to calm him down! We knocked him down.
> In the future, do not climb into someone else's sky!

There was also an article titled 'Playing with fire is dangerous', and the first details of the incident were published. The article entitled 'The Air Pirate was shot down', contained photographs of 'soldiers of the N-th division', namely Major M. Voronov, Sergeant A. Fedorov, Private A. Bayborodin, Corporal A. Kuznetsov, Private V. Turkin and Private B. Kondratiev. The official version of events was also given there:

> Pervomay morning was just getting started when the alarm sounded in the unit. As always, the warriors, who were entrusted with formidable equipment to protect the air space, instantly prepared to perform the combat task. And now the radar antenna was already in motion, and the radio operators received the first reports of the flight of an unknown aircraft that had penetrated into Soviet territory from the southern border. The soldiers

at the command post are working hard. It is becoming clearer by the minute that there is a foreign plane in the Soviet sky and that its intentions are hostile. Its course is clearly plotted on the screens.

The order was received: 'Destroy the enemy aircraft!' Everything is ready for this task. Here, Corporal V. Nekrasov and A. Khabargin skilfully act at their combat posts. They are both communists, true masters of their craft. Understanding their responsibility, warriors act especially clearly. Their actions are skilfully led by Sergeant V. Yagushkin. Time seems to have stopped – so slowly are the last seconds preceding the completion of the combat mission. The specialist soldiers, commanded by Senior Lieutenant M. Mitin, were at their combat posts. Sergeant A. Fedorov, Corporal A. Kuznetsov, privates V. Turkin, B. Kondratiev and other soldiers are confident that complex and formidable equipment will not let them down. The battle did not last long. Soon it became known to all its participants: the target was destroyed!

The bandit got what he deserved. This will happen to anyone who tries to penetrate the clear Soviet sky in the future.

On 7 May, the newspaper *Pravda* published an article entitled 'Photo documents expose', in which images of items seized from Francis Powers during the search were printed. Among them was a pistol with a silencer and three boxes of cartridges for it, several knives, three wristwatches (including two ladies' watches!), a bundle of Soviet money, six women's gold rings and other small utensils. The newspaper wrote:

> This is what equipment the pilot of the American aircraft that invaded the territory of the Soviet Union on May 1, 1960 and was shot down near Sverdlovsk received from his owners. Small arms and an edged weapon, money, precious metals … It is unlikely that the pilot needed it, as the US State Department is trying to claim, to explore the upper atmosphere.

And it was hard to argue with that! In addition, a note in fourteen languages, including Russian, was seized from Powers. It read: 'I am an American and I don't speak Russian. I need food, shelter, and help. I won't hurt you. I have no evil intentions against your people. If you help me, you will be rewarded for it.'

Powers' set of belongings caused confusion and laughter among Russian citizens. Why would a reconnaissance plane pilot need all these things (especially ladies' rings and watches)? Was it really in order to sell them in the first pawnshop that came along in case of an emergency landing on Soviet territory, and then use the money to travel around the territory of the USSR? Or was all this intended to bribe Soviet border guards? And the gun with a silencer with almost 200 rounds of ammunition also looked a little ridiculous in the context of the Powers flight mission. All this equipment was more suitable for saboteurs, or even for simple robbers and criminals. In short, the Soviet people had a reason to laugh, as if they had caught not an American pilot, but a seasoned bandit. Powers himself explained during the interrogation that the pistol with a silencer was intended for hunting animals.

Among other things, it turned out that Francis Powers smoked Kent cigarettes. In any case, the half-smoked pack was also on the list of 'physical evidence' …

The famous Soviet poet Samuil Marshak breathed all this into a poem called 'What does a meteorologist need?' …

> So, to study Air flow
> You need a sharp pin,
> Dulles will give it to you,
> And what is it saturated with,
> – You guessed it yourself.
> You need a gun, Take the silent one with you,
> So that the population of the planet does not wake up
> with gunfire …

On 8 May, the Soviet media reported for the first time that the American pilot was alive and gave his surname, which is still known in Russia no less than the first astronaut, Yuri Gagarin. Photos of Senior Lieutenant S.I. Safronov, Captain K.I. Neludko and Major M.R. Voronin were also published. It was reported that for the successful completion of the combat mission of the Soviet government to protect the inviolability of the Soviet Union and the destruction of an aircraft that penetrated into the territory of the USSR, they were awarded the Order of the Red Banner. So these previously unknown men from the Urals became national heroes. Safronov received a posthumous award but it was not reported that he had been killed. Only Francis Powers went down in history, while the names of those who operated the anti-aircraft missile system were quickly forgotten.

Khrushchev expected Eisenhower, whom he had pinned to the wall with irrefutable evidence, to repent and at least apologise. Until the last moment, he considered the president to be a genuine peacemaker, who was cunningly deceived by his military. However, to the utter disappointment of the Soviet leader, nothing of the kind happened. Meanwhile, Soviet newspapers continued to criticise the United States without touching on Eisenhower's personality. The *Izvestia* newspaper published an article 'The brazen and cynical statement of the State Department':

The State Department, with amazing audacity, is trying to explain the aggressive act of the United States by the need to collect information to protect the United States from a surprise attack, since, allegedly, the United States has no other way to obtain information of this kind. In an attempt to somehow justify the aggressive actions of the United States, the State Department slanders other countries, claiming that such provocations are practised by all states. Naturally, the State Department does not provide any arguments to confirm this ridiculous fiction. Moreover, the State Department cynically admits that American reconnaissance planes 'have been flying along the borders of the free world in recent years'.

After that, as was customary in the Soviet Union, mass rallies and gatherings took place throughout the country, in factories, universities and institutions. Even children in the most remote rural school discussed the sneaky trick of the Americans, and painted red rockets soaring into the sky and a black plane splitting apart from the explosion. The article 'Uralians angrily condemn the aggressors' reported:

Today, crowded meetings were held in the workshops of the factories of the city of Sverdlovsk. At a meeting in the machine shop of large units of the Uralmash plant, the innovative tooth cutter Arseniy Danilovich spoke.

'We, the workers of Uralmash plant,' he said, 'have been living all these days under the impression of the session of the Supreme Council that has just ended. Well, things are going great in our country! The new laws once again convincingly show what great social gains the Soviet people have achieved under the leadership of the Communist Party. We clearly see that the party has no other concerns except for the prosperity of the Motherland and the welfare of the people.'

In their decisions, the Uralmashevites declare their unanimous support for the peaceful foreign policy of the Soviet government and express their anger at the provocative actions of the American military. The general and unanimous opinion of the workers and employees of the Uralmash plant was well expressed by draftsman Lev Baranov. He said: 'In the eyes of many Uralians, a pirate plane that flew into the Sverdlovsk region became a pile of debris in an instant. So, it will be with every uninvited guest. Don't mess with fire, gentlemen aggressors!'

In Stalingrad, a 100,000-strong protest rally was held on the Square of Fallen Fighters, at which speakers attacked the 'banditry of the American military' and 'robber speeches of responsible US figures', and also approved the decisive measures of the Soviet government. Huge rallies were held in Odessa, Kiev, Minsk, Tbilisi, Novosibirsk, Vladivostok and other cities. The *Pravda* newspaper wrote:

Indignant resolutions, letters and telegrams strongly condemning the machinations of the enemies of peace are being sent to the Pravda newspaper in a continuous stream. Individual Soviet citizens write, families write, collectives of factories and construction sites, collective farms and state farms, institutions, military units and educational institutions write. The words of popular indignation and protest come from the very heart.

'We, the Soviet people, stigmatise the provocateurs, the champions of the Cold War. Caught red-handed, disgraced in the eyes of the entire world community, the warmongers expose themselves.' This is how the head of the workshop, engineer M. Yablonsky, expressed the feelings and thoughts of a team of thousands of workers at the Moscow Dynamo plant. 'Our hearts were filled with anger when we heard with what a vile espionage Mission the Americans sent their spy into our sky,' locksmith N. Akhmedzhanov said at a citywide rally of the Tashkent Locomotive and Wagon Repair Plant October Revolution.

On 10 May, Soviet citizens for the first time learned the name of the mysterious aircraft, which many immediately associated with the famous Soviet Polikarpov U-2 (y-2) biplane. TASS news agency reported:

> According to Japanese radio, today at a meeting of the special commission of the lower house of parliament to consider the new Japanese–American 'security treaty', Minister Fujiyama, answering questions from opposition deputies, said that the Japanese government would again request information from the command of the American armed forces in Japan regarding the purposes of Lockheed U-2 aircraft staying at military bases in Japan.

For the first ten days, the whole scandal around the U-2 shot down over the Urals took place at the level of statements, mutual accusations and more and more details being thrown into the press. Only on 10 May, did the Minister of Foreign Affairs of the USSR Andrei Gromyko, summon the American ambassador and hand him an official note of protest. The document stated:

> On 1 May, at 5.36 am Moscow time, a military aircraft violated the USSR border and invaded the Soviet Union at a distance of more than 2,000 kilometres. The government of the USSR, of course, could not leave unpunished such

a gross violation of Soviet state borders. When the nature of the intruder's intentions became apparent, it was shot down by Soviet missile forces in the Sverdlovsk region. When experts studied all the data at the disposal of the Soviet side, it was irrefutably established that the invading aircraft belonged to the United States of America, was permanently based in Turkey and was sent through Pakistan to the Soviet Union for hostile purposes ... This aircraft was specially equipped for a reconnaissance flight over the territory of the Soviet Union. It had on board equipment for aerial photography, for detecting the Soviet radar network and other special radio equipment included in the USSR air defence system ...

The pilot said that he did everything in full accordance with the mission assigned to him. The route map selected from him clearly and clearly records the entire route assigned to him after departure from the mountains. Adana (Turkey): Peshawar (Pakistan)–Aral Sea–Sverdlovsk–Arkhangelsk–Murmansk with subsequent landing at the Norwegian airfield in Bodo. The pilot also said that he serves in unit 10-10, which, under the cover of the National Aeronautics and Space Administration, is engaged in military intelligence from high altitudes.

It is worth noting that this note, which began with accusations, ended quite amiably:

The Soviet government would like to sincerely hope that the US government, in the end, recognises that ending the cold war and searching through joint efforts with the Soviet Union and other interested states for a mutually acceptable solution to unresolved international problems is in the interests of maintaining and consolidating peace between nations, including the interests of the American people themselves.

The next day, Foreign Minister Gromyko held a large press conference attended by about 500 Soviet and foreign journalists. There he again discussed Herter's 'brazen statement', but immediately called on Americans for peace and friendship.

Meanwhile, an entire exposition dedicated to the U-2 was organised in the Gorky Central Park in Moscow (such exhibitions had not been organised since the Second World War). Along with the wreckage of the plane and various pieces of physical evidence, a large stand was erected called 'The pilot of the downed US aircraft Francis Gary Powers'. Three photos of the main character were posted on it, in a helmet, full-length in a pilot's suit and in civilian form (in a jacket and tie). These were enlarged images of photographs seized from Powers. There was even a book of reviews in which everyone could express their indignation at what they saw.

The scandal continued in the United States, and the White House was looking for a way out of the situation. At the same time, Eisenhower received a variety of offers. For example, Allen Dulles offered to resign in disgrace, after which he would publicly apologise to the people and declare himself guilty of what happened. However, the president did not accept and took full responsibility himself. On 11 May, as if in response to the Soviet note of protest, Eisenhower spoke at a press conference and made an open statement. He officially admitted that he personally gave permission to conduct an intelligence operation. The president stated that 'no one wants a second Pearl Harbor', so the U-2 mission had only one goal – to prevent a surprise attack by a potential enemy. In addition, he accused the Soviet Union of excessive closeness and secrecy, which, in his opinion, carried the threat of a surprise attack. From these words, it was clear that Eisenhower was not addressing Khrushchev, who was waiting for an apology from him, but the Americans and Western countries.

On 12 May, the United States also published a response note to the Soviet government:

In its note, the Soviet government stated that the collection of intelligence information about the Soviet Union by American aircraft is a 'calculated policy' of the United States. The United States Government does not deny that it is pursuing this kind of policy solely for defensive purposes. However, it categorically denies that this policy has any aggressive purpose or that the flight of the unarmed U-2 aircraft on May 1 was undertaken in an attempt to damage the success of the upcoming meeting of heads of government in Paris or 'return the state of American-Soviet relations to the worst times of the Cold War'. And it is precisely the actions of the Soviet government in connection with this case, however, that may cast doubt on its intentions regarding these issues.

The Americans said they would take part in the Paris meeting anyway, and also said that the best way to avoid such incidents was to develop mutual guarantees against a surprise attack.

In the USSR, of course, this note was considered to be another insult, and the famous poet Sergei Mikhalkov immediately composed a fable called 'The Answer of the Burglar'. He compared the United States to a criminal whom the owner found in his own apartment during the theft:

- Why did you climb over someone else's fence?
- Your gate, neighbour, was closed!
- And why did you break the lock on the door?
I didn't have a key! – read the bandit's reply.
The State Department has given the same answer
What the world is outraged about today!

Soviet writers did not doze off either. In just ten days, a team of authors wrote and published (under the auspices of the Union of Journalists of the USSR) a book entitled *Aggressors – to the pillory. The truth about the provocative invasion of the American aircraft into the airspace of the USSR.*

Meanwhile, on 13 May, Foreign Minister Gromyko handed over an official protest note to the Norwegian ambassador to the USSR, O.H. Gundersen. The content of its first part exactly copied the note to the Americans, but the second part described in detail the established role of this country in the U-2 missions. The document stated that Powers confessed he had repeatedly flown this aircraft to the Norwegian Bodø airfield and knew that it had been used repeatedly for secret flights over Soviet territory. At the same time, unlike the actually conciliatory protest composed for Eisenhower, the note to the Norwegians contained direct threats:

> The Soviet government considers it necessary to warn that if such provocations are repeated from the territory of Norway, it will be forced to take appropriate retaliatory measures. It is known that the Soviet Union has weapons at its disposal that, if necessary, can completely neutralise the air bases used to commit aggressive actions against the Soviet Union.

The last Soviet protest note, on 20 May, was finally received by another unwitting accomplice of the U-2 project, Japan. Gromyko also recalled the previous September's incident with the forced landing of a reconnaissance aircraft in the country, revealing the full role of the Japanese in escalating tensions.

> Deliberately going to complicate the situation, the Japanese government enters into military collusion with a power that proclaims espionage and sabotage, violation of sovereignty and inviolability of borders of other countries as its state policy. The Soviet government, of course, cannot ignore the fact that the conclusion of a new military treaty between the United States and Japan is precisely designed to provide conditions for aggressive actions against the USSR and friendly states from Japanese territory.

Gromyko clearly hinted that Japan, unlike the United States, was located very close to the Soviet Union and that it would not be difficult to influence it.

Interestingly, Khrushchev initially decided not to go to the meeting in Paris. On 16 May, his message addressed to French President Charles de Gaulle, British Prime Minister Harold Macmillan and US President Eisenhower was published in the Soviet media (to a greater extent, it was still addressed to Eisenhower). This appeal explained the reasons why the Soviet leader would not go to the summit and actually summed up the reaction of the Soviet leadership to the U–2 incident:

> It goes without saying that if the US government had stated that in the future the United States would not violate the state borders of the USSR with its aircraft, condemns provocative actions taken in the past and punishes the direct perpetrators of such actions, which would ensure equal conditions for the Soviet Union with other powers, I, as head of the Soviet government, am ready to accept participate in the meeting and make every effort to contribute to its success ...

However, Khrushchev changed his mind at the last moment. On the morning of the same day, when Soviet citizens were reading these lines, Khrushchev nevertheless appeared in Paris. There he insisted that he be the first to be given the floor. Then the Soviet leader delivered an emotional diatribe, at the end of which he personally demanded an apology from Eisenhower and guarantees to stop aerial espionage. The US president replied that reconnaissance flights had been stopped and would not be resumed, but he did not apologise. Nikita Sergeyevich eventually swore at those present and left, effectively disrupting the meeting.

In addition, as a result of the U-2 incident, Eisenhower's upcoming visit to the Soviet Union was disrupted. It was scheduled for 10 June, and preparations for it were in full swing. At the same time, the president himself, despite the changed conditions, did not formally refuse to go, and his press secretary in every possible way avoided direct answers about this. But in the USSR, after rallies and letters from people to newspapers, Eisenhower's visit would not have looked appropriate. Khrushchev stated in this regard:

Unfortunately, as a result of provocative aggressive actions against the USSR, such conditions have now been created when we are deprived of the opportunity to receive the president with the proper cordiality with which Soviet people receive welcome guests. We cannot show such cordiality towards the US president right now ... The Soviet people do not know how to dissemble and do not want to. Therefore, we believe that the US President's trip to the Soviet Union should now be postponed and an agreement on the timing of this visit should be reached when the conditions for this are ripe. Then the Soviet people will be able to show due cordiality and hospitality to a distinguished guest representing a great power with which we sincerely want to live in friendship and peace. I think that both Mr Eisenhower and the American people will understand me correctly.

The statement was friendly enough. Khrushchev did not accidentally use the words 'postpone' (not cancel) and 'great power' (not 'decaying imperialists'). These were hidden curtsies, hinting that, despite the American 'pranks', the Soviet Union still hoped to be friends with them.

On 20 May, the Soviet leader delivered a speech to the German communists in East Berlin during a tour of Eastern European countries. Most of the long speech was predictably devoted to the U-2:

They sent a military reconnaissance aircraft to our country on 9 April. As I said, we decided not to protest then, so as not to please our opponents. They probably reasoned like this: if you did not shoot down the plane, then you are not able to protect your sky from our invasions. It was pressure, pressure on us. The Pentagon officials decided to repeat the aggressive act by timing the next departure of the spy plane for the international proletarian holiday on May 1. But then, as they say, they thought one thing, but something else came out. The plane took off, but did not arrive at the base [loud applause]. The plane was shot down, and now its wreckage is on a reliable 'base' – in Moscow – at the exhibition. And the pilot will appear before the court [stormy, prolonged applause, cheers]. How the sharks of imperialism have played out here! The aggressors should apologise at this moment, as is customary, condemn the violation, make assurances that this will not happen, and the perpetrators will be punished. But anger blinded the aggressors' eyes. They announced that planes used to fly to us and will fly in the future, because such actions are in the interests of the national security of the United States.

However, in this speech, Khrushchev, who wanted to show his allies determination and firmness, also said that he was ready to make peace and make friends with the Americans.

It would not be an exaggeration to say that after 1 May 1960, the world changed beyond recognition. What only a limited circle of people had known until recently suddenly became the property of the entire world community. Everything that was covered with the halo of secret information (the name and purpose of the aircraft, the airfields where they were based, flight routes, cover legends) was now discussed even by housewives and schoolchildren. The only thing that the Americans managed to conceal was the fact that British pilots participated in the missions.

The Trial of the Worker's Son

In the American film *Bridge of Spies*, Francis Powers' stay in Soviet captivity was shown very dramatically. The American pilot is not allowed to sleep, they pour water on him and mock him in every possible way. At the same time, during interrogations, he stubbornly remains silent and behaves like a hero, and meanwhile Dulles in America argues that 'this good

guy knows too much'. None of this had anything to do with
reality.

Powers had been cooperating with the Russians from the
first day. At the very first interrogation, he described in detail
his biography before joining the CIA. And then he said that in
April 1956 he was offered the opportunity to carry out special
reconnaissance missions in specially equipped high–altitude
aircraft. Powers said:

> During the recruitment process, the tasks that I had
> to perform were explained to me. I was informed
> that my main job would be to fly an aircraft along the
> borders of the USSR in order to collect information on
> radar installations and radio stations, as well as other
> information. I was also informed that in the future, maybe
> I will be assigned other tasks, provided that everything
> goes well. After that, I signed a secret contract with the
> US Central Intelligence Agency, headed by Allen Dulles,
> and signed a subscription to keep this cooperation secret.
> I was warned that for violating my subscription and
> disclosing data on the activities of American intelligence,
> I would be criminally punished in the form of ten years
> in prison or a fine in the amount of 10 thousand dollars,
> or both at the same time.

Powers said that he received a monthly salary of $2,500,
whereas during his service in the US Air Force he was paid
$700 per month. He also immediately revealed to the Russians
the location of the secret air base where the U–2 pilots were

trained. Powers said it was located in the Nevada Desert near a nuclear test site, and training flights were carried out over California, Texas and the northern part of the United States.

Powers spoke in full detail (and without any torture or bullying) about the preparation and objectives of the Grand Slam mission:

> On the night of May 1, two and a half hours before departure, I received from Colonel Shelton the task to fly over the territory of the USSR from south to north at an altitude of 20,000 metres along the route: Peshawar, the Aral Sea, Sverdlovsk, Kirov, Arkhangelsk, Murmansk and land in Norway at the Bodo airfield. According to the instructions I received, when flying over the territory of the Soviet Union, I had to turn on special equipment on board the aircraft in certain places for aerial photography and recording the operation of radar stations of the air defence system. According to Shelton's instructions, I needed to pay special attention to several sections of my route and to two target areas, one of which was supposed to have been a launch pad for launching missiles, and the other a new missile range.

The prisoner described in detail the circumstances under which U-2 was shot down and he was captured. At the same time, Powers honestly stated that at the time of the explosion of the anti-aircraft missile, the plane was flying at an altitude of 68,000ft (approximately 20,500m). It was these detailed statements, which the prisoner had already given on 2 May, that allowed Khrushchev to learn the circumstances of the Grand Slam mission and other similar missions so quickly and in full detail. On 17 May, Powers was brought to Gorky Park, where the wreckage of U-2 was on display. During this 'investigative experiment' he identified his aircraft and gave various explanations on its technical details. Powers also gave out the names and surnames of his commanders and colleagues. He did not hide almost any information from the Soviets.

Most of the devices and mechanisms of the U-2, despite falling from a height of 20km, were well preserved and Soviet experts were able to study them in detail. They compiled a detailed report on photographic equipment, radio signal detection equipment, recording devices, the aircraft detonation unit and others. All this information was very useful for creating similar devices and developing more advanced radar stations. The Russians even carefully studied the needle with poison, making a detailed report about it. The document stated:

A needle extracted from a pin was injected under the skin of an experimental dog in the area of the upper third of the left thigh. One minute after the injection, the dog fell on its side, while there was a sharp weakening of the respiratory movements of the chest, cyanosis of the tongue, visible mucous membranes appeared, and a minute and a half after the injection, breathing stopped. Three minutes after the injection, the dog's cardiac activity died out and death occurred.

The same needle was inserted under the skin of a white mouse. Twenty seconds after the injection, death from respiratory paralysis occurred. After that, the remnants of the poison from the needle were washed off with distilled water; the resulting solution was used to establish a lethal dose. At the same time, it turned out that the lethal dose for rabbits with intravenous administration is five gamma per kilogram of weight; for white mice, ten gamma per kilogram of weight. As you know, gamma is equal to one thousandth of a milligram. Thus, as a result of the study, it was found that the needle in the pin contains a substance that, judging by the nature of its effect on animals, by its toxic doses and physical properties, can be attributed to the curare group – the most strongly and rapidly acting of all known poisons. Given the very high toxicity and nature of the poison's effect on animals, as well as the relatively large amount of it on the needle, it can be assumed that when a person is pricked with this needle, poisoning and death will occur as quickly as in animals.

The only thing that had not been established was the purpose of the mysterious piece of black cloth, textile that was discovered in the cockpit of the U-2. It was carefully studied in laboratories and shown to a variety of specialists, but no one was able say what it was used for. No encrypted messages, no poison, no hidden geographical map. In fact, it was just a black rag! Powers himself said that Colonel Shelton handed him it before the flight. At the same time, he said that after landing in Norway, a piece of black cloth should be given to the American personnel of the air base. What this rag was intended for has remained a mystery!

Taking avantage of Powers' willingness to cooperate and interact with the Soviets, Khrushchev decided to hold a public trial. At the same time, it had to be held in accordance with international standards so that no one would have doubts about the fairness of the sentence. In July 1960, Mikhail Grinev, a lawyer, visited Powers. He was an experienced Moscow lawyer who took part in many high-profile and scandalous lawsuits. Several times he represented the interests of foreign spies and Soviet people accused of espionage. Grinev informed the surprised pilot that his trial would be open and public. At the same time, Powers was allowed to write letters to his family. Grinev said that Powers' wife Barbara and other relatives would be able to attend the trial. At the same time, the lawyer questioned Powers in detail about his youth and social background. After learning that the pilot came from a poor family, and that his father had previously worked as a miner, Grinev said that this was very important. He also asked Powers for his relatives to take pictures of the house where the family lived and bring these pictures to the USSR. The lawyer said it was very important for the trial.

Surprised, Powers complied with all these requests. In fact, social origin was very important from the point of view of Soviet morality and justice. In the USSR, the American capitalist system was considered unfair. From the point of view of Soviet ideology, it was an exploitative political regime in which capitalists and financiers profited from poor workers and exploited them. Since the Powers family was poor and did not exploit anyone (no hired labour was used on their small family farm), it turned out that the pilot was also a 'victim of exploiters', and it was not greed for profit that pushed him to serve in the CIA, but poverty and hopelessness.

When the Powers family arrived in the Soviet Union in August, Grinev met with them. He asked them in detail about the pilot's biography, about his life in the United States, took the photos from them and promised that the trial would be fair. Shortly before the start of the trial, a meeting was arranged between Powers and his wife. She was surprised to see that her husband looked great and was in a good mood. He did not look at all like a prisoner of war or someone who had been tortured. Even then, Barbara Powers wondered if her husband had betrayed the United States by cooperating with the Soviets. He looked really good and well fed.

Especially for the trial, an elegant blue classic suit was made for Powers, at the same sewing factory that sewed classic suits for Khrushchev and other leaders of the Soviet state!

The trial took place from 17 to 19 August 1960 in the Columns Hall of the House of Unions. The House of Unions (originally called the House of Noble Assembly) was built at the end of the seventeenth century. The main room in this building was a large, pillared hall. There were twenty-eight Corinthian columns along its perimeter, which illuminated multi-row chandeliers. The hall area was 600 sq m, the ceiling height, painted with mythological scenes, was 14.5m. The hall could accommodate more than 2,000 people and was famous for its impressive acoustics. Since then, the Columns Hall has seen many historical and cultural events. In the second half of the nineteenth century, famous Russian composers Pyotr Tchaikovsky, Sergei Rachmaninov and Nikolai

Rimsky-Korsakov performed concerts there. On 30 March 1856, Emperor Alexander II made a speech at the House of Noble Assembly on the need to abolish serfdom, and in the summer of 1912, the 300th anniversary of the Romanov dynasty and the 100th anniversary of victory in the Patriotic War of 1812 were celebrated there.

After the Bolshevik Revolution, the building was renamed the House of Unions. Mass events and congresses of various Soviet organisations were regularly held there. Vladimir Lenin spoke in the Columns Hall about fifty times. A funeral ceremony was held there after his death. After that, the funeral of all the leaders of the USSR began with a farewell ceremony in the Columns Hall. These included Felix Dzerzhinsky, Sergei Kirov, Mikhail Kalinin, Andrei Zhdanov and Joseph Stalin. Starting in 1928, the Soviets began using this huge room for public trials. In parallel, New Year holidays, chess tournaments and musical concerts were held there. In general, the building of the House of Unions was sacred to the Soviet Union, and it is no coincidence that the trial of Powers took place there. This fact testified to the great importance and political significance of this event.

The trial was presided over by the Deputy Chairman of the Supreme Court of the USSR Lieutenant General of Justice Viktor Borisoglebsky. The prosecution was supported by the Prosecutor General of the USSR, the actual state Adviser of Justice Roman Rudenko. Lawyers and advocates from the USA, India, Denmark, Scotland, Greece, Finland, France, Canada and Belgium, diplomats, American tourists, as well as 140 journalists and correspondents from 30 countries were present in the hall. Also present at the event were Powers' father and mother, his wife, mother-in-law and family friend Solomon Carey. During the trial, Powers fully confirmed his previous testimony and answered questions from the judges and the lawyer in detail. The defendant fully admitted his guilt, repented and asked for forgiveness for his actions. Powers also stated that he regretted that his flight and the failure of the mission had aggravated the international situation. The details given by the pilot shocked many people present in the hall, especially foreign journalists. For the first time, the covert activities of the CIA and the United States were described publicly and in great detail. What had been so carefully hidden was now printed on the pages of dozens of newspapers and broadcast on radio stations. The Americans themselves were shocked by Powers' revelations and the fact that he gave the real names of his commanders and colleagues, and talked about the training system for American pilots and secret air bases. From now on, even children knew that the mysterious Area 51 was located in Nevada next to the nuclear test site! And during the reading of the results of his interrogation, the names of many American companies that developed secret equipment for secret intelligence were announced. America had never known such a complete failure of secrecy.

The morning session on 19 August began with Prosecutor Rudenko's accusatory speech. At the beginning, he said:

The real trial of the American spy pilot Powers exposes crimes committed not only by the defendant Powers personally, but also reveals to the end the criminal aggressive actions of the ruling circles of the United States – the true inspirers and organisers of monstrous crimes against the peace and security of peoples. In this process, it was once again proved that the reactionary forces of the United States in the fight against the forces of peace do not disdain any means, criminally flouting the elementary norms of international law, violating the national sovereignty of other states in order to pursue a bankrupt policy of balancing on the brink of war.

In conclusion, Rudenko stated that Powers was a dangerous criminal, and that his actions were qualified under Article No. 2 of the Law of the USSR 'On Criminal Liability for State Crimes', which provided for the death penalty. But, given the defendant's remorse and his cooperation with the investigating authorities, the prosecutor asked the court to sentence him to fifteen years in prison.

After that, Powers' lawyer Mikhail Grinev made a long speech. He said that he had to do a difficult job – to defend in court an American pilot who committed an act of aggression against the USSR. He said that was to protect the real enemy. Grinev said that the main criminals were those who prepared secret missions and sent U-2s into Soviet airspace. Powers was a simple executor of someone else's will. The lawyer dwelled in particular on Powers' social background and the motives that led him to join the CIA. The fact that the pilot grew up in a poor family, could not get a good academic education and find a permanent job was a mitigating circumstance. The lawyer explained that it was the social problems of American society that forced Powers to enter into a risky contract and carry out criminal orders. In addition, Grinev called Powers a victim of anti-Soviet propaganda that portrayed Russians as cruel and insidious enemies. In conclusion, the lawyer asked the court to commute the punishment.

The defendant's last word was extremely brief. Powers said:

I am aware that I have committed the gravest crime and deserve to be punished for it. I ask the court to weigh all the evidence and take into account not only the fact that I committed a crime, but also the circumstances that prompted me to do so. I also ask the court to take into account the fact that no classified information has reached its destination. All this information ended up in the hands of the Soviet authorities. I am aware that the Russian people consider me an enemy. I can understand that. But I would like to emphasize the fact that I personally do not and have never harboured any hostility towards Russian people. I am asking the court to judge me not as an enemy, but as a person who is not a personal enemy of the Russian people, a person who has never been brought to court on any charges and who has deeply realised his guilt, regrets it and deeply repents. Thank you.

As a result, Powers was sentenced to ten years in prison. The pilot went to serve his sentence in the famous Vladimir Central Prison in the city of Vladimir, 200km east of Moscow.

The prison was built in 1783 by order of Empress Catherine II. The building was erected near the Vladimirsky Tract, a long road that led from Moscow to the eastern provinces and Siberia. Convicts, political exiles and other prisoners usually moved along this road. The phrase 'go along Vladimirsky' has been synonymous with the phrase 'go to prison' for centuries. This gloomy prison, located on the outskirts of Vladimir next to an ancient cemetery, housed political prisoners and especially dangerous enemies of the tsarist regime. In 1906, this institution was named 'central', that is, 'central prison'. After the October Revolution, the Bolsheviks created a so-called political isolation ward in this prison, a special area for political opponents of the new government. Subsequently, in this building, from which no one has ever escaped, especially dangerous state criminals (spies, saboteurs, terrorists, anarchists, etc.) were imprisoned there. At various times these included German Field Marshal Ferdinand Schörner; Vasily Stalin (the son of Joseph Stalin); a well-known employee of the Soviet special services, Pavel Sudoplatov; and Soviet dissident Vladimir Bukovsky. In Russia, most people did not know about the existence of this special prison until the famous singer Mikhail Krug sang a song called 'Vladimir Central' in 1998, in which the chorus went:

Vladimirsky Central (North wind)
The phase from Tver (There is a lot of Evil)
Has a heavy burden on my heart …

In general, Powers was in prison with a rich historical past. The court ruled that while he was serving his sentence, his wife had the right to come to the USSR, settle near the prison and meet her husband regularly. No Soviet prisoner had such comfortable conditions of stay. The distance from the prison to Moscow was only 200km, so Barbara could live in the Soviet capital and periodically visit her husband. However, Mrs Powers, since known for her addiction to alcohol and for living a bohemian life, did not want to go to Vladimir. During the trial, she had been shocked by her husband's confessions and apologies. She was also confused by his beautiful and well-groomed appearance, as if he was spending time not in prison, but at a resort! Like many Americans, Barbara decided that her husband was a traitor and a coward who had given American military secrets to the Russians. Immediately after the end of the trial, Barbara Powers left the Soviet Union for good.

Chapter 6

The Nuclear Dragon

The Battle Over the Barents Sea and Nixon's Withered Hand

The loss of U-2C No. 360 marked the cessation of aerial reconnaissance over the USSR. Firstly, the inability of the Russians to fully track the flight route and the U-2's invulnerability to air defence had been the main requirements of the Aquaton project. Secondly, by that time, the Corona secret programme for the creation of space spy satellites was already nearing completion.

Despite the Soviet notes of protest, the Americans were in no hurry to evacuate the U-2 from foreign airfields, but subsequent events forced their hand. On 27 May, a coup took place in Turkey and the government of Adnan Menderes was overthrown. Thus, the agreements reached with the US government on the operation of secret flights were also cancelled. Three of the four U-2s at Incirlik airfield were disassembled and taken home in a Douglas C-124 transport aircraft. Nevertheless, the Americans decided to leave one reconnaissance aircraft there and put it in a strictly guarded hangar, where it stood for several years in a mothballed state. Later, this U-2 was taken to the USA.

The Japanese government had tolerated protests and damning articles in the press for some time. But on 8 July, it nevertheless appealed to the United States to eliminate Detachment C. Soon, the U-2s were disassembled, loaded on to C-124s and shipped overseas. Then, at Edwards Air Force Base, from the pilots of the disbanded Detachments B and C, a new Detachment G was formed. It consisted of eleven pilots. The main tasks of the unit were defined as flights over Cuba and North Vietnam. In total, twenty-four flights over the territory of the USSR were carried out within the framework of the Aquaton project over four years, including fifteen by Detachment B from Turkey and Pakistan; six by Detachment A from Germany; and three by Detachment C from Japan and Alaska. During this period, 391,000m of photographic film were obtained and 33.6 million sq km of Soviet territory were photographed. At the same time, the Aquaton project, originally designed for two years, lasted twice as long.

Meanwhile, the situation in the sky after 1 May 1960 was extremely tense. The Soviet air defence forces received categorical instructions to mercilessly shoot down all border violators. At the same time, Eisenhower, having formally banned flights over the territory of the USSR, did not extend it to reconnaissance aircraft flying along the borders or in the airspace of the allied states. Such flights were conducted daily along the entire Iron Curtain from the Adriatic Sea to the Arctic in order to photograph border areas, monitor the air and survey the area using airborne radars. However, the air border is a very relative concept, because it is not marked by any lines or flags. At transonic speeds, this milestone was even less noticeable. It is clear that such flights greatly unnerved Soviet pilots and the military throughout the curtain perimeter. Therefore, new incidents were not long in coming.

On 20 May 1960, an American C-47 Skytrain transport aircraft (registration number 43-15544) from the USAF, taking off from Copenhagen, accidentally flew into the airspace of the GDR. There it was immediately intercepted by a pair of MiG-17s (pilots Captain L. Shkaruba and Senior Lieutenant M. Krylov) and, under threat of being fired on, made an emergency landing in a field 15 miles north of the town of Grevesmulen. The command of the Russian Air Force, due to confusion with the definition of the type of aircraft, reported to Moscow about the detention of a 'RV-47E air reconnaissance aircraft'. Later, six crew members and three passengers (obviously accompanying the cargo) were handed over to the American authorities.

A much more serious incident occurred on 1 July. A USAF ERB-47H Stratojet electronic reconnaissance aircraft (registration number 53-4281, according to other sources 53-0482) from the 38th SRS (55.SRW) took off from Brize Norton Air Base in the UK in the direction of the Barents Sea. After refuelling off the coast of Norway from a KC-135 flying tanker, the aircraft rounded Cape Nordkapp and set a course parallel to the coast of the Kola Peninsula. At 17.30, a Soviet fighter suddenly appeared in the area of Cape Svyatoy Nos (Holy Nose) to the right of the Stratojet. It was a MiG-19P of Captain Vasily Polyakov from the 174th GIAP (10th Separate Air Defence Army), which had taken off from Amderma airfield. For some time, the interceptor flew a parallel course, and the pilot reported to the base about the course of the target and its probable intentions.

When the ERB-47H reached the return point and was 50 miles from the Soviet coast, the crew commander, navigator Captain John McCone, ordered a left turn. Polyakov perceived this manoeuvre not as a U-turn, but as a turn on a course to Novaya Zemlya, where the main Soviet nuclear test site was located. After the pilot's report, the headquarters of the 10th Separate Air Defence Army decided that an American reconnaissance aircraft was flying to Novaya Zemlya, and Polyakov received an order to attack. When the crew of the ERB-47H saw flashes from shots from the MiG-19, the second pilot, Major Bruce Olmsted, returned fire from a remotely controlled tail turret. During the battle, a third of the ammunition was used up, but to no avail. The shooting allowed Polyakov to finally convince himself of the aggressive intentions of the Americans. After expending 111 23-mm shells, the left engines of the reconnaissance aircraft caught fire. The pilot, Captain William Palm, was able to level the plane for a while, but it soon began to descend. At 18.03, ERB-47H fell into the Barents Sea. Palm, Olmsted and McCone ejected, but Palm was tangled in the parachute and drowned. Radio operators Captain Eugene Posey, First Lieutenant Oscar Gotthort and First Lieutenant Dean Phillips were killed. After six hours at sea in a lifeboat, McCone and Olmsted were rescued by the Soviet fishing trawler RT-291 Tobolsk (in some sources called the patrol ship SKR-56).

The reaction of the Soviet leadership was predictable. Vasily Polyakov received the extraordinary military rank of major and was awarded the Order of the Red Banner. Khrushchev personally presented the award to him in the Kremlin. For ten days, the USSR Foreign Ministry paused, apparently expecting that the Americans, as had been the case with the Powers incident, would concoct a new story about a 'weather explorer' or some kind of off-course transport. Only on 11 July, an official statement followed that 'another American RB-47 spy plane' was shot down, and Olmsted and McCone were arrested. Khrushchev said that this new aggressive act showed that all Eisenhower's assurances about stopping reconnaissance flights over the USSR 'are not worth a damn', and that the United States was provoking a serious military conflict. Foreign Minister Gromyko also demanded the convening of an emergency meeting of the UN Security Council to discuss new aggressive actions by the United States.

At the same time, Soviet reports said that the RB-47 entered Soviet airspace, where it was shot down, and Olmsted and McCone admitted that they were carrying out a spy and sabotage mission. During the meeting, US representatives presented a map compiled according to radar data, which showed that the ERB-47H did not even come close to the border. And then they themselves accused the USSR of provoking a war. Heated discussions began, although these did not have serious consequences. During Security Council voting on the resolution, the majority of participants sided with America. Palm's body was found on 25 July and subsequently handed over to the Americans.

In general, unlike the U-2 incident, the hype raised in the USSR subsided quite quickly. This time there were no crowded rallies and poems in the newspapers. This fact was explained by the upcoming presidential elections in the United States. The Eisenhower era was coming to an end, and Khrushchev hoped that if the Democratic candidate, John F. Kennedy, won, the foreign policy course of the United States would change radically.

Kennedy built his election campaign on criticism of the foreign and domestic policies of the Republican leadership. He reproached Eisenhower for 'squandering presidential power', and for entrusting the solution of all issues to his entourage, while he 'rested on the ranch'. Therefore, he said, America was ruled by Herter, Dulles, Nixon and others. Kennedy said that this collegiality had led to shame in the U-2 incident. In addition, Kennedy stated that Eisenhower had reduced America's prestige and 'allowed the Soviet Union to get ahead of it'. This phrase about the Soviet Union was taken literally in the Soviet Union, exclusively in a positive context for itself and as proof of the advantages of communism. Khrushchev decided that he would definitely make friends with this 'kind guy'.

Republicans campaigned under the slogan 'Vote for the invincible Nixon Lodge team!' They embarked on a two-week tour on a special train that travelled day and night across the country from one state to another. In addition to Nixon and his wife, there were more than 100 advisers, political strategists and journalists from the Republican Party media. As a result, the indefatigable candidate went all over the United States, setting an unbroken record to this day. And the train itself travelled a total of 64,000 miles. During endless rallies, speeches, and meetings with thousands of residents of cities and towns, Nixon lost a lot of weight and became hoarse. As if taking an example from Alexander Kerensky (one of the leaders of the Russian Revolution of 1917), who liked to personally shake hands with entire divisions, he greeted thousands of Americans. As a result, the candidate's right hand swelled up and he had to say hello with his left. Suffering fatigue and insomnia, at one of the rallies, to laughter in the audience and the horror of his advisers, Nixon called Henry Cabot Lodge Jr, the vice presidential candidate, a liar and a hypocrite, confusing him with Kennedy. Nixon's nerves were also giving out. In the town of Grand Rapids, a tomato was thrown at him from the crowd. 'In some places, in other places, stones were thrown at me!' the tired candidate shouted back. As for foreign policy, his main thesis was the statement: 'I know how to talk to Khrushchev.' For clarity, this phrase was even placed on posters that had a photo of Nixon talking with the Soviet leader. Nixon often said that he knew Russia first-hand, as a child he had lived there for a while, and in 1959 he had visited the country. Nixon had visited the Urals and, ironically, drove very close to the place where the U-2 would soon be shot down. 'I know everything about the Russians and I will settle all issues with them,' Nixon promised voters. The outgoing president also helped his successor as much as he could by going on his own tour of America. 'Nixon brought the largest-calibre artillery into battle,' was a typical headline in the press.

John F. Kennedy won the election by a narrow margin. The Soviet leadership perceived this as a worldwide celebration and, perhaps, the end of the Cold War. The Soviet newspapers were full of joy and winning headlines. *Izvestia* wrote:

> The lively responses of the English press to the election of John F. Kennedy as president of the United States reflect the main question that worries the English people today: will the US foreign policy course change, will the new president take into account the ardent desire for peace of millions of ordinary Americans? The *Ayanida* newspaper writes: The American people voted to abandon the policy on the brink of war, to defuse international tensions, and to normalize relations with the Soviet Union ... The Communist Party of Japan regards Kennedy's victory as the result of the increasing demands of the American people for the establishment of lasting peace, as an expression of the American people's distrust of the Cold War policy and aggression carried out by the Republican Party led by Eisenhower ... Explaining the failure of the Republicans in the elections, the influential Melbourne newspaper *Age* writes that American foreign policy for a long time was too rude.

On 20 January 1961, Kennedy took office as president, after which Khrushchev decided to give him a gift. This gift was the release of two crew members of the same ERB-47 shot down on 1 July over the Barents Sea. Without any trial, McCone and Olmsted were transferred to the Americans on 25 January. With this gesture, the Soviet leader wanted to demonstrate his friendly intentions and start a new page in Soviet–American relations. As the near future would show, all these arguments about Eisenhower's 'aggressiveness' and Kennedy's 'kindness' turned out to be naive. It was Kennedy who brought the world to the brink of war, and nuclear war at that! Against the background of the future Caribbean crisis, Eisenhower's 'tricks' soon began to look like harmless childish pranks. The U-2 aircraft played an almost decisive role in these events.

U-2 and the 'Emigrant Landing'

Khrushchev's first disappointment in the new president came after the notorious events of the spring of 1961. In 1956, a civil war began in Cuba, which ended with the victory of the revolutionaries led by Fidel Castro. In January 1959, they took control of the country's largest cities, Havana and Santiago. At first, the American leadership reacted positively to the overthrow of the Batista military dictatorship and even tried to be friends with the new authorities. But soon Castro announced a course towards building socialism and friendship with the Soviet Union, which forced Eisenhower to quickly change his mind. On 17 March 1960, he approved the decision to carry out an operation to overthrow the Castro regime. The training was entrusted to CIA Director Allen Dulles. The immediate development of the plan was carried out by his deputy for planning, Richard Bissell. The main condition set by the president was the implementation of the operation without the direct participation of the United States but by rebel forces operating on the island and Cuban emigrants in America.

It should be noted that the operation almost 100% copied a similar operation to overthrow Guatemalan President Jacobo Árbenz Guzmán, which the CIA carried out successfully in June 1954. Guatemala also had a revolution, then numerous reforms were carried out there, including the free distribution of plantations to the poor and nationalisation. Árbenz came to power in 1951 during democratic elections. This politician was wrongly accused by the Americans of having sympathies with communism and ties with the Soviet Union. On the territory of Honduras, an anti-communist government junta was formed under the leadership of the CIA, which began an insurgency in Guatemala that was actually openly supported by the United States.

One of the points of the Cuban plan drawn up by the CIA, of course, was a thorough preliminary reconnaissance of all important military facilities on the island. On 26 and 27 October, U-2s from Detachment G conducted their first sorties over Cuba. However, there was cloud cover over the island, and aerial photography from high altitudes did not yield results. The next flights were undertaken on 27 November, then on 5 and 11 December. This time, the CIA received detailed images of airfields, military bases, ports and the coast.

Meanwhile, preparations for the operation were slow, which was primarily due to the change of government. During his election campaign, Kennedy strongly criticised Eisenhower for being interested in exploring 'distant lands' (hinting at U-2 flights over the USSR), but at the same time overlooked the appearance of the communist threat just 90 miles from the United States. This criticism added voters to him (perhaps even deciding the outcome of the campaign). Therefore, after moving to the White House, Kennedy had practically no choice but to continue preparing for the Cuban operation.

When Dulles and Bissell introduced him to the details of the plan, code-named Trinidad, the president generally approved them, but offered to familiarise Pentagon experts with it. In general, the new US leadership did not really like the practice that had developed under Eisenhower, when the CIA planned and carried out a number of operations, such as Aquaton and Robin Hood (an attempt to overthrow the Sukarno regime in Indonesia in 1958) on its own, without involving the military.

Already on 26 January, immediately after Kennedy took office, an amended plan was approved. However, this was more of a pure adventure and hooliganism than a serious mission. Thus, air support was supposed to consist of strikes by outdated Douglas B-26 Invader bombers in the insignia of the Cuban Air Force. The marine landing force consisted of emigrants who had previously undergone special training in secret military camps. At the same time, to raise morale, the rebels were promised the support of the Marines and other elite American units, although in reality the use of such on a large scale was not envisaged. The landing was to be preceded by massive sabotage on Cuban territory, which was supposed to distract Castro's troops from the bridgehead and encourage Cubans into a general uprising (in fact, the only serious action was the arson of the capital's department store). The so-called Cuban Revolutionary Council was formed in advance from Cuban emigrants to Miami, whose members were supposed to land on the island almost immediately after the landing in order to lead the uprising.

On 19 and 21 March, new U-2 flights were flown over Cuba, during which the deployment of troops, aircraft and bombing targets were clarified. On 4 April, Kennedy approved the final version of the operation. On 14 April, just before the air attack, a U-2 from Detachment G took another picture of the Cuban airfields. As a result, the Americans established the exact location of fifteen Cuban aircraft. In total, the Cuban Air Force numbered twenty-four aircraft: fifteen B-26s, six Sea Furies (a British piston-engined fighter) and three T-33 (a two-seat training version of the American F-80 jet fighter). The U-2 operated from Laughlin Air Force Base in Texas.

On the morning of 15 April, eight 'rebel' B-26C bombers, piloted by pilots of the Alabama National Guard, took off from an airfield in Nicaragua and carried out an air attack against three Cuban airfields. However, the raid ended in complete failure. Only three aircraft were destroyed, but the Cuban air defences knocked out two Invaders. One fell into the sea 50km north of Cuba (the crew of two died), while the second reached the Key West air base and made an emergency wheels-up landing.

Another B-26 returning from a mission landed at Miami International Airport. One of the pilots, who was wearing a Cuban uniform, stated in broken Spanish that he was a deserter who, along with his comrades, had rebelled against the Castro regime, after which he appealed to the US authorities for political asylum. However, the reporters who arrived noticed that the paint and especially the Cuban identification marks on the bomber were too fresh, and the pilot did not look very much like a Castro soldier (he looked too glamorous).

As a result, Kennedy was forced to cancel a repeated airstrike on targets on the island.

On the evening of 16 April, a solemn funeral for the victims of the bombing took place at Havana's Colon Cemetery. These were seven Cubans who died as a result of the air attacks. A crowded rally was held near the cemetery, at which Fidel Castro spoke. He compared the B-26 raid to the attack on Pearl Harbor, called the bombing an 'insidious and despicable attack' and compared the United States to the German Nazis. At the end of the speech, Castro said: 'Long live the socialist revolution! Long live free Cuba! Homeland or death! We will win!' These words, broadcast on the radio, caused an ovation and an emotional upsurge. Castro accused his enemies of wanting to steal sugar cane plantations, mines and factories from the Cuban people again.

CIA planners believed that the air attacks would scare civilians, inspire Castro's opponents to fight, and that the bomb explosions would be a kind of signal for an uprising. In fact, the bombing was used by the revolutionary to turn public opinion in his favour and mobilise his supporters. A French journalist described the situation in the Cuban capital:

Last night, Havana looked like a fortified camp, the militias mobilised on Saturday conducted strict monitoring of the situation in the city. Willis SUVs with armed men are driving around the streets. The security of large enterprises, power plants, radio stations, and newspaper offices has been strengthened. Barricades are stacked in the shopping district, sandbags are stacked at intersections.

Meanwhile, in the afternoon of 16 April, at a distance of 65km from the coast of Cuba, the invasion fleet of the 'Cuban expeditionary forces' (two landing ships and five cargo ships) met with a detachment of the American fleet consisting of two destroyers and two aircraft carriers. At about midnight on 17 April, the landing of 2506 Brigade, consisting of five infantry battalions, the 4th Tank Battalion and an artillery division, began simultaneously at three sites.

At 03.15, the Cuban leadership learned about the landing, martial law was imposed on the territory of the country and general mobilisation was announced. At dawn, seven Cuban aircraft unexpectedly attacked the beachhead and ships, sinking two transport vessels (including the *Rio Escondido*, which contained most of the ammunition and heavy weapons of the 2506 Brigade) and two landing barges. There was a huge explosion of 145 tons of ammunition and 3,000 gallons of fuel. According to Cuban information, the 38-year-old pilot of a Fury fighter, Enrique Carreras Rojas, sank the *Houston* transport with a volley of four unguided rockets. The ship was carrying the 5th Battalion of the 2506 Brigade. After that, he shot down a B-26C bomber with his 20-mm cannon together with Lieutenant Douglas Rood Mole. T-33 pilots Alvaro Prendes Quantana, Albert Fernandez and Rafael del Pino Diaz also shot down one B-26C each.

At 07.30 hours, 6 transport planes dropped 177 soldiers of the 1st Airborne Battalion, 2506 Brigade, in the San Blas area. However, by the middle of the day on 17 April, the offensive of the Cuban expeditionary forces had been foiled, and by the evening of 18 April, the so-called rebels were trapped in the triangle Playa Girón–Cayo Ramona–San Blas. At the same time, the Americans continued to provide them with moral support. For example, A-4D-2N carrier-based aircraft from the aircraft carrier *Essex* with painted-over markings flew several times at low level over the beachhead, but neither bombs nor missiles were dropped.

The Whole World Knows

After the presidential election, the Soviets were very friendly towards the United States. A typical sign of this was the complete disappearance of anti-American articles from newspapers. And in mid-April, the main topic was the first manned space flight. On 12 April, cosmonaut Yuri Gagarin flew around the globe for the first time in the Vostok spaceship. For the Soviet leadership, the primacy in the exploration of near-Earth space was a matter of prestige, for which they were ready to take any measures. After all, what could demonstrate the superiority of socialism over decaying capitalism even better and more clearly than the launch of a manned spaceship from Soviet soil? At the end of March, the Soviets received secret information that on 20 April the Americans were going to send a man into space. In this regard, Khrushchev had no choice but to schedule the launch of the Vostok spaceship for the period between 11 and 17 April. All information about this was strictly classified. Immediately before the launch, all Soviet media received three secret envelopes with numbers 1, 2 and 3, as well as instructions to open at a special signal only the envelope whose number would be indicated from

Moscow on 12 April. The remaining envelopes were to be destroyed immediately. Envelope No. 1 contained a solemn version of the launch of a spaceship with a man on board into low–Earth orbit, the second held a message about the failure of the spaceship to orbit and its emergency landing, and the third was a message about the tragic death of an astronaut. When confirmation of Gagarin's safe landing came in the afternoon of 12 April, all the media received an order: 'Open envelope No. 1!'

These events caused a storm of rejoicing in the Soviet Union. At that moment, in a burst of euphoria, it seemed to people earthly affairs such as road repairs, housing construction and harvesting were no longer as relevant as yesterday. Why bother with such outdated 'little things' when tomorrow it will be necessary to build spaceports and pave roads on Mars, Saturn, on the planets of other stars' galaxies? Soviet newspapers wrote:

> The time has come for the practical implementation of projects that previously seemed fantastic – the time for the creation of extraterrestrial scientific stations-observatories, human space travel to the Moon, Mars, Venus and other planets of the Solar system. This is an era of colossal expansion of the sphere of life and activity of mankind, the era of man's conquest of the near-solar space.

In April 1961, almost all parents were sure that their children, or at least their grandchildren, would definitely fly into space.

A young engineer, Lara Novikova, who was walking with her four-month-old daughter, told reporters:

> I am a contemporary of the first human exit beyond the Earth, into the universe. Marishka will still be a child when a Soviet man goes to explore the planets of the Solar system. Well, when she becomes an adult, she may have to become a crew member of a spaceship flying along interstellar routes. We will try to educate Mariska so that she can become a real astronaut.

Everyone was passionate about space and dreamed of future space travel. However, just five days later, the mood of Khrushchev and the Soviet leadership deteriorated greatly. On 18 April, articles appeared in the newspapers such as 'The United States is behind the rebels', 'Intervention against Cuba', 'Vile attack', 'Anger of the Soviet people', and 'The perpetrators of the crime have been exposed'. The Soviet Union immediately blamed the United States for the intervention in Cuba. An article in *Pravda* stated:

> Thus, we are talking about organised and controlled planned aggression from one centre. The reactionary press in the United States is in a hurry to present the case in such a way that such a centre is allegedly the notorious 'revolutionary council' headed by the defector Cardona. This council supposedly directs the 'liberation army', put together by no one knows where, no one knows with whose money, armed by no one knows who

and arrived from no one knows where … The whole world knows that the troops of mercenaries who landed in Cuba were assembled in the United States, armed with American weapons, trained under the guidance of American officers.

On the same day, the Soviet Government issued an official statement accusing the United States of organising aggression against Cuba. And Khrushchev sent a threatening message to President Kennedy. He hinted that a small war in a particular region could cause a chain reaction, and modern weapons were so long-range that such events could lead to disaster. 'As for the Soviet Union, there should be no misconceptions about our position: we will provide the Cuban people and their government with all necessary assistance in repel ling an armed attack.' In fact, Khrushchev was threatening Kennedy with nuclear war.

—Meanwhile, rallies in support of Cuba were held in all cities of the USSR. Thousands of workers and peasants went to these meetings after the end of the working day, during which angry speeches and threats were heard. Here is what journalists wrote about the rally in Tbilisi:

A working day has just ended at the Kirov machine tool plant. Hundreds of workers, engineers and technicians headed to the factory rally. Locksmith Beridze spoke: 'It is difficult to express in words the feeling of anger and indignation that we feel after learning about how Cuba was attacked by a pack of bandits and traitors supported and financed by the American aggressors. We are confident that justice will prevail, and the victory will be for revolutionary Cuba.'

A huge rally was held in Moscow near the American embassy. Crowds of people actually blocked the building, shouting anti-American slogans and curses. 'Don't play with fire, aggressors!' one of the banners read.

Mass anti-war demonstrations took place on this day in American cities, including in New York near the UN building. Inside the building, the Foreign Minister of Cuba Raúl Roa García, made an accusatory speech, showing the audience various proof of direct US participation in the 'landing of emigrants'. But the most painful consequences for the White House were the anti-American demonstrations that took place in Latin American countries: Mexico, Venezuela, Bolivia, Chile, Guatemala and Colombia. They were accompanied by massive burning of American flags, attacks on American embassies and urban riots. During these hours, some American politicians and congressmen, as well as military officials, exerted strong pressure on Kennedy. They demanded that the US Army openly side with the rebels, provide them with direct military support and begin a naval blockade of the island. However, the president hesitated. He was afraid of dragging the United States into a protracted conflict with unpredictable consequences.

At 18.00 on 18 April, the text of Khrushchev's message to Kennedy was broadcast in Havana and other Cuban cities. At that time, mass arrests of people suspected of having ties to the emigrant government and even sympathies with it were taking place throughout Cuba. The detainees were mostly handed over to the Committees for the Protection of the Revolution, which handed down sentences within a few hours.

On the morning of 19 April, five 'emigrant' B-26s with American crews raided the positions of Cuban troops. According to the plan, the Invaders were supposed to accompany jet fighters from the aircraft carrier *Essex*, but they did not appear in the specified area, and they had to carry out the attack without any cover. As a result, two more B-26s were shot down by Cuban fighters. A third aerial victory was won by Quantana, and the second by Rojas, who was nicknamed 'Grandfather'. Already in the evening of that day, it became clear that the operation had failed, and two American destroyers approaching the coast in order to evacuate the paratroopers were driven away by the firing of Cuban T-34 tanks!

At 17.30 on 19 April, the battle ended. The losses of the Cuban expeditionary forces amounted to 114 people killed and 1,202 prisoners, 5 tanks and 10 armoured personnel carriers. Twelve aircraft were also lost, at least eight of which (seven B-26s and one C-46) were shot down by Cuban fighters. Such a rapid failure of the emigrant landing came as a complete surprise to both Cubans and Americans. The Soviets also did not expect such a quick outcome. The confirmation of this in a Havana radio broadcast on the morning of 20 April shocked literally everyone.

Even bigger sensations happened in the following days. Hundreds of rebels surrendered to the Cubans and willingly told the details of the preparation for the mission. One of the prisoners told reporters:

> The Americans landed us here; they cunningly deceived us. The Americans said that in Cuba we would fight the Russians, the Chinese and the Czechs, and the Cuban people would immediately join us. We were told that the Cubans were already fighting an insurgency against Fidel and we were going to support these guerrillas.

Photos of the captives, many of whom turned out to be mercenaries from different Latin American countries, were published in the world's press and interviews with them were broadcast on the radio. The captured rebels willingly told everything they knew, hoping thereby to ease their fate.

In general, the landing in Cuba caused the same scandal as the shooting down of the U-2 in the Sverdlovsk region on 1 May 1960. The *New York Daily News* wrote: 'Allen Dulles has been fooled again. They squandered the $600 million that we allocate to him annually for cloak and dagger operations.' In fact, these events became the First Cuban Crisis, which became the prologue (forerunner) for the Second Cuban Crisis, which happened a year and a half later. Khrushchev openly supported Fidel and won. He was sure that it was precisely because of the protests from the USSR and other countries that Kennedy did not decide on an open military intervention. After that, relations between the Soviet Union and Cuba became even more friendly. Russians began to perceive Cubans as close friends, and schoolchildren even came up with their own interpretation of the name of this country, 'Communism Off the Coast of America' (Communism U Beregov Ameriki – CUBA). This phrase was also popular in the 1980s, when the author of this book was in school.

Detachment G performed fifteen sorties over Cuba during the operation and immediately after it. Later, U–2s flew regularly over the island, at least twice a month.

The First Cuban Crisis again strained relations between the USSR and the United States and provoked a new round of tension. The Soviets suspended the process of further planned reduction of the army, and military budget expenditures were increased by 3 billion rubles (for 1961). Khrushchev authorised the development and testing of new, more powerful types of weapons, primarily thermonuclear bombs of enormous power.

At the Vienna Summit on 4 June 1961, Khrushchev met with Kennedy for the first time and demanded a faster settlement of the East and West Berlin conflict. The Soviet leader threatened that the Soviet Union would unilaterally sign a peace treaty with the GDR, which would annul the 1945 agreement of the four victorious powers and make the presence of NATO troops in West Berlin illegal. Khrushchev issued an ultimatum, setting a deadline of 31 December 1961.

On 25 July, Kennedy gave a long-televised speech in Washington, which was broadcast nationwide. The president stated that there was a threat to West Berlin from the Soviet Union. In this regard, he called on NATO countries to increase military spending and military-strategic partnership. He also announced that he would ask Congress to allocate an additional $3.25 billion for military spending. Kennedy promised from eight to six new divisions (six for the army and two for the Marines), and announced plans to triple the draft and call up reservists. Kennedy ordered the postponement of the planned withdrawal of several ships and battleships from the fleet, as well as the postponement of the decommissioning of B-47 Stratojet bombers. The president especially stressed that the USAF should be able to organise air bridges (with a hint of the blockaded West Berlin). At the end of the speech, Kennedy said, 'We seek peace, but we shall not surrender.'

Khrushchev interpreted this speech as a rejection by the United States of disarmament and demilitarisation, as well as direct military blackmail by Kennedy. In the following days, articles appeared in Soviet newspapers with the headlines 'No time to rattle weapons', 'Dangerous game with fire', and 'Nations condemn military hysteria'. In fact, Kennedy's speech led to two consequences. First, Khrushchev ordered Walter Ulbricht to immediately begin blocking West Berlin. Secondly, the Soviet leader ordered the resumption of nuclear tests, suspended in 1958.

At midnight on 12 August, the East German border police, the East German army and units of the Soviet Army began blocking the border, and by morning the process was over. On the border of West and East Berlin, the installation of barbed wire fences for 97 miles had begun. Following this, the construction of concrete barriers began. This is how the history of the famous Berlin Wall began. This event caused another political crisis, culminating in the confrontation between American and Russian tanks at Checkpoint Charlie on 27–28 October. Kennedy actually came to terms with the new reality and declared, 'It's not a very nice solution, but a wall is a hell of a lot better than a war.' Khrushchev was also pleased and abandoned the idea of signing a peace treaty with the GDR.

While these dramatic events were developing, nuclear explosions were thundering in the Soviet Union almost every day. On 1 September, a 16-kiloton bomb dropped from an aircraft was detonated at the Semipalatinsk test site. Then, during September, fifteen more nuclear and thermonuclear (hydrogen) bombs were detonated over Kazakhstan. Another nine tests were conducted in the Novaya Zemlya archipelago. In October, the Soviet Union conducted twenty-three nuclear tests. And on 31 October, a 58.6 megaton thermonuclear bomb (the so-called 'tsar bomb') was detonated over Cape Sukhoy Nos. It was the most powerful nuclear explosion in history, which demonstrated to the whole world the fact that the Soviet Union had created weapons of incredible destructive power. In November, the USSR carried out ten more tests. In total, almost sixty nuclear explosions occurred in three months. In fact, it looked like a small nuclear war. Most of the tests were conducted in the atmosphere, however, a large amount of radioactive fallout was released on to the planet. After that, Khrushchev felt that he had scared everyone enough, and the Soviet Union again paused testing nuclear charges.

At the end of 1961, relations between the USSR and the United States unexpectedly improved again. This was due to the fact that during the XVI session of the UN General Assembly, the representative of the Soviet Union made a proposal to create a Committee on Complete and General Disarmament. This idea was unexpectedly supported by the United States, Great Britain,

France and other countries. The United Nations (UN) General Assembly accepted the decision of the major powers to create the Eighteen Nation Committee on Disarmament (ENCD) through resolution 1722 (XVI) on 21 December 1961. The first meeting of the committee was to begin on 18 March 1962. Khrushchev perceived this event as a turning point in international foreign policy. On 7 February 1962, the Soviet leader received a joint message from President Kennedy and Prime Minister Macmillan. In this letter, the leaders of the United States and Great Britain expressed hope for the successful start of ENCD's work and hoped that this committee would become an effective platform for negotiations on universal demilitarisation. The message contained many warm words addressed to Khrushchev and concerns about the arms race. The document stated:

> We are confident that every effort must be made and that the three of us must assume a single degree of personal responsibility for finding any ways to limit the arms race. In the event that a way is not found to control the increasingly escalating arms competition, events may take an unpredictable turn and result in a tragedy that will affect both the people of the Soviet Union and the people of Great Britain and the people of the United States … The menacing nature of modern weapons is so terrifying that we cannot consider it as a common problem or as a problem in the field of propaganda.

Khrushchev was very touched by this message. He ordered it to be published in the newspapers. In addition, the Soviet leader ordered the reimposition of a moratorium on nuclear tests and the immediate release of Francis Powers.

In Steven Spielberg's film *Bridge of Spies*, negotiations on the exchange of Powers for the Russian spy Rudolf Abel, who was arrested in the United States in 1957, are shown very dramatically. In this film, Abel (real name William Fisher) is shown as a super spy, and lawyer James Donovan as a superhero who held all the threads of negotiations with the Soviets in his hands. Powers is also depicted as an American hero, whom the Russians did not want to return. But then they finally agreed to a secret deal to get Abel. In fact, neither Powers nor Abel were of any value to the Soviet Union at that time. The Russians knew for sure that Abel had not confessed to working for Soviet intelligence and had not given away any secrets. Also, Powers had already fulfilled his propaganda role and, conversely, has given away absolutely all the Americans' secrets.

Khrushchev decided to give up Powers only for the sake of improving relations with Kennedy. One very important coincidence points to this fact. On 10 February, Khrushchev's reply to the US president and the British prime minister was published. In it, the Soviet leader thanked them for their mutual understanding and expressed hope for the success of the Eighteen Nation Committee on Disarmament. On the same day, on the Glienicke Bridge connecting East and West Berlin, there was an exchange of Powers for Abel. The next day, *Pravda* published a message:

The Presidium of the Supreme Soviet of the USSR considered the petition of relatives of the American pilot Francis Powers, convicted in the USSR. Taking into account Powers' confession of committing the gravest crime, as well as being guided by the desire to improve relations between the Soviet Union and the United States, it was decided to grant Powers amnesty and transfer him to the American authorities.

'We Are With You, Cubans! We Are With You!'

In the spring of 1962, relations between the USSR and the United States seemed to be getting better again. Anti-American articles disappeared from Russian newspapers, and there was complete silence at the nuclear test sites. Unfortunately, however, this did not last long. Several events took place at once, increasing the threat of nuclear war.

During the first month of the meetings of the Eighteen Nation Committee on Disarmament, the Soviet Union presented a draft Treaty on General and Complete Disarmament, which provided for the complete abandonment of atomic weapons by all countries, the cessation of nuclear tests and the phased elimination of accumulated nuclear arsenals and all means of delivery of nuclear warheads (strategic bombers, intercontinental ballistic missiles and cruise missiles). This was to be carried out under mutual control. The committee also received a memorandum from eight neutral states, which proposed to completely abandon further nuclear tests and create nuclear-free zones in the world. However, representatives of the United States and Great Britain did not agree with these proposals, offering in response a vague concept of phased and controlled disarmament.

At the same time, the White House officially announced the resumption of nuclear tests in the atmosphere and the beginning of a series of tests of nuclear weapons in outer space. On 25 April, the United States launched Operation Dominic. On this day, a 190-kiloton nuclear explosion was carried out on the Pacific Kiritimati atoll (Christmas Island). Two days later, a B-52 bomber dropped another 410-kiloton bomb on this island. These facts were perceived by Khrushchev as the West's rejection of disarmament and demilitarisation, as well as another attempt by the United States to achieve military superiority over the Soviet Union. At the same time, intelligence officials informed Khrushchev that information had emerged about the United States preparing a new invasion of Cuba. And at about the same time, Khrushchev learned that American ballistic missiles with nuclear warheads were stationed in Turkey.

And it was true. In early 1961, the Pentagon concluded that the intercontinental strategic missiles already in service could not ensure the security of the United States. These bulky structures were still imperfect and, most importantly, due to the complex refuelling technology (fuel had to be constantly drained and refilled, as in a space rocket), they could not always be on combat duty. The PGM-19 Jupiter missile did not have such disadvantages, but it could hit targets at a distance of no more than 2,400km. The Jupiter was equipped with the Mk 3 combat unit, equipped with a thermonuclear charge with a capacity of 1.44 megatons. Then the idea arose to secretly place them on the territory of Turkey, thereby covering the entire western part of both the USSR and the countries of the Eastern Bloc. Soon, fifteen Jupiters were secretly stationed in the Izmir city area.

However, as has often happened, the secret did not stay that way and Khrushchev found out about it. He considered this act by Kennedy a personal insult and another pressure on the USSR. In mid-May, when the first round of the work of the Eighteen Nation Committee on Disarmament reached an impasse, and the Americans carried out ten more nuclear tests in the Pacific Ocean, Khrushchev decided to act. On 21 May 1962, at a meeting of the Defence Council, he proposed secretly sending Soviet troops and nuclear weapons to Cuba. On 30 May, Fidel Castro agreed, and on 10 June, at a meeting of the Presidium of the Central Committee of the CPSU, USSR Defence Minister Rodion Malinovsky presented a preliminary draft of the operation to transfer missiles to the island. It provided for the deployment of two types of ballistic missiles in Cuba – the R-12 with a range of about 2,000km and the R-14 with a range twice as long. Both types of missiles were equipped with 1-megaton thermonuclear warheads. In addition to missiles, it was decided to send to Cuba a helicopter aviation regiment, a squadron of fighters, forty-two Il-28 bombers, two units of cruise missiles with nuclear warheads with a capacity of 12 kilotons (range 160km), several units of anti-aircraft guns, as well as twelve S-75 anti-aircraft missile systems (144 missiles). In addition, the Russians wanted to send several tank battalions equipped with the latest T-55 tanks to Cuba. The operation was prepared in the strictest secrecy. At the same time, anti-American publications began to appear in Soviet newspapers again. The USSR accused the United States of refusing to disarm, threatening the proliferation of nuclear weapons in space and provoking a new round of the arms race.

On 1 August, the Soviet Union broke the pause and resumed nuclear tests. During the month, the Soviets carried out nineteen explosions. The record was set on 22 August, when the Russians detonated three nuclear bombs in one day.

Despite all this, Khrushchev tried to maintain the appearance of good relations with Kennedy. For example, on the eve of 4 July, he had personally congratulated the president on the Independence Day of the United States. And the return thanks from Kennedy were even printed in Soviet newspapers.

But, soon the hour came when the U-2 aircraft again played an important role in world history. On 28 August 1962, during another duty flight over Cuba, the U-2 photographed new, previously unknown military facilities, which, after decrypting the images, were identified by the American military as SA-2 (S-75) anti-aircraft missile systems. However, there were no missile launches on the reconnaissance aircraft. This information quickly became known to the American military and politicians.

On 4 September, President Kennedy told Congress that there were no offensive Russian missiles in Cuba. Nevertheless, the CIA received information that Soviet missiles with nuclear warheads, the range of which covered the entire southern coast of the United States, could soon be deployed on the island. The Pentagon suspected that the S-75s were specially prepared to protect some other, much more dangerous weapon. This prompted the intensification of U-2 flights over Cuba. However, due to bad weather, only three of these were carried out by the end of September, as a result of which only poor-quality images were obtained.

Meanwhile, soon after Eisenhower's departure, the USAF command sought to remove the CIA from conducting reconnaissance flights and transfer this function (along with the aircraft) to them. The first U-2s entered the 4028th Strategic Reconnaissance Squadron, part of the 4080th Strategic Reconnaissance Wing (4080th SRW), in July 1957. But since then, these aircraft had not participated in any serious operations. This was due to the restrictions that existed regarding the use of American troops. According to them, USAF aircraft could be used against targets outside the United States only in the event of an open military conflict, or with the consent of third countries. Cuba did not fit these parameters, so until the autumn of 1962 only CIA or 'Cuban rebel air force' planes flew over it.

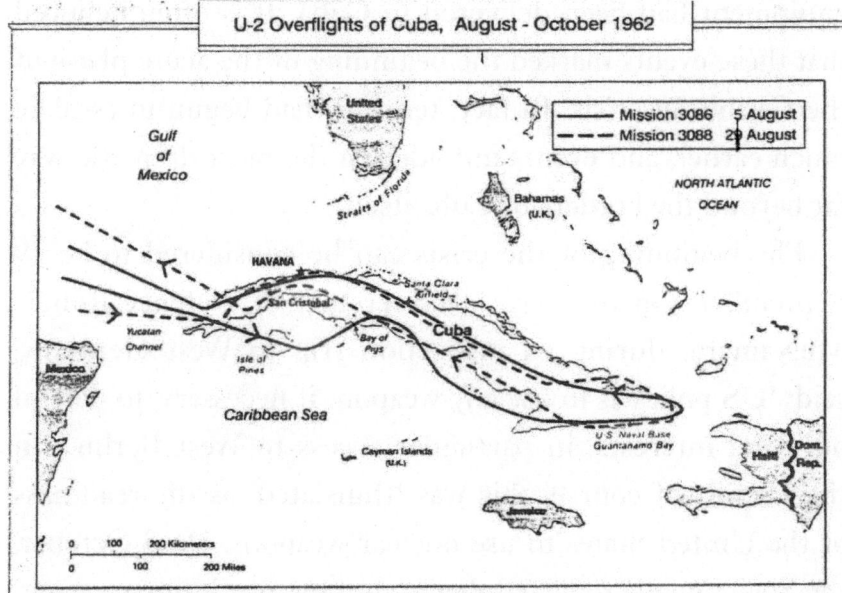

The U-2 flights plan over Cuba on 5 and 29 August 1962.

From 5 September to 14 October, Kennedy banned U–2 flights over Cuba altogether. This was due to bad weather, as well as fears of an escalation of the conflict if the American plane was shot down by a Soviet anti-aircraft missile.

In fact, back in early August, in an atmosphere of strict secrecy, the first Soviet ships approached Cuba with a highly secret cargo and troops on board. On the night of 8 September, the first batch of R–12 and R–14 ballistic missiles was unloaded in the port of Havana. Their positions were located in the west of the island in the area of the village of San Cristobal and in the area of the port of Casilda in the central part of the island. Along with the missiles, a contingent of troops arrived in Cuba to protect them. Several cruise missiles and a motorised infantry regiment were stationed in the eastern part of the island. By 14 October, all forty missiles and most of their equipment had been delivered to Cuba. It is often believed that these events marked the beginning of the acute phase of the Caribbean crisis. In fact, tensions had begun to escalate much earlier, and events unfolded in the most dramatic way far beyond the borders of Cuba itself ...

The beginning of the crisis can be considered to be 29 September. On this day, US Secretary of Defence Robert McNamara, during an inspection trip to West Germany, said: 'US policy is to use any weapon, if necessary, to defend our vital interests, in particular access to West Berlin.' In the USSR, of course, this was 'translated' as the readiness of the United States to use nuclear weapons. On 3 October, the Soviet media reported that a 'counter-revolutionary gang' engaged in the murders of Cuban workers and peasants had been defeated in the Cuban province of Las Villas. In addition, the newspapers wrote about how the American imperialists continued provocative actions against Liberty Island: 'In recent days, four American military aircraft and three warships have violated the airspace and territorial waters of the republic.' On the same day, the United States conducted another nuclear test on Johnson Island in the Pacific Ocean.

On 5 October, NATO manoeuvres began in Greece. In the USSR, this was perceived as a direct challenge and threat of attack, including a nuclear strike (after all, American medium-range missiles were very close in Turkey).

On 7 October, the Central Committee of the CPSU published the so-called 'calls for the 45th anniversary of the Great October Socialist Revolution'. They mainly concerned foreign policy, and item No. 12 read as follows: 'The peoples of all countries! Be vigilant, expose the imperialist arsonists

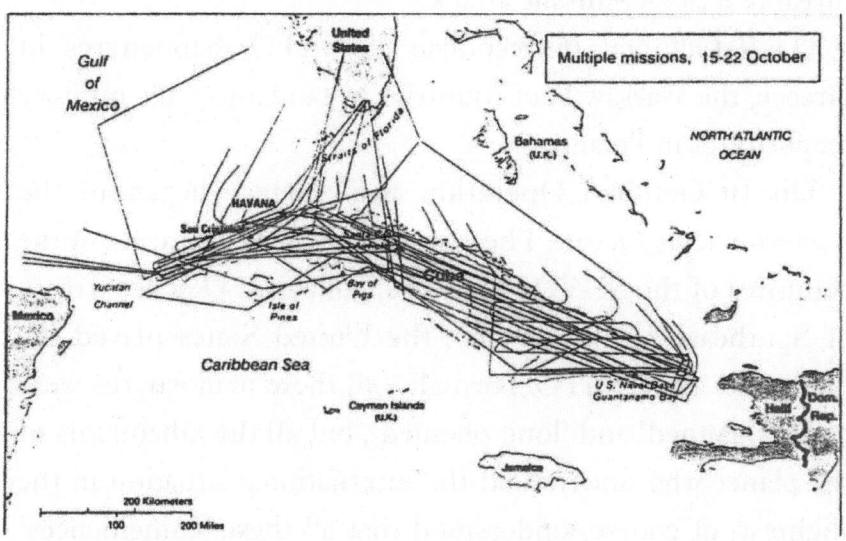

The U-2 flight plan over Cuba from 15–22 October 1962.

of the war! Fight harder to ensure lasting and indestructible peace!' This was followed by greetings to fraternal peoples, and China stood in first place (although relations between the two countries were already far from ideal). For some reason, the heroic people of Cuba were given only twelfth place.

The next day, for the first time, Soviet newspapers directly hinted at the threat of world war. All the newspapers quoted the words of US Vice President Lyndon Johnson: 'Those who advocate the blockade of Cuba obviously do not realise that the detention of a Russian ship is an act of war.' On the same day, TASS published reports on the upcoming tests of 'powerful launch vehicles of space objects without the last stages'. Two areas in the Pacific Ocean were designated where ballistic missiles launched from the territory of the USSR were supposed to fall. In America, this was perceived as a threat of a Soviet missile attack.

On 9 October, in response to NATO manoeuvres in Greece, the Warsaw Pact countries began large-scale military manoeuvres in Poland.

On 10 October, Operation Sea Surface began in the western Pacific Ocean. These were large-scale exercises of the countries of the SEATO bloc (the Collective Defence Treaty of Southeast Asia), in which the United States played the main role, as in NATO. Formally, all these manoeuvres were called 'planned' and 'long planned', but all the inhabitants of the planet who understood the international situation in the slightest, of course, understood that all these 'coincidences' were not accidental at all.

On 13 October, large-scale military manoeuvres involving the Soviet, Romanian and Bulgarian armies began in Romania. Dozens of military units, divisions and aviation regiments were suddenly put on alert.

The turning point came on 14 October. At 03.00, Major Richard Heizer's U-2 from the 4028th Squadron took off from Edwards Air Force Base in California and headed towards Cuba. The flight to the target took five hours. After flying around the island, at 07.31 the aircraft entered the airspace of Cuba and crossed its course from south to north, flying over the cities of Taco Taco, San Cristobal and Bahia Honda. After spending twelve minutes over Cuba, Heizer turned to an air base in Florida.

On 15 October, after analyzing the photographs obtained, CIA specialists made a terrifying discovery: Soviet SS-4 medium-range ballistic missiles (according to the NATO classification) were now stationed in Cuba. In the evening, the information was received by the Pentagon. On the same day, more 'planned' joint manoeuvres of the Hungarian and Soviet armies began in Hungary. In fact, under the guise of exercises, both sides carried out the gradual deployment of their ground forces, fleets, aircraft and missile units in different parts of the world.

At 08.45 hours on 16 October, photographs of the rocket launch pads were shown to President Kennedy during breakfast. The president immediately authorised the continuation of U-2 flights over Cuba with an intensity of at least six missions daily.

During 16–17 October, the USSR successfully launched a multistage rocket into the central Pacific Ocean at a distance of 12,000km. The official cover for this operation was 'preparation for flights to the moon'. Meanwhile, U-2s from the 4028th SRS had discovered sixteen positions of Russian nuclear missiles in Cuba by 18 October.

On 18 October, Soviet newspapers published an order from the Minister of Defence of the USSR, Marshal Rodion Malinovsky:

> Comrades soldiers and sailors, sergeants and petty officers! Fellow officers, generals and admirals! This year marks the 150th anniversary of the Patriotic War of 1812 – the immortal epic of the heroic struggle of the Russian, Ukrainian, Belarusian and other peoples of our country against the invading Napoleonic army. In the war of 1812, the spirit of freedom of the peoples of Russia, their anger and hatred of foreign enslavers were vividly manifested ... The great victories won by our Motherland over numerous aggressors serve as a terrible warning to all lovers of imperialist adventures.

The next day, an artillery salute was given in many cities of the USSR. It should be noted that the anniversary of the Battle of Borodino, in which the Russian army fought the army of Napoléon Bonaparte, was actually celebrated on 7 September. However, most of all, this event was remembered during the Caribbean missile crisis. Thus, the Soviets, as it were, drew historical analogies. A favourite Russian saying is 'Those who comes to us with a sword [rocket], will die from the sword [rocket].'

On 19 October, another U-2 flight over Cuba revealed several more mounted missile positions, as well as a squadron of Soviet Il-28 bombers and the latest MiG-21 fighters at air bases. In addition, the positions of cruise missiles aimed in the direction of Florida were photographed. On this day, American

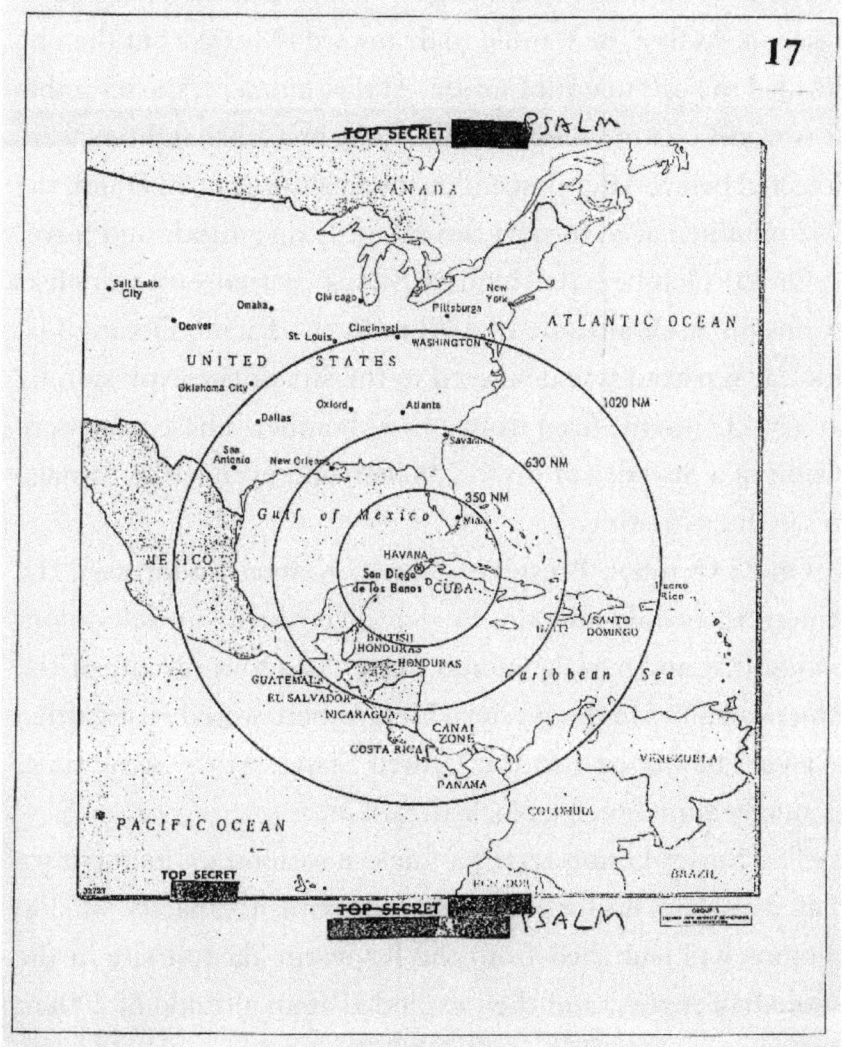

Calculated radius of destruction by nuclear missiles from Cuba.

strategic bombers switched to the constant patrol mode, during which several groups of B-52s carrying nuclear bombs were continuously in the air. Soviet bombers also constantly patrolled in the sky. During this period, several critical situations occurred during the U-2 flights. One of the reconnaissance planes over Havana had an engine failure and the pilot had to descend. At first, he wanted to fly towards Mexico, but then he decided to head to until Florida. At that moment, the scramble of two MiG-21 interceptors and flying by Cuban fighters were detected below. After descending to an altitude of 12,000m, the U-2 pilot managed to start the engine, gain altitude and leave.

On 20 October, the United States carried out a nuclear explosion at an altitude of 147km in the Pacific Ocean. The nuclear warhead was delivered to the site of the explosion by an XM-33 missile fired from a B-52 bomber. These tests were visible at a distance of up to 2,000km and even led to damage to satellites in orbit.

On 22 October, President John F. Kennedy addressed the American people and the Soviet government on television, noting that any missile launch from Cuba towards any of the American allies in the Western Hemisphere would be regarded as an act of war against the United States. At the same time, Kennedy announced a blockade of Cuba.

The Soviet Union tested a nuclear weapon on its territory that day. The K-3 nuclear missile with a capacity of 300 kilotons was launched from the Kapustin Yar test site in the Astrakhan region, and then exploded at an altitude of 290km above Kazakhstan. The test was conducted during the day so as not to blind people. The electromagnetic pulse resulting from the explosion caused interference in the radars of the missile defence system at a distance of about 1,000km from the point above which the explosion occurred. At the same time, damage was caused to an underground electric cable with a length of 1,000km that was buried at a depth of 90cm and connected Tselinograd with Alma-Ata. The impulse caused numerous fires due to short circuits in electrical appliances, the largest at the Karaganda thermal power plant. More than 570km of telephone lines running above the surface were also damaged.

On 23 October, Soviet citizens (those who did not secretly listen to foreign radio broadcasts) learned that the world was on the verge of war. The editorial of the *Gorky Worker* newspaper described the morning of that day at the machine tool plant 'Kuybyshev' (the newspaper itself was published in the evening):

Mikhail Ananyevich Kuzmin, the foreman of the collectors, entered the workshop in the morning and was even surprised: it seemed to him that everything here was the same as yesterday, as if nothing significant had happened in the world. As usual, some assemblers were swarming around the workbenches, preparing tools, others were bringing the necessary parts to the workplaces, and only those who apparently came early gathered in the recreation area and, sitting on benches, smoked in silence. But Mikhail Ananyevich soon realised that he was mistaken: his fellow workers were no less excited than he was. There is a stamp of anxiety, anger and indignation in their eyes.

Such scenes of indignation and at the same time fear of nuclear war were observed that day all over the country – in factories, universities, and schools. One newspaper reported: 'The city of Gorky people, like all the peace-loving Soviet people, angrily protest against the actions of the American military in relation to Cuba. The working people of the city warmly support the Soviet government and declare: "Hands off the Island of Freedom!"' All the editorials gave similar information.

On 24 October, Khrushchev sent Kennedy a letter in which he blamed him for setting 'ultimatum conditions' and called the blockade 'an act of aggression pushing humanity to the abyss of a global nuclear war'. Meanwhile, numerous rallies and gatherings dedicated to Cuba were held throughout the country. 'We, like all Soviet people, in response to the machinations of the American aggressors, will triple our efforts on the labour front,' said Ivan Pavlovsky, foreman of shipyards, during such a gathering at the Krasnoe Sormovo shipyard. But in the eyes of his colleagues, he saw fear rather than determination. This plant secretly produced submarines, and MiG-21 fighters, which were now at the forefront of the Cold War, were being built at the nearby aviation plant No. 21. Everyone understood that Gorky city would probably be one of the first to become a target for American nuclear strikes. 'We are peaceful people, but at any moment, at the call of the Motherland, we are ready to change the steering wheel of a combine harvester to a machine gun, a milling machine to a missile system. If necessary, we are ready to defend the Cuban Republic!' said Tukmakov, a milling cutter at the Gorky Automobile Plant, at a rally. Along the way, newspapers, as was then customary, printed poems by folk authors, such as this one:

'We are with you, Cubans! We are with you!' – that's what our country says.
Let Cuba's free banner burn over the glorious island!
The United States is threatening war, but the truth lives on earth,
Pirates of the twentieth century will not be able to defeat her.
We will not let our enemies extinguish the hot flame of our hearts.
We are with you, Cubans! We are with you! We will stand up! We will win!

The photographs preserved from those rallies clearly show that behind the determination it was not possible to hide the fear and horror of war. The women looked especially confused. After all, only seventeen years had passed since the end of the previous massacre – and again you will have to send your sons to the front? Or maybe we won't have to: what if we're all going to be incinerated tomorrow, like in Hiroshima?

And that terrible tomorrow was approaching inexorably. On 25 October, President Kennedy ordered the combat readiness level to be raised to DEFCON 2 (preceded by maximum combat readiness for a nuclear attack). Mass civil defence exercises were held in all cities of the Soviet Union, and children were told in detail how to behave in the event of a nuclear explosion. All the bomb shelters were kept unlocked, and responsible workers were constantly on duty there.

On 26 October, Khrushchev sent a second, less belligerent letter to Kennedy, in which he offered to remove Soviet missiles from Cuba in exchange for guarantees of non-aggression on the island. Meanwhile, in France, a 'state of alert number 2' was declared, which corresponded to the pre-mobilisation situation. This decision was made at a meeting of the Supreme Council of Defence, chaired by Charles de Gaulle. In the Soviet Union, this act was regarded as preparation for a large-scale war in Europe.

The Cuban Missile Crisis culminated on 27 October. In the morning, U-2F No. 343 56-6676 of Major Rudolf Anderson from the 4028th SRS carried out another flight over Cuba. At the same time, due to bad weather and a tropical storm in the area of the island, it was impossible to conduct aerial photography from a high altitude this time. Therefore, Anderson was instructed to act according to the circumstances, a fatal order for him. Soviet radar stations detected the aircraft when it was flying in the area of the American base of Guantanamo, although they could not identify the target. The chief of staff of the S-75 Dvina anti-aircraft missile division, Captain Antonets, called the headquarters of the commander of the Russian military contingent, Army General Pliev, and asked for instructions on further actions. But the commander was not at his workplace. Pliev's deputy for combat training, Major General Leonid Garbuz, ordered Antonets to wait for further instructions. Several more unsuccessful calls followed. When the U-2F was already over Cuba, Garbuz ran to the headquarters and personally gave the order to destroy the target. According to other sources, the order was given by the Deputy Commander for Air Defence Lieutenant General Stepan Grechko, or the commander of the 27th Air Defence Division, Colonel Georgy Voronkov. Whoever it was, at 10.22, the missiles were launched.

About thirty seconds later, an explosion occurred about 200m from the nose of the U-2F, when it was over the city of Banes. Apparently, the pilot was flying without an oxygen mask, in violation of all instructions. Fragments hit the cabin of the aircraft and caused decompression of the cabin, from which the pilot lost consciousness. After that, the unguided plane continued flying for a long time before crashing on the northern coast of the island. When Kennedy was informed that the reconnaissance plane had been shot down by the Russians, he fell into prostration for a while. The military surrounding him had additional arguments in favour of an attack against Cuba. They told him that 'while we are thinking here, the Russians are already shooting at our planes'. In fact, the U-2 flight over Cuba was an act of aggression and formally the Soviets had the right to destroy it.

The Chase Over the Magadan Region

No less dangerous was another, much less well-known episode that happened on the same day in a completely different area of the globe. And this was also connected with the U-2.

While in the eastern United States millions of Americans were waiting for a nuclear strike and shaking with fear, with many of them holed up in bunkers, at the opposite end of America – in Alaska – life, one might say, went on as usual. At 04.00 summer North American Eastern Time (in Alaska it corresponded to midnight), WU-2A 56-6715, flown by Captain Charles Maultsby, took off from Eielson air base. In total darkness, the plane gained altitude and headed for the North Pole.

The fact is that part of the 4080th SRW, while their colleagues were flying over Cuba, was performing another responsible mission – collecting air samples in the Arctic after Soviet nuclear tests on the Novaya Zemlya archipelago. The tests went on as usual, despite the events in the world, and on 26 October, American seismologists recorded another explosion, the power of which they estimated at 260 kilotons. These routine missions full of dangers usually lasted for eight hours. At the same time, in the conditions of the polar night in the Arctic, it was completely dark, and the pilots had to navigate only by the stars and using the gyrocompass. Interestingly, to Barter Island, located off the northern coast of Alaska, the WU-2A was accompanied by amphibious rescue aircraft, a GA-1 Duck and a GA-22 Drake.

Halfway to the pole, Maultsby was blinded by the aurora borealis and lost his bearings for a while. In addition, the gyrocompass on the U-2 was not disconnected from the magnetic compass. Whether this was due to a technical malfunction or whether the pilot himself forgot to switch the device, it has not been precisely established. The fact is that the northern magnetic pole, unlike the geographical pole, periodically changes location, and in 1962 it was located near the Canadian island of Bathurst. This point is located almost a 1,000km from the North Pole. In other latitudes, this phenomenon does not have a serious impact on orientation, but during flights over the icy Arctic, such an error could play a fatal role. And in this case, it could even lead to a nuclear war!

Maultsby completely lost his bearings in the night sky and eventually got lost. According to the mission plan, at exactly noon North American Summer Eastern Time (08.00 Alaska time), the U-2 was supposed to land in Eielson. Instead, the plane set a southeasterly course, flew west of Wrangel Island and entered the airspace of the USSR in the area of the Long Strait. The mysterious object flying over the Magadan region was soon detected by radar stations of the 11th Separate Air Defence Army. The Russians had doubts about where this mysterious target could have come from but they decided to intercept it anyway. A pair of MiG-19Ps was scrambled from Anadyr air base, and a pair of MiG-17PFs took off from Ureliki. Targeting was hampered by zero visibility and a weak object signal on radars. As a result, only one MiG-19 pilot managed to approach the U-2, still without visual contact with the target.

Meanwhile, Maultsby was negotiating with his base, trying to restore orientation. The operators turned the map of the starry sky in front of them, comparing it with the descriptions of the pilot, and eventually realised with horror that the plane was flying over Soviet territory, and heading for Anadyr. Maultsby was instructed to turn slowly to the left until he clearly saw the constellation of Orion behind the right wing.

It pointed exactly south at this time of day. Over the Gulf of the Cross, U-2 finally turned towards the United States, but was still over Soviet territory. At the same time, a secret radio interception station in Alaska intercepted the negotiations of the Soviet pilots with their command. It became clear from them that the U-2 was being chased (Maultsby himself did not suspect that the MiG-19 was flying 5km below him). However, they could not give this information to the pilot. Listening to Soviet radio signals was considered a national secret, and if the pilot had received the radio interception data, there was a risk that they, in turn, would be overheard by the Russians and they would guess that the Americans were listening to them.

Meanwhile, the situation was heating up. By order of the Alaska Air Defence Command, a pair of F-102 fighter jets took off from Galena air base, each carrying a pair of AIM-26 Falcon air-to-air missiles with nuclear warheads. They had a power of 0.25 kilotons and were designed to destroy formations of Soviet bombers. Upon entering the airspace over the Bering Strait, the interceptor pilots reported to the base that they saw targets on radar and asked for further action. There was a real possibility of a nuclear strike where it was least expected at that moment – in Chukotka! However, there was no response, the pilots heard only 'oohs and sighs' in their headphones, and then the F-102 received an order to return to base.

The MiG-19P escorted the U-2 for eighteen minutes, but, a little short of reaching American territorial waters, turned back. However, for Maultsby, the troubles didn't end there. The aircraft had been in the air for more than nine hours and had used up all its fuel. As soon as the plane left Soviet airspace, the engine stalled. The pilot had to glide for about an hour towards the shore. After ten hours and twenty-five minutes of flight, at 14.25 Washington time, the WU-2A landed safely in Alaska.

However, at that moment, this achievement turned out to be, to put it mildly, not very timely! Even at the moment when the plane was in the air, the commander of the 4080th SRW, Colonel John A. des Portes, received a call from the Headquarters of the Strategic Air Command (SAC), who in a rude, hysterical form asked: 'What the hell was this idiot doing on a plane over Russia? Did you decide to start a war there yourself, cretins?' At 13.41 Washington time, the incident was reported to US Secretary of Defence Robert McNamara ... Needless to say, one can only imagine what impression this news made on him at a time when another U-2 had just been shot down over Cuba, and a missile attack was expected at any moment in the White House. According to eyewitnesses, for a moment McNamara turned white and was speechless, but then he pulled himself together. At 13.45, he reported the incident to the president, and two minutes later to the State Department. After that, according to USAF General David Burchinal, McNamara ran out of the Pentagon covered in sweat, tearing his hair and shouting hysterically: 'This means war with the Soviet Union! The president must contact Moscow right now!'

The irony of military fate had played a truly cruel joke on the Americans. In 1956, in case the top-secret U-2 reconnaissance aircraft was shot down by the Russians, the CIA developed a cover story that such aircraft were engaged only in meteorological research and collecting air samples in the upper atmosphere. When Powers' U-2 was actually shot down, this ruse did not work, and all the aircraft's carefully guarded secrets became the property of the entire world community. But the incident did not have any serious military consequences, which were so feared in the White House. Now it was exactly the opposite! The plane was indeed performing a legal and peaceful flight, collecting air samples, but at the same time it accidentally ended up in Soviet airspace. And, as it seemed to the American command, the incident could now actually provoke the outbreak of the Third World War!

On the evening of 27 October, another incident occurred. A pair of RF-8A naval reconnaissance aircraft were fired on by conventional anti-aircraft guns during a low-altitude flyby of Cuba. One aircraft was damaged, but both aircraft returned safely to base.

The evening of this day, which went down in world history as 'black Sunday', was not boring. Kennedy's military advisers tried to convince him before it was too late to order an attack against Cuba before Monday. The president hesitated, but still hoped for a peaceful resolution of the conflict. And Fidel Castro, who was sure that the bombing of missile bases would begin in the morning, persuaded Soviet Ambassador Alexeyev to put pressure on Khrushchev to order a pre-emptive nuclear strike against the United States. At the same time, he stated that 'the Cuban people are ready to sacrifice themselves for the sake of defeating American imperialism'. Of course, the Cubans themselves did not conduct opinion polls on whether they agreed with such a decision, and there was no time to organise one. Khrushchev, in response, said that 'Comrade Fidel Castro has lost his nerve', and that ongoing negotiations with the Americans to solve the crisis were proceeding well.

On the morning of 28 October these talks reached a conclusion and Soviet newspapers published a statement by President Kennedy: 'I welcome Khrushchev's wise decision to stop the construction of bases in Cuba, dismantle offensive weapons and return them to the Soviet Union under UN supervision. This is an important and constructive contribution to the cause of peace.' Cuba, it turned out, had Soviet 'offensive weapons'. Previously, nothing was reported to the Russian people about Soviet missiles on the island! Khrushchev himself later summed up the Caribbean missile crisis in a speech:

> There are smart people now, and there are always more smart people when danger passes than at the moment of danger. And if we hadn't conceded, maybe America would have conceded more? Maybe so. But it could have been like a children's fairy tale when two goats met on a crossbar over a precipice. They showed goat wisdom, and both fell into the abyss. That's the thing.

As for the incident with the U-2 flight over Chukotka, then, contrary to McNamara's panic, the Soviet leadership did not pay any attention to it and did not even write any protest notes. The American leadership was confident that the Russians were only looking for an excuse to attack, and the Soviet leadership believed the same of the Americans. But, ultimately, no one wanted to fight and die.

After the crisis ended and an agreement was reached on the removal of Soviet missiles from the island, U-2 aircraft continued to fly over Cuba. This time, their goal was to photo-monitor the dismantling of missiles and their loading on to ships as part of the fulfilment of the terms of the Khrushchev–Kennedy agreement. On 20 November, U-2C No. 350 56-6683 pilot Joe Hyde of the 4028th SRS crashed off the south-west coast of Florida for an unknown reason while returning from a reconnaissance flight to Cuba. The pilot was killed but this incident did not provoke any reaction. The 102nd and last U-2 flight over Cuba was performed on 16 December 1963.

Conclusion

The U-2 reconnaissance aircraft became one of the symbols of the Cold War, along with the Berlin Wall, boycotts of the Olympic Games and nuclear tests. Probably no aircraft has played such an important role in political events as this brainchild of the CIA. The author of this book was also born in the Cold War era. I belonged to a generation of children who were afraid of American presidents and nuclear explosions from infancy and drew these explosions during school classes. In 1980, my grandmother said that if Ronald Reagan was re-elected for a second term, he would definitely start a nuclear war. When the news of Reagan's victory became known in November, I cried with fear. My classmates and I often discussed the question of whose house was more durable, which building would be able to withstand the shockwave of a nuclear explosion, and which one would not be able to. We also calculated the time it would take us to reach the nearest bunker.

In the late 1980s, the Cold War ended unexpectedly, after which a joyful period of Russian–American friendship began. In that era, Russians really fell in love with America and American flags. It seemed that the old enmity and political tension were gone forever. This happy and optimistic era lasted only ten years. It ended in March 1999, when the United States and NATO launched a military operation against Yugoslavia. In fact, it was this fateful event that became a psychological turning point, after which many Russians became disillusioned with America and began to perceive it as an enemy again. Even in my own family there was a split in 1999. One half of the family angrily condemned the bombing of Yugoslavia (in Russia they were called the Slavic brothers), the other expressed neutral assessments. This crack, which split Russian society, gradually began to widen over time. Many Russians rejoiced at the terrorist attacks of 11 September 2001. They considered it a just revenge for Yugoslavia! Later there were 'orange revolutions' in Georgia and Ukraine, which Russians also perceived as an invasion of the West into their post-Soviet and Slavic world. Russians increasingly felt their national greatness violated and trampled upon. The reason for this phenomenon is actually much deeper and more philosophical than it is perceived in Europe and America. Unfortunately, the Cold War has returned, and now our children are also forced to remember about the protective bunkers.

The history of the U-2 aircraft clearly shows how political ambitions, mutual misunderstanding, inability to negotiate and recognise mutual interests almost led to a nuclear war. Unfortunately, sixty years later, history repeats itself in many ways.

Index